# Renewing Birmingham

## Economy and Society in the Modern South

edited by Philip Scranton and Douglas Flamming

During the past half century, the American South has undergone dramatic economic and social transformations. Gone is the South of cotton fields and cotton mills, of monocrop agriculture and rudimentary industries, of desperate poverty and stultifying racial segregation. Gone is the South that Franklin Roosevelt saw as "the Nation's Number One economic problem." But if that South is gone, how can we explain the rise of the "Sunbelt," and what has economic change meant to southerners—their daily lives, their attitudes, their culture? This series aims to answer these critical questions through a multidisciplinary analysis of the region's economic and social development since World War II. It seeks to present the best new research by historians, economists, sociologists, and geographers—fresh scholarship that investigates unexplored topics and boldly reinterprets familiar trends.

Christopher MacGregor Scribner

# Renewing Birmingham

## Federal Funding and the Promise of Change, 1929–1979

THE UNIVERSITY OF GEORGIA PRESS *Athens & London*

Athens, Georgia 30602

Designed by Walton Harris
Set in Carter & Cone Galliard by G&S Typesetters, Inc.
Printed and bound by Thomson-Shore, Inc.

The paper in this book meets the guidelines for permanence and durability of the Committee on Production Guidelines for Book Longevity of the Council on Library Resources.

Printed in the United States of America

06 05 04 03 02 C 5 4 3 2 1

Library of Congress Cataloging-in-Publication Data

Scribner, Christopher MacGregor.
Renewing Birmingham : federal funding and the promise of change, 1929–1979 / Christopher MacGregor Scribner.
p. cm. — (Economy and society in the modern South)
Includes bibliographical references and index.
ISBN 0-8203-2328-4 (alk. paper)
1. Urban renewal—Alabama—Birmingham. 2. Grants-in-aid—Alabama—Birmingham. 3. Federal aid to community development—Alabama—Birmingham. 4. Federal-city relations—Alabama—Birmingham. 5. Social change—Alabama—Birmingham. 6. Birmingham (Ala.)—Social conditions. 7. Birmingham (Ala.)—Economic conditions. 8. Birmingham (Ala.)—Politics and government. I. Title. II. Series.
HT177.B57 S27 2001
307.3'416'097617810904—dc21 2001034726

British Library Cataloging-in-Publication Data available

*For Peaches Yeilding Scribner*

# Contents

# Acknowledgments

In writing this book I have accumulated many debts. I could not have completed it without the love, support, and generous spirit of my wife, Peaches. Also, my parents, Dick and Inez Scribner, provided a strong foundation and encouragement during the time I worked on this project and long before that.

*Renewing Birmingham* began as a research paper in Hugh Graham's modern America seminar at Vanderbilt University. Graham's energy, insight, and guidance convinced me that I was onto a topic that deserved more attention than a single research paper. I can only hope to repay Graham by providing the same example to students in the future. Also at Vanderbilt, Jimmie Lewis Franklin and David Carlton taught me about Birmingham and the South. This book flows, in part, from what I learned as a Princeton undergraduate. Writing my senior thesis, under Sean Wilentz, first showed me how to approach the past as a scholar.

This book was made possible in large measure because of Birmingham's rich historical archives. Some of the discoveries were my own, such as the Birmingham Housing Authority files in a spare room in the city's Metropolitan Gardens housing development, but most were in collections organized by able archivists. In particular, I enjoyed working with Tim Pennycuff of the University of Alabama at Birmingham and Marvin Whiting and Jim Baggett of the Birmingham Public Library. I hope they and other archivists who assisted me see their efforts reflected here. Many others deserve credit as well. They include: Kyle Kirkwood, Brooks and Martha Jayne Yeilding, Chris Lynch, Steve Boyle, Lauren Mazow, Mike McCann, Jim and Cherie Cannon, Bill and Becky Smith, Mike Emerson, Rob Dunham, Clay Bailey, Tim Bassler, Ronnie Kann, Ted Green, Darby Ray, Ray Clothier, Alex and Colin Carter, and Foster and Ceilidh Scribner.

Malcolm Call of the University of Georgia Press has been a stalwart editor as this project moved toward publication. Thanks to his care—and the efforts of many others—this book is better than my original draft. I am thankful for the help, but in the end I am responsible for the pages that follow.

I explored some of the themes in the book in essays in *The Alabama Review* 48 (1995) and Byron Daynes et al., *The New Deal and Public Policy* (St. Martin's Press, 1998).

# Renewing Birmingham

# Introduction

Observers struggled to make sense of Birmingham during its year of infamy, 1963, when it stood as the symbol of southern white defiance toward the civil rights movement. Not only did events in Birmingham seem to elude simple explanations, but the city seemed different from the rest of the region. Writers called it a place of paradox: a southern industrial city; a New South town that had inherited the worst aspects of the Old South. It lurched menacingly and violently between two eras, wrote James Reston of the *New York Times.* The Pulitzer Prize–winning columnist found Birmingham "engaged in a remarkable and hazardous experiment: it is trying to back full speed into the future." Reston's arresting image captured the frantic urgency—and the seeming lack of foresight—that marked events in Alabama's largest city. Amid the uneasy chaos, Birmingham did pass from one period into another.[1]

In the early 1960s, a series of factors converged in Birmingham to cause the wrenching change. For the most part, scholars have given most of the credit to the homegrown civil rights protest and its intersection with the wider national movement for racial justice. Beneath the more visible rights revolution, other forces also shaped the events and began to undermine the traditional order in Birmingham: the city's economic decline, the movement of its citizens to the suburbs, and the belief of business leaders that federal development aid could help to rebuild their city all helped to undermine the traditional order in Birmingham. Although historians have begun to study federal economic policy in the post–New Deal South, their research still tends to slight or ignore its role in the political and social changes that occurred in the region. Some scholars have even argued that it reinforced the status quo. A thorough examination of federal grant policy, however, offers insights about the political, economic, and social pressures in Birmingham from the Depression forward. It also suggests that Washington's array of grant programs, far from reinforcing the status quo, actually stimulated and supported groups with alternative visions of Birmingham's future development and that, contrary to the common understanding, the transforming role of the federal government in Birmingham—and by implication elsewhere in the country—began well before 1963.

The multiplying power of the federal government, especially its growing role in everyday affairs, forms a dominant motif of twentieth-century America. Washington's activism escalated in response to the economic crises of the 1930s. Wartime mobilization, for example, institutionalized certain aspects of New Deal policy and expanded the federal government's role in stabilizing the economy. As Washington's policy reach extended, the nature of its intervention, particularly in America's cities, shifted as well. In addition to the traditional economic assistance begun during the Depression years, Washington (both the Congress and the executive branch through its administrative agencies) attached numerous conditional requirements that in time became instruments of social as well as fiscal policy. Social reform quickened during the 1960s, and by the end of the decade, a comprehensive regulatory state had been constructed.

Grant-in-aid legislation, largely devoid of social requirements, served as the initial policy agent of the American government. Beginning in the Depression, Congress relied on grants to underwrite improvements to the nation's infrastructure, including the building of roads, hospitals, and government-subsidized housing and urban renewal. Congress preferred grants because they tended to sidestep troubling questions about federal power. If grants, which transmitted the most basic policy objectives, simplified national debates during the drafting of bills, their implementation at the local level could become complicated. An examination of the effects of national grant programs clarifies why the nature of federal intervention shifted and also helps to explain the transformations at the local level. Thus Washington's expanded funding role and Birmingham's acceptance of that aid contributed to epochal changes in Alabama's principal city.[2]

This evolution in Birmingham—quieter and less apparent than the dramatic civil rights confrontations—hollowed out the core of the old order and helped establish new elites. Federal power expanded locally as well. This growth, however, came in a peculiar way: not in the traditional hierarchy of linear administrative control but through collaboration punctuated by complex bargaining and coalition-building. Local bargaining refashioned policies drafted in Washington. Furthermore, bargaining decentralized authority; it opened politics by energizing public and private groups seeking to influence legislation. Coalitions formed among clientele groups, experts, local officials, and national bureaucrats who administered the programs. These coalitions fortified Washington's leverage in local matters and altered its views regarding intervention. Birmingham's blacks, for example, benefited as they found allies and advantage in the federal presence.

In Birmingham, the outlines of federal spending policy emerged during the 1930s as New Deal policymakers sought to stimulate economic recovery. Right from the start certain elements of Birmingham's African American community realized that Washington's involvement in local affairs provided new opportunities for protest. The early aid programs coexisted naturally with the Jim Crow South and did not challenge the status quo. Nonetheless, they created fissures in customary social relations.

Congress institutionalized Washington's public investment role during and after World War II. Birmingham's participation in federal programs deepened in the two decades following the war. It spurred an unplanned transition during the 1950s. Hospital construction and urban renewal aid did more than build the city's infrastructure. In unexpected ways they nourished new elites—modern entrepreneurs in medicine, biomedical research, and education. Acceptance of the grant programs elevated other economic elites, especially participants in real estate, construction, and service businesses, who sought to profit from national policies. At the same time African Americans began to establish coalitions with federal bureaucrats in an effort to press their own grievances. These protests had uneven success, but they drew Washington closer into local affairs and drew blacks together in new ways.

By the mid-1950s competing visions for the city's future existed. A battle for Birmingham ensued. It pitted medical elites and economic modernizers against city politicians who had the backing of the manufacturing interests and white working-class voters. Forming the backdrop for these debates was the city's attempts to build on its wartime prosperity and find an economic niche as its industrial economy began an inexorable decline. Business leaders tried several times to link Birmingham and its upper-middle-class suburbs to give them a stronger political base. Although the factions did not always openly debate federal funding, past and future opportunities for economic development (stimulated by aid from Washington) framed the disagreements. Urban renewal had social as well as economic meanings. To be sure, the modernizers were not social liberals, but they were willing to overlook the possibility of new regulations to participate in select federal programs.

To break the political impasse the modernizers staged a structural coup d'état (the change-in-government drive) that removed an impediment to change. Both local and national civil rights protests heightened the pressure, primarily because they showed the existing commission government's willingness to impale the city on the dagger of segregation. The modernizers' capture of city hall in 1963 allowed the two Birminghams to converge. Mayor Albert Boutwell's government, as well as subsequent administrations, understood the importance of linking the future of the city to the emerging medical center. The confusion surrounding the political transition, in addition to the city's formidable segregationist past, made it an inviting target for the national civil rights movement. By then, however, Eugene "Bull" Connor represented a defeated faction of the city. The new leadership wanted "good business, even if it ha[d] to obey the Federal law to get it," in Reston's words.[3]

A new Birmingham arose that would leave behind parts of its paradoxical past and become less distinguishable from other American cities. The city had changed, although it would not shed all of its old inequalities or the hateful ways that had earned it the well-deserved reputation as "integration's hottest crucible." Understanding the ways that Washington-based grant programs helped shape the city's evolution also helps us to appreciate how the South has been both a region at odds with America and one that participates in national trends. Southern states and cities remained wary of Washington's intervention even as they became reliant on federal funding sources. This dependence injected new pressures into local affairs and made the region vulnerable to shifts in national policy.[4]

CHAPTER ONE

# Public Housing and the Promise of Reform

In the late 1920s Birmingham seemed poised to fulfill the promise of its industrial founders. A 1927 *American Mercury* article captured the optimism pushing the restless growth of Alabama's largest city. H. M. Walker described a dynamic city, illuminated by blast furnaces and smelters at night and sparked by aggressive salesmanship during the day, ready to wrest regional superiority from Atlanta. The city's Chamber of Commerce, Walker reported, "ropes in new industries with such rapidity that it is now possible for a Birminghammer to speak without envy and with some condescension of Atlanta." Civic confidence soared as the region created jobs and lured new residents in the 1920s faster than its rival 130 miles to the east. Walter Henley, president of First National Bank and chairman of the Chamber of Commerce, compared Birmingham to earlier urban upstarts Chicago and St. Louis, commercial boomtowns that had become dominant in their regions. Speaking to fellow Chamber members in 1929, Henley indicated that the upcoming census would confirm Birmingham as the South's greatest city.[1]

Birmingham's economy appeared robust at the start of 1929, suggesting that trouble never strayed too far from success in this Alabama city. The area's unemployment rate held steady at 6 percent, and steel output, which next to pig iron production stoked the region's economy, peaked at 1.5 million tons. The city had just completed a three-year run in construction starts at a pace that exceeded Atlanta's, and it also had outpaced the Georgia capital in job creation in the decade, 34,000 to 31,000. Nonetheless, slackening nationwide demand for iron and steel manifested the country's economic ills even as output remained high. Local coal production fell in 1929, hinting at the rapid industrial collapse to follow. By 1931, the steel and iron mills ran part-time schedules. The Tennessee Coal, Iron and Railroad Company (TCI), Sloss-Sheffield Steel Company, and Woodward Iron Company, among the largest employers in the district's iron and steel economy, switched to three-day workweeks, then scaled back to a full shift every two weeks. Steel production declined by half in 1931 compared to the 1929 peak. The next year it fell by half again and coal production matched the 1900 level, less than half the 1926 high. In the 1930s, Birmingham's robust population growth slowed; it grew by 4 percent while Atlanta, Memphis, and New Orleans averaged 12 percent.[2]

Workers suffered. Districtwide manufacturing employed 45,000 workers in 1929 but fewer than 25,000 in 1934. Times were tough even for those with jobs. By 1933, TCI, a U.S. Steel subsidiary, had cut workers' wages by 50 to 70 percent. A majority of employed factory workers averaged just two-thirds of the federal "minimum maintenance" income of $1,179, and a mere 8,000 of the area's 108,000 wage earners received pay equal to their pre-Depression paycheck. All segments of the economy slowed. In the early 1930s, unemployment in the building trades reached 60 percent and retail jobs in the city declined by one-third. Construction expenditures dropped to 1906 levels. Segregated job patterns meant that African Americans were let go before whites, and about three-fourths of Birmingham's black workers lost their jobs in the first half of the decade. Department store owner Louis Pizitz observed the desperation creeping into the city. "When I gave my Thanksgiving Dinner," Pizitz wrote Mayor James Jones in December 1930, "I saw with my own eyes people taking bread from the table and putting it in their pockets, and you could see that some of them had not eaten in a day or two." Such sentiments scarcely shook Jones's confidence that private charities, facing peak caseloads by 1932, could provide enough relief for the needy. Ever the optimist, Jones decided to move the lighted motto, "Birmingham: The Magic City," to the front of the railroad station.[3]

A 1937 *Harper's* profile—a decade after the *American Mercury* piece—found little magic, but it noted elements of change. During the lean years of the Depression, George Leighton tagged Birmingham as the city of "perpetual promise" because absentee ownership dominated the area's industry and the costs of Jim Crowism and racial tension were immeasurable. The Depression worsened Birmingham's misery, thwarting its potential yet again. According to a rueful Birmingham adage that Leighton repeated, "hard times come here first and stay longest." The Depression struck Birmingham hard. Tough times, nonetheless, cracked the old order, and Leighton noticed fissures in the city, in particular the unionization of miners and manufacturing workers. Thanks to the celebrated Section 7a of the National Industrial Recovery Act and subsequent labor legislation, for instance, the United Mine Workers (UMW) had formed ninety-three locals with twenty-three thousand new members by 1934. By January 1937 another breakthrough came when TCI, the city's largest employer, entered negotiations with the steelworkers' union. Working-class organization continued to erode the political authority of local business leaders. Moreover, despite efforts to retain limited government in Birmingham, the New Deal's legislative agenda fostered unaccustomed debates about Washington's role in trying to restore the economic vitality of the region. For the first time, public housing entered the local lexicon in the form of proposed federal aid for slum clearance and replacement housing.[4]

When the Depression came, the three-member city commission—which had a history of meager public spending in flush times—cut the municipal budget. Fiscal restraint meant passing responsibility to federal agencies. In 1931, Jones and fellow commissioners William Downs, a former TCI employee and county sheriff, and Lewey Robinson, a onetime newspaper reporter, had passed a $500,000 bond issue for work relief, transient care, and hot meals for the jobless. Subsequent efforts, however, followed initiatives from the nation's capital. By 1932, the city appeared to have come to a halt; weekly commission meetings lasted just ten minutes because there was no business to transact, the *Birmingham Post* reported. The commissioners slashed the city's budget by nearly one-third from its 1928 high and shifted twenty thousand relief cases to the temporary Federal Emergency Relief Administration. Roosevelt administration programs, like those run by the Civil Works Administration (CWA), carried more dollars to Birmingham and put thousands of the city's jobless to work repairing public buildings, fixing roads, and building parks. Likewise, thanks to the New Deal, public health expenditures doubled between 1935 and 1940 even as local funding dwindled.[5]

If Mayor Jones and his political allies first invoked traditional policies to answer the economic distress, others in Birmingham recognized the epoch-making nature of the federal intercession. Emory Q. Hawk, an economics professor at Birmingham Southern College, compared the New Deal to the era after the Civil War: "Once again the federal government now undertakes to reconstruct the South." The pro-business *Birmingham News* approved of Washington's activism, citing the need for remarkable measures during the deep economic malaise. "It becomes increasingly apparent that the problem calls for attention by local, state and national governments. It is not a problem for local authorities only, or for state or national authorities only," went a not atypical *News* editorial of the period. Washington's intervention meant a fairer system of relief but it did not mean fundamental reform of local customs. CWA programs, forerunners of Works Progress Administration (WPA) efforts, hired blacks, 40 percent of the city's population, in proportionate numbers. Whites and blacks nonetheless received unequal wages, and when in 1936 the Workers Alliance, a group of radical labor activists, protested the discrimination, Alabama's WPA director threatened further cuts in wages for blacks. The UMW organized whites and blacks, but in racially mixed locals, meetings were segregated and only whites gained leadership positions. Thus federal programs served to reinforce the clear and defined boundaries of segregation.[6]

While the New Deal targeted economic recovery and did not seek to challenge local social customs in any fundamental way, the question of whether to accept federal money provoked strong disagreements in Birmingham. Following the *News*'s lead, the business community prodded the commission to pursue federal aid that advanced its narrowly defined agenda, especially capital projects that supported commercial and industrial development. The centerpiece of the city's industrial growth campaign was a $7 million request in 1934 to dam the Warrior River, thirty-two miles north of Birmingham, to create an industrial water supply. Officials nonetheless proved reluctant to seek grants that lacked clear business goals and that threatened to reverse stingy social welfare spending. Thus the commission requested dozens of Public Works Administration (PWA) construction grants while rejecting money for school improvements. (In 1936, for example, the commissioners stopped a proposed bond issue to finance the 55 percent local share needed to match $7 million in construction funds for the cash-strapped public schools.) Public housing took center stage in these debates because it was a hybrid policy that mixed pump-priming capital spending with make-work and social welfare goals.[7]

The issue of public housing gathered momentum in the fall of 1933 after the PWA formed a Housing Division, which sought to remove dilapidated urban homes and to build government-subsidized replacements. In many American cities, but not Birmingham, such discussions had antedated the New Deal, pitting "housers," as those who favored government intervention to assist the working poor called themselves, against business groups that believed the private market sufficed. Once started, those debates and the subsequent implementation illustrated how the pull of Washington's orbit reoriented priorities in Birmingham. In 1934, following several aborted attempts, city officials moved ahead on a housing project for blacks. The Smithfield project, quickly enmeshed in a series of controversies, showed both how African Americans gained bargaining leverage through Washington's role and the circumscribed nature of the federal intervention. Washington bureaucrats, called upon to mediate local disputes, supported fair housing conditions at Smithfield, but they did not challenge segregation. Thus in 1936 they ignored a plea by local black activists for African American administrators in the completed project. While the protests, which helped to ensure that government-subsidized housing remained controversial in Birmingham throughout the 1930s and afterward, energized the black professional class, they emphasized economic divisions in the African American community. When black workers fought in 1939 and 1940 for the benefits of the national housing agency's job quotas at Birmingham's second New Deal housing project, Elyton Village, the National Association for the Advancement of Colored People (NAACP) ignored them. Federal officials made cursory inquiries on their behalf, but those failed.

Frank Spain cast his support for public housing in the early 1930s in pragmatic social welfare terms that implied that prompt government intervention would reduce the need for later action. The government's role rested on the "premise that substandard housing is a breeding place of crime and disease and results in excessive public spending for health, police, and fire services," according to Spain, a former city attorney who had married into a prominent Birmingham family and opened a private practice that represented many of the city's largest insurers. Other fiscal conservatives also linked subsidized housing and public spending. A study by Birmingham Southern's Hawk found that in one low-income neighborhood the city received $10,000 in property taxes but spent $178,000 on public services. Hawk's report prompted several leading industrialists to agree that the razing of slum areas might lessen the city's outlays on services. W. B. Moore, president of the American Cast Iron and Pipe Company, told the Birmingham Real Estate Board in 1935 that slum removal and public housing might balance the city's books. A *News* editorial noted that slum clearance followed by government-subsidized housing could reduce the spread of blight, strengthen the tax base, and raise property values, all goals of real estate interests.[8]

In opposing public housing, Sam Clabaugh, president of Protective Life Insurance, the largest insurer in Birmingham, offered a more conventional business outlook, one in keeping with the position held by the city's real estate interests. The head of Birmingham's Chamber of Commerce and later chair of the national organization's committee on housing, Clabaugh opposed plans that undermined the private market. Slums should be checked by stricter code enforcement or private rehabilitation; furthermore, public housing sapped private initiative. (The agency, with the assistance of local groups, would buy and condemn property and then operate demonstration housing projects. The PWA's policy, intended to create jobs and to upgrade unsuitable living conditions, required that the number of new homes must equal the number of razed houses.) As he later testified to a congressional committee considering housing legislation, the government's proper role is "to stimulate the building by private enterprise of new housing for persons in middle-income groups and into the acceptable second-hand housing vacated by such persons, the dwellers in the present unsafe dwellings would move."[9] Yet Clabaugh supported some of Washington's economic initiatives. He backed development projects like the Warrior River proposal. After a PWA review board rejected the city's bid, eliciting howls among Birmingham's leaders, Clabaugh maintained that a project of long-term economic impact should not be thwarted because the city had an adequate drinking supply. The argument swayed PWA chief Harold Ickes, who supported Birmingham's appeal. Construction began in 1937.[10]

Spain's goals, nonetheless, fit squarely within the framework of segregation. While public housing opponents argued that government subsidies sapped private will, housers believed that the grant program could improve Birmingham by reducing economic disadvantages (such as substandard housing that caused poor health conditions) and create a more equitable, if still separate, community. This economic paternalism depended on the continuation of distinct black and white neighborhoods. The miserable conditions in the city's black communities, where nearly 90 percent of homes were substandard, meant blacks could benefit from the economic and social possibilities of public housing. Moreover, canny developers could see that by manipulating the location of African American residents they could increase the value of existing black neighborhoods by developing them for purposes other than houses for blacks.

Thus city real estate interests accepted Washington's programs if the plans could subsidize private operators. Executives of prominent property development firms worked with the groups that made the earliest proposals to the PWA's Housing Division but with agendas often at odds with those of federal bureaucrats. Entrepreneurs such as Hill Ferguson and Robert Jemison Jr. primarily sought to push the slum clearance bill in similar directions as the National Housing Act of 1934, which provided mortgage guarantees and also created the Federal Housing Administration (FHA). The Chamber, under Clabaugh's direction, actively backed the FHA and advised property owners to seek money from the agency's rehabilitation program. The effort, which subsidized repairs to existing homes, proved far too limited to cure Birmingham's housing ills. By June 1936, the FHA had distributed some $90,000 in loans to the Alabama city, less than 1 percent of the

$20 million that Clabaugh estimated city property owners needed to fix Birmingham's shoddy housing.[11]

Jemison, the director of Alabama's FHA division, proposed the most aggressive plan to the PWA and one at cross purposes with the agency's rules because it focused on downtown renewal rather than public housing. "It seems a pity for Birmingham to sit idly and let other cities secure appropriations for slum clearance development," he wrote a friend. Two decades earlier, his firm had developed a company town for TCI in Fairfield. While Jemison's company built several downtown office buildings, it made its mark developing suburban subdivisions in the 1920s, in particular, Mountain Brook, on the south side of Red Mountain, where several thousand of the city's wealthiest residents moved. Mountain Brook's growth slowed in the 1930s, forcing Jemison to search elsewhere for projects, and he saw the federal bill as an opportunity to energize his company. In concert with new housing for middle-class blacks on the city's outskirts, he advocated clearing slums that surrounded the Jefferson County courthouse in downtown Birmingham, an area he considered to be better suited for commercial building. To find a suitable area for the new black neighborhood, Jemison wrote TCI officials asking about vacant land he could buy. Housing bureaucrats ultimately rejected Jemison's application because it lacked public housing. His bold stroke—submitting a proposal that avoided a central feature of the legislation, public housing—proved ahead of its time. Not until the 1950s did federal housing shift its focus to commercial redevelopment. [12]

Other submissions had specific plans for new homes. In October 1933 a newly formed ministerial alliance, the Jefferson County Interracial Committee, proposed a sixteen-hundred-unit housing project for blacks. Also, an Episcopal charity, the St. Mark's Housing Association, wanted to build single-family homes near an existing middle-class black neighborhood. "Our principal object," noted Ferguson, a St. Mark's member, "is to set a pace for colored housing in Birmingham which will have the effect of speeding up the destruction of the old type quarters and gradually improve the class of housing throughout the city."[13]

Although each plan derailed, the proposals brought the city's decaying housing stock to the attention of PWA bureaucrats, who pushed for a demonstration project in Birmingham. In the spring of 1934, after a cursory investigation of city neighborhoods that found nearly half the homes substandard, the Housing Division's Eugene Klabber asked the Birmingham area's public health officials to form a local committee. The agency would set aside $4 million for a PWA-owned project, he told J. D. Dowling, the county health officer. To increase the likelihood of federal approval for the project, the committee should be "divorced from the real estate companies with commercial interests in the [housing] proposition" and represented by "disinterested, civic-minded organizations." The all-white committee combined social welfare activists and two prominent Chamber of Commerce members so as to ensure support from segments of the business community. The group included Dowling; J. C. deHoll; Rev. Graham Lacey, the pastor at St. Mark's; Rabbi Morris Newfield, of the city's largest Jewish synagogue, Temple Emmanuel; Mrs. Paul Lanier of the State Federation of Women's Clubs; Mrs. Roderick Beddow, a member of the Jefferson County Tuberculosis Society and wife of a prominent trade union leader; James Mills, publisher of the *Post;* and John Persons, a vice-president at First National Bank.[14]

While the program's impetus came from Washington, government-subsidized residences were also local political issues because federal rules required the city to pay for a housing survey. By a two-to-one margin the city commission approved the expenditure. The vote came over the protests of real estate interests, although the largest newspaper backed the plan. "It is to be hoped that Birmingham's appeal for federal slum clearance will meet with favorable consideration, especially since that is probably the only possibility for such a project," a *News* editorial went, continuing that "the city itself cannot spend money on a housing project." Heavy lobbying by Mills and Persons helped convince commissioners Robinson and Downs to support the idea. Mayor Jones, more closely allied with real estate interests, opposed the initiative. The committee would use the survey to select a project site and to offer a basic rebuilding plan, additional local responsibilities under the federal law.[15]

After completing its survey in September, the committee, following advice from Washington, selected an African American neighborhood for clearance and rebuilding. Federal housing director Horatio Hackett wrote one of Alabama senators that the "need of a slum clearance project for Negroes was much more acute." In December 1934, the PWA tentatively approved a $2.5 million housing project. The grant would pay land acquisition and construction costs. Almost four hundred families resided in the twenty-eight-acre section of Smithfield designated for demolition. The replacement development, called Smithfield Court, would include 544 rental homes. In all, the committee's report had identified twenty-two blighted areas with deplorable housing conditions. The study of nine white and thirteen black neighborhoods covered 817 blocks, nearly one-tenth of the city and home to one-quarter of Birmingham's 260,000 residents. Those communities had double the citywide rates of infant mortality and tuberculosis and three times the number of illegitimate births, the survey found. These conditions were by no means unique. Atlanta officials, for instance, estimated that about 15 percent of their city could be classified as a slum because of overcrowding, lack of sanitary facilities in homes, or an extensive need for repairs.[16]

The conditions were worse in the black neighborhoods studied. Nearly half the city's black population, about 52,000 people, lived in those blighted districts. (In comparison, the nine white areas held 7,500 people, or 5 percent of the city's white population.) By one estimate, more than three-fourths of all the homes occupied by blacks were substandard, and just 15 percent of black families lived in homes that they owned. These figures were similar to those for other southeastern cities. In Atlanta, planning for its first public housing project, Techwood Homes, 70 percent of blacks lived in substandard units. About one-third of Birmingham's black families lacked indoor plumbing—only Columbia, South Carolina, among major southern cities registered worse figures—and one-third also lacked electric lights. Rabbi Newfield described the typical black slum as a place where

> shotgun houses devoid of beauty . . . are thrown almost against each other around a block. The house faces outward on a dirty, unpaved street. At the back they look out on a "compound" in the center of which is a water hydrant which supplies water for all the houses. The "compound" is also likely to contain three or four shabby little outhouses comprising the sole sanitary facilities for the homes in the block. Beside the hydrant, a piece of concrete pipe rises above the ground and into this the waste water is supposed to be thrown. Weeds abound, and debris. Pig pens, with their filth and stench, are likely to be found backed up against some of the houses.

The city needed upward of seven thousand new homes to meet the demand properly, the survey concluded.[17]

In selecting Smithfield, reformers revealed not only that they had no intention of attacking residential segregation but that public housing was not—as it would later become—for the most destitute either. Birmingham had worse black slums than Smithfield, a neighborhood with a substantial middle-class population one mile northwest of the downtown business district. According to an index of blight developed during the housing survey, sixteen areas—including seven white neighborhoods—were worse. In fact Smithfield, along with nearby Enon Ridge, was one of two significant middle-class black communities populated by professionals and schoolteachers. Adjacent to Industrial High School, Smithfield was near transportation and employment centers. Still, about one-fourth of the residents in the project area received public assistance. The "housers" believed that Smithfield's middle-class enclaves made it easier to rehabilitate. Moreover, the original intent of the federal program was not to provide homes for the hard-core poor but to improve the lot of the working poor, viewed as worthy of reform efforts. This aim becomes evident after creation of the salary schedule regulating qualifications for the project, in which black elementary school teachers barely passed the minimum income threshold for occupancy.[18]

The city's black community, a *News* reporter wrote in 1936, was a "city within a city," a "city apart from Birmingham." A 1926 zoning ordinance that divided the city by race codified that separateness. The law prescribed thirty-seven residential districts for blacks. Those neighborhoods—Tuxedo Junction, Kingston, Brown's Hill, Titusville, and Tip Top Alley, for example—were scattered throughout the city. Despite the Supreme Court's *Buchanan v. Worley* ruling, a 1917 decision that had declared racial zoning unconstitutional, cities such as Birmingham, Atlanta, Richmond, New Orleans, Dallas, and Miami continued the practice, their efforts coinciding with increased attention to urban planning in the 1920s. Most laws did not survive legal challenge, but Birmingham blacks did not take the city ordinance to court until the 1940s. The races did not always follow the rigidly segmented zoning lines, and exceptions abounded. The housing survey, for example, noted that a majority of blacks lived in districts zoned for whites and next to popular white communities. The absence of enough homes for blacks in black districts meant that "Negroes have moved into [these areas] in growing number during the past four years on account of the dilapidated conditions of the buildings." In the first half of the 1930s, for example, thirty-two thousand people moved into Birmingham, but the city added just a thousand new homes.[19]

At the center of Birmingham's downtown African American entertainment and business district stood the Masonic Temple. Located at 1630 Fourth Avenue North, the building housed the NAACP headquarters and the offices of several fraternal organizations, numerous insurance agencies, several physicians, two dentists, the Black Eagle detective agency, and the weekly *Birmingham Reporter*. The dual society's black professional class had grown, and in many ways its conservative outlook mirrored that of the white professional elite. Grand Chancellor of the Knights of Pythias and editor of the *Reporter* Oscar Adams, a prominent member of the black middle class, was cast from the mold of Booker T. Washington. In Adams's favorite speech, titled "salesmanship," he praised the insurance business as the best occupation and lectured about thrift, hard work, and the evils of laziness. Adams's occasional column in the *News*, written under the banner of "What Negroes Are Doing," provided the paper's rare coverage of the black community.[20]

Segregation's heaviest toll resulted in an uneven economy that restricted the earnings and opportunities for blacks because of the color of their skin. In 1935, 97 percent of black families earned less than $1,000 a year compared to just 46 percent of white families. At the start of World War II, the average salary for a white public school teacher was $1,466 while the school system paid black teachers $682, according to a study by the sociologist Charles Johnson. In other areas, especially politics, segregation meant exclusion. In the 1930s, just several hundred of Birmingham's one hundred thousand blacks were registered to vote.[21]

Within segregated Birmingham the races had occasional contact, although usually within well-defined boundaries. Many social welfare groups, such as the city's Community Chest, an umbrella outfit that oversaw the distribution of money to charities, had Negro divisions. Industrial TCI even funded a black newspaper, the *Weekly Review*, to push its antiunion ideas. Few whites countenanced challenges to racial customs. In 1938, when the Council for Interracial Cooperation held its Southern Conference for

Human Welfare in Birmingham, local police, led by public safety commissioner Eugene "Bull" Connor, disrupted the meeting after First Lady Eleanor Roosevelt called for integrated seating. Connor was reported to have told the First Lady that in Birmingham "whites and Negroes are not allowed to segregate together." The malapropian comment, which Connor denied, caused local newspapers to mock his uncouth performance; nevertheless, those attacks represented social snobbery more than sentiments of racial moderation.[22]

A federal court ruling altered—and delayed—the Smithfield project. In January 1935 federal district judges in Louisville ordered that the PWA could not condemn property. Land acquisition costs increased without condemnation, which essentially stymied the PWA housing program. In the short term, Birmingham would have to shift the way it handled Smithfield. Eventually, Congress responded with the United States Housing Act of 1937, establishing the United States Housing Agency (USHA) to support public housing through local housing authorities, who would own and manage the projects. (Washington would loan 90 percent of capital costs, repaid with low-interest loans at sixty-year terms, and subsidize the operating costs of the projects.) Birmingham's housers, anticipating the new direction of federal legislation, scrambled to form an official agency with the appropriate powers. In February, the state legislature passed a bill creating the Housing Authority of the Birmingham District (HABD), a five-member public agency to plan for and administer local public housing.[23]

Although the city government could exercise political control over the board through its designated powers to appoint the members and approve new projects, the commissioners were content to distance themselves from the sensitive subject of public housing. The HABD, Mayor Jones made clear, borrowed money from the federal government, not Birmingham's citizens. (The lion's share of the authority's budget would come from its ongoing operations.) The three commissioners nonetheless sought to balance the political voices in the HABD when they named its five board members in July 1935. The selections included social welfare, labor, and downtown business interests, and Jones appointed school board member deHoll the HABD chairman. DeHoll had spent most of his career as a banker, first with the Federated Savings Bank and then for the Southern Bank and Securities Company, which catered to working-class clients and had been closed by the Depression in 1933. During the 1930s deHoll had become more active in civic affairs, earning a spot on the school board and a local health council and becoming a vocal advocate for public housing. When he became HABD chairman, deHoll worked as an agent for the Girard Fire and Insurance Company. Joining deHoll on the board were lawyer Spain; Charles P. Marks, an executive with the real estate firm W. B. Leedy and a former vice-president for Jemison's real estate company; Guy Snavely, former president of Birmingham Southern College; and Charles P. Thiemonge, president of the Birmingham Trades Council.[24]

Besides the administrative and legal delays, other disputes hounded the project, hinting at the new political pressures that accompanied the arrival of federal dollars in Birmingham. HABD officials, for instance, had hoped that PWA chief Harold Ickes, visiting the city in May 1935 to discuss the Warrior River project, would dedicate the start of work at Smithfield Court. Ickes's trip came and went without a ceremony because officials had yet to acquire all the property for the project. Several Smithfield homeowners rejected the city's offers for their land. The recalcitrant blacks did not quarrel with the goals of slum clearance. To the contrary, Sallie Russell, who had balked at the sale of her home and had organized twenty-seven other property owners, told deHoll that "home ownership is the most important institution in making good citizens." Russell's group objected because Birmingham's limited black housing market would make it difficult for its members to find suitable replacement homes. Several of the houses were worth $6,000, Russell noted, and Birmingham's restrictive 1926 zoning law would make it impossible to find comparable property elsewhere. Russell's group also charged that the housing committee misinformed local residents about its plans. Despite the earlier existence of an auxiliary black group, Russell contended that many of the property owners had to rely on newspaper articles to learn about the city's plans.[25]

Unhappy with what she viewed as deHoll's slow responses, Russell took the group's protests beyond the local community—directly to the PWA administrator in charge of the project. "Being of the colored race," Russell wrote PWA housing chief Hackett, "we are without political weight and influence to make our objections felt in official quarters." Local blacks could not make a difference at the polls. In 1935, for instance, just 456 of Jefferson County's 28,000 registered voters were black. By August, twelve property owners, eight blacks and four whites, still refused the HABD's offers.[26]

Rebuffed, deHoll and fellow committee members countered with a mixture of irritation and bewilderment. They talked tough, threatening condemnation proceedings, but ventured softer approaches too. They worried that "unless these property owners come to terms, the Government will withdraw and turn the funds over to some other city." In addition to linking the housing project to improved facilities for Industrial High School, local housing officials considered upping the purchase prices to ease relocation pressures. The PWA balked because the incentives would have pushed the land acquisition costs above the New Deal agency's $450,000 allotment. The conflicting pressures put the HABD in a peculiar bind, caught between local blacks demanding fair treatment and federal bureaucrats requiring adherence to national guidelines.[27]

To ease the stalemate, the HABD conceded to several of the blacks' demands. To lobby the Smithfield holdouts, deHoll reassembled the auxiliary division, a cross section of the city's black middle class, a group that included Bishop B. G. Shaw, leader of the state's African Methodist Episcopal Church; Dr. E. W. Taggart, the president of the local NAACP chapter; Rev. B. J. Anderson; and leading clubwomen Mrs. H. C. Bryant and Mrs. R. M. Neely. The group convinced the Smithfield residents to sell to the authority, arguing that the project would create jobs, provide modern homes for those without decent housing, and improve the area's recreational facilities. DeHoll also pushed through a meaningful zoning change, convincing the city's zoning boss to shift the racial designation of the west side of Center Street, Smithfield's western boundary, from white to black. The change allowed property owners to buy their homes from the demolition contractor and move them across the street. Over time, the zoning shift proved significant because it gave blacks a foothold in the adjacent white neighborhood. A decade later, blacks were still trying to move just beyond this area and whites responded with bombs, heightening racial tension and black activism.[28]

Neither side viewed the interplay over the Smithfield project as a challenge to the basic tenets of segregation. Nevertheless, Birmingham's black community expected improved treatment within the confines of a separate society. Whites remained more wedded to tradition—a position emphasized by the groundbreaking for the Smithfield project. While Mayor Jones shoveled the first dirt, local politicians and dignitaries crowded the reviewing stand, and the PWA's housing chief, A. R. Class, gave the dedicatory address. The Industrial High School band furnished the music and a black minister, P. J. Watkins, led the opening prayer. The symbolism was too pregnant, however, for the NAACP's Taggart, who wrote deHoll that he regarded the "singing and praying role as a mere gesture a kind of 'sop' that must be regarded as the same kind of paternalism that characterizes most efforts requiring cooperation of the races." DeHoll fired back, chastising Taggart for questioning the HABD's motives when the all-white housing committee had selected a project for blacks first and had proceeded despite criticism "by white people of this community who are, as you are, always ready and anxious to play tweedle dee and tweedle dum with the race question."[29]

The exchange eroded feelings of goodwill between the housing committee and its supporters in the black middle class. The mistrust deepened after newspaperman H. D. Coke, editor of the city's black biweekly, the *Birmingham World,* uncovered the authority's plans to abandon central heating for the homes. Coke complained to PWA officials, but the bureaucrats backed the local decision, calling central heat a frivolous expense in the South. (Several years later, federal housing officials stood by this decision for a housing project for whites in the city.) In response, the NAACP organized a special committee to monitor events at Smithfield Court, and the watchdogs soon found reasons to question the HABD. DeHoll's group planned to eliminate a community center and several apartment buildings and to jettison certain conveniences, the NAACP claimed. Indeed, the authority had decided in April 1936 to replace gas ranges with coal stoves and to require tenants to buy and install their own refrigerators. The NAACP group, which included former auxiliary committee members such as Taggart, Dr. Charles McPherson, and Oscar Adams, considered the proposals unsatisfactory. In addition, special committee members believed their reputations had been tarnished by the changes. After persuading homeowners to sell, it now appeared that they might have made empty promises. They charged that the changes amounted "to a breaking of faith and confidence [that] destroys the influence of Negroes to be of any kind of service to the government whatsoever in projects of this kind, especially in Birmingham."[30]

The two sides held a series of meetings in September but failed to resolve any issues, so the NAACP leadership reached beyond Birmingham. DeHoll said the switches had been made to keep the project within budget, especially, he noted, because the decision to include the community building, at the urging of black leaders, made it essential to cut costs elsewhere. The protesters rejected his logic. "If you can't give us respectable, decent houses," Mrs. C. W. Brooks told deHoll in one exchange at the agency's office, "don't give us anything." "If you don't meet our demands," she went on, "we will send a committee to Washington and get what we want." And they did.[31]

On the subject of the household amenities, the NAACP committee found a receptive audience when visiting PWA officers in October 1936. The delegation lobbied Robert Weaver, Harold Ickes's Negro Affairs adviser, arguing that the purposes of slum clearance were to "clear away a large area that was a blight in the life of our people" and to provide decent housing at an affordable price. Committee members also presented their petition to Lawrence Oxley, another special assistant to the secretary of labor. Walter White, the civil rights organization's executive secretary, weighed in too, contending that Birmingham's planners had engaged in "Jim Crowism" and "as always a segregated Negro project is inferior."[32]

The combined protest, bypassing traditional constraints in Birmingham, brought results. Agency officials, who had final say because the PWA paid the construction costs, demanded that the HABD's plans match the NAACP's requests. Smithfield Court apartments would include both gas ranges and electric refrigerators—and the project would have a community center. The special committee also should feel fortunate because the federal agency had increased the play areas next to the community center, the PWA's Howard Gray wrote newspaper editor Coke. In a cost-cutting concession, however, the PWA allowed the housing authority to abandon the multistory homes.[33]

The NAACP special committee spurred and redirected black activism in Birmingham. A petition drive that ultimately amassed one thousand signatures broadened its community backing and helped spark the reorganization of the local office. McPherson, catapulted into the top post, wrote the national headquarters that his election symbolized that the "young

Turks were replacing the insincere apologetic leadership of the past." The disputes invigorated Birmingham's NAACP branch, and its membership peaked at eight hundred in 1939, a pre–World War II high. The group, moreover, broadened its focus, targeting racial zoning and voting rights cases along with fights against police brutality and unfair prosecutions. Participants in the protests saw the power of political leverage and attempted to build a loyal Democratic base among Birmingham's African American community. In the fall of 1936, W. C. Patton, a school administrator, and Arthur Shores, a lawyer, organized the Jefferson County Negro Democratic Club, hoping to add to the few hundred blacks who had registered to vote in the 1930s. Before the New Deal, many of those few hundred voters regularly supported the GOP. In 1935, a year after receiving his law degree from the University of Kansas, Shores opened his Birmingham practice and soon would become the city's leading civil rights litigator. A *News* editorial surmised that blacks found the "tangible good will" of the New Deal superior to "illusory Republican promises." As Shores later remembered, "The participation of blacks in New Deal programs prompted black leaders to look increasingly toward the federal government for support."[34]

The completion of Smithfield Court's 540 apartments in November 1937 did not end the protests at the thirty-acre site. Newspaper coverage of the dedication emphasized the modern facilities, one headline announcing that "Smithfield Court Proves Uncle Sam's Ability as a Housekeeper Is Top Notch." Under the terms of the new federal housing law, responsibility for uncompleted PWA projects, like Smithfield Court, transferred to the USHA and the local agency would manage it. Blacks soon found fault with the HABD's operations. The civil rights group, as in the earlier protest, involved Washington bureaucrats in its disputes. This time, however, the group received less satisfactory answers because the federal government's mandate was less clear. Most of the postconstruction disagreements centered on employment at the housing project. African American housing activists, for instance, wanted a black resident manager at Smithfield Court, the employment of competent black personnel, equal salaries for black employees, and a comparable wage scale for blacks in subsequent public housing projects. The *World*'s Coke outlined the request in a January 1938 letter to Donald Jones, a USHA administrator. A factional dispute within the black community undermined the effort. Bishop Shaw and Oscar Adams split away from the housing group to nominate separate candidates for manager, bookkeeper, and other office staff. More important, the special committee's protest lacked the teeth of the earlier effort because federal officials no longer had the leverage of the purse strings or clear regulatory guidelines to act. Weaver, the top Negro Affairs officer at the USHA, informed his boss that the USHA did not have the authority to intervene in staff appointments at a project. Furthermore, the agency's prevailing wage guidelines included laborers, not managers.[35]

HABD officials did not want a black manager because they had their own candidate: deHoll. USHA administrator Jones agreed with Spain's request, writing to his superior that in Birmingham "the philosophy of employing people is to have a white man over Negro employees." The agency, deHoll wrote, would hire a black bookkeeper for Smithfield Court and a black aide, and it would consider paying equal wages to black and white employees. Equal wages, he wrote USHA chief Nathan Strauss, would break with tradition in a city where economic discrimination was customary. The disputes did prompt Birmingham's housing authority to form a Negro Advisory Committee, but its members included none of the participants in the Smithfield Court protests. DeHoll justified their exclusion by calling the activists "trouble-makers . . . disappointed in their efforts to get jobs in the operating personnel."[36]

The Smithfield protests bequeathed a divided legacy. While deferring to local standards on social issues, the presence of Washington bureaucrats allowed blacks, for the first time, to enter into real negotiations with Birmingham's white leaders. The special committee was not a powerless auxiliary group. Nevertheless, challenges by the NAACP's oversight committee had been most successful when federal guidelines were clearest and fared less well when it more directly challenged the racial status quo. For the most part, PWA officials were color-blind regarding the technical requirements for public housing. Federal officials, like deHoll's housing committee, which first had selected a project for blacks, wanted to improve the standard of living in Birmingham. Allowing for particular local differences (such as climate), housing division bureaucrats wanted a public housing project in Buffalo for whites to be indistinguishable from public housing for blacks in Birmingham. Yet Washington's reliance on local implementation circumscribed the boundaries of protest; thus the special committee's demands for jobs and patronage floundered. USHA bureaucrats lacked clear directives on the issue, and they also wanted to defer to the local group that would operate the project. National officials avoided any action that would undermine the Birmingham authority's community standing, such as putting blacks in management positions—a clear challenge to the segregated order. Social policy remained a local concern.

The building of Smithfield Court failed to settle the rancorous political debates surrounding public housing. The HABD pushed a second project, an eight-hundred-unit development for whites two miles west of the downtown commercial district called Elyton Village after the original Jones Valley settlement. While "housing is usually regarded as a Negro problem," a 1934 survey had noted, "these studies clearly establish the great need of better housing for whites in the low income group." Again, the authority needed local government approval to win federal aid. The politicians faced fierce lobbying. City real estate interests derided the proposal as socialism. Labor groups counted the jobs the new project would bring, and social welfare activists talked about the benefits of new homes. During one stormy commission meeting, Mayor Jones demanded Spain's resignation as head of the local housing board. Spain refused.[37]

Real estate groups continued to oppose government-subsidized housing. Besides their ideological opposition to New Deal activism, they worried about competition from public housing. Federally subsidized housing would put adjoining property owners and renters at a disadvantage, Mark Hodo, president of the powerful Birmingham Real Estate Board, told the commissioners. Quite simply, the government might provide nicer homes at lower rates. Hodo and other major property owners, including Sidney Smyer, formed the Real Estate Owners Association, which claimed to represent fourteen thousand city residents. Slum clearance assisted the middle class, not the destitute, one association petition asserted; it also depressed property rates and created a political racket.[38]

Conversely, Birmingham's trade unions viewed public housing as a bread-and-butter proposition. Public housing construction, unlike WPA employment, brought needed jobs at prevailing wage rates (a requirement of the Davis-Bacon Act of 1931). The potential jobs mattered because times remained tough. Through most of 1937, coal mines stayed closed, steel production faltered again, and more than forty thousand workers were without full-time jobs. In addition, the Depression still idled about half to three-fourths of the city's building tradesmen. Federal construction projects could stimulate "broader economy without costing the city a penny," according to Roy Copeland, secretary of the Birmingham Building Trades Council.[39]

As unions grew in numbers and power throughout the 1930s, they eroded the political authority of the local business elite. Working-class political strength had been on the rise in Birmingham since 1910, when the Greater Birmingham Movement annexed several industrial and residential suburbs. Leading industrialists fought the land-grasping downtown merchants, and TCI officials managed to keep the company's main mill in Fairfield, outside city limits. White workers, skilled and unskilled alike, gained power in the 1920s by linking their workday concerns with social and cultural conservatism. On the job, whites used union job classifications to retain a superior position to black workers. Before the Depression, the working-class electorate and the middle-class merchants who held political office held a shared faith in low taxes, balanced budgets, and limited government. Irascible James Jones, who served as the city's mayor from 1925 to his death in 1940, personified the convergence of mass and elite politics in Birmingham. After losing a leg in a December 1904 railroad accident, Jones became a bookkeeper. He then entered politics, first as tax collector in East Lake, a suburb annexed into Birmingham in 1910, and then as comptroller in Mayor Nathaniel Barrett's administration in the 1920s. A member of the Ku Klux Klan and also of the True Americans, an anti-Catholic political club, Jones also embraced the fiscal conservatism and civil service platform favored by Birmingham's wealthier residents.[40]

Both sides aimed their political artillery at Mayor Jones, who held the swing vote on the new city commission elected in 1937. Jones's colleagues, first-time commissioners "Bull" Connor and James Morgan, who would both serve in municipal government for the next two and a half decades, had staked opposite positions: Connor against public housing, Morgan for it. Connor had the backing of the "local gentry," a result of his support of civil service reform and his fiscal conservatism during consecutive terms, starting in 1934, in the state legislature. In time, this support would wane, but then "he had the backing of . . . the strictly corporate interests more than 100 percent in his race," one challenger wrote Senator Hugo Black.

The winning candidate interpreted his victory as a vindication of his opposition to higher taxes, while one newspaper attributed it to the voters' anti-incumbent leanings and their eagerness to end the rows among Jones and fellow commissioners Downs and Robinson. Whatever the cause, Connor, born in Selma in 1897 and a Birmingham resident since 1922, was a well-known figure in the town. He became the popular announcer of the city's Southern Association baseball team, the Birmingham Barons. As a radio broadcaster, Connor earned his nickname, "Bull," partly because of his constant chatter during games and also because of a contemporary *News* editorial cartoon about Dr. BUL Conner.[41]

Showing the divided political base in Birmingham, Morgan's victory had been helped by the endorsement of labor groups, who had not backed Connor. Born in 1891 in West End, another community annexed into Birmingham in 1910, Morgan, a minor league baseball player in Anniston and Bessemer, opened a radio dealership and repair shop near his boyhood home in 1922. Turning to politics in 1933, he had lost his bid for the commission by five hundred votes. By 1937, the *Post* called Morgan the city's top amateur promoter. "I propose to establish," Morgan announced during his campaign that year, "a department of the city government to give full-time cooperation to the Chamber of Commerce in a drive to build a bigger and better Birmingham." His boosterism made him a favorite of downtown merchants and businessmen as well as labor leaders.[42]

It was not uncommon for working-class and upper-income whites to support the same candidates in local races for they had broad areas of political common ground. Labor, for example, regularly backed fiscally conservative local government—unless it cost jobs. In 1938, for instance, real estate executive Smyer, elected that year to the state legislature, led the successful drive against an $8 million education bond that would have benefited the city's fiscally strapped schools. Working-class voters, one political analyst noted, showed the strongest opposition to the bond. The vote count "showed that [working-class] precincts like Pratt City, Wylam, West End, Ensley, East Lake, North Birmingham, and Acipco hit the proposed spending program harder than the city's so-called 'silk stocking' sectors."[43]

Reflecting its growing political strength, labor won the battle over public housing. In August 1938 Mayor Jones joined Morgan in backing the $4.2 million Elyton Village housing venture. To help sway Jones, the HABD agreed to pay between $15,000 and $16,000 annually in lieu of lost property taxes. Support for Elyton Village, where work began the next year, coalesced around its employment opportunities. "In building the slum clearances, we are helping labor conditions by putting men to work and giving business to lumber dealers and others handling building supplies," Morgan wrote Spain. The *News* estimated that the eighteen-month project would employ seventeen hundred workers. Jones signaled another link between public housing and labor when he named George Leigh, president of an AFL-affiliated organization, to replace the departed Snavely on the HABD's board, giving labor two of its five seats.[44]

The construction of Elyton Village again pulled Birmingham into Washington's funding vortex, opening up avenues of protest for the city's African Americans. This time, without an interest in housing conditions of the whites-only complex, black opposition centered on job opportunities. As part of an established policy to assist black workers, federal officials required that blacks receive their fair share of the work. In September 1933 Interior Secretary Harold Ickes had issued an order banning discrimination in all PWA projects. In 1934, Ickes, with Robert Weaver's assistance, had developed a labor quota system based on the federal occupational census. Local contractors needed to employ a fixed percentage of available skilled and unskilled black workers. Again, the issues focused more on economic matters than social concerns. Weaver believed that including blacks in the economic bounties of New Deal construction would transform American society. Like New Dealers and housers, he contended that attacking economic (and class) inequity could solve racial troubles in the South. In this case, the push came as much from Washington as it did from local black groups. Noticeably absent from the protests was Birmingham's NAACP branch, the main driver of the Smithfield controversies. Matters at Elyton Village concerned working-class blacks, and the NAACP's absence showed that socioeconomic distinctions within the black community could be powerful dividing forces.[45]

From the start, Elyton Village contractors proved unable or unwilling to meet the hiring quotas. Firms had to hire black laborers for 70 percent of the unskilled and 20 percent of the skilled work, according to USHA regulations. When the president of the Wreck-A-Pair Building Company asked for a release from the obligation, asserting that the local carpenters union informed him there were no blacks available, federal bureaucrats recognized the union's attempt to exclude black labor. The immediate past proved the union's claims false. During the work at Smithfield Court, contractors had employed twenty-seven black carpenters with union membership or permits; in fact, African Americans were represented in six of the twenty-three crafts and accounted for one in four skilled or semiskilled workers at Smithfield. Historically African Americans had not participated in the city's building trades unions; nonetheless, black carpenters formed a union in 1936. It remained intact for about a year and a half, or for the duration of the Smithfield Court construction.[46]

Arm-twisting by national housing officials seeking compliance with the agency's standards caused promises of change but few results. At first, Birmingham's white carpenters, bowing to pressure, agreed to sanction a separate black union. Paul Jackson, the union president, indicated that black workers would be available by mid-April. The HABD's Spain objected to Washington's direct intervention in the union's affairs. Despite the agreement and the flurry of letters and labor reports by USHA investigators, local contractors did not change their practices at the work site. As the rock drilling, steam shovel operations, and foundation work began, skilled black labor remained scarce at Elyton. The Perusini Construction Company worked three weeks with no skilled blacks before USHA district officials asked their superiors for advice about how to intervene. Furthermore, continuing delays in organizing black workers troubled USHA bureaucrats and prompted Walter Price, the agency's director of labor relations, to suggest that the local carpenters union either accept black members or issue work permits without charge to qualified black carpenters.[47]

The agency's full-scale inquiry into the matter revealed the tensions between white members of craft unions and black workers; it also showed the limits of federal intervention. One investigator, racial relations officer Clarence Johnson, contended that despite willing black leadership and a "sufficient Negro labor market in Birmingham to meet present contract specifications," few blacks found work at Elyton. Moreover, Johnson noted that HABD officials had merged skilled and semiskilled laborers on its compliance form in order it appear that it had met the quotas. Jefferson County Carpenters District Council leaders had resisted black membership and a separate union because they wanted the jobs for white workers, according to Leon Wofford, the USHA's labor inspector. Union leaders claimed that blacks had abandoned the organization in the years between the Smithfield and Elyton projects. They maintained that "they had spent [too] much time and money to get a slum clearance program in Birmingham" to lose jobs on the project. Besides fearing that nonunion or permit workers at Elyton might push down wage scales, labor leaders were loath to open their rolls to black workers when the union bosses had recently denied membership to white applicants because of job shortages.[48]

Even a series of deals to make union membership easier for blacks failed to alter the labor status quo. Wofford threatened to withhold future projects in an effort to force labor to the bargaining table. Three locals agreed to substantial reductions in their initiation fees, causing Wofford to advise the HABD and its contractors that they should soon employ black workers. Black carpenters forwarded twenty-seven names to the Birmingham locals; however, in late August with 85 percent of the foundation completed, the carpenters union officials claimed they could not provide black workers to the subcontractors at the site. Yet Wofford no longer blamed the union. He contended that he had "gone thoroughly into the Negro carpenters' trouble and as I see it there is nothing that can be done. The white carpenters have done everything humanly possible to get the Negro carpenters to join their locals. The Negroes just will not avail themselves of the opportunity in spite of the large amount of work in prospect."

Nonetheless, in the final year of the project, he expected that skilled black plasterers, cement finishers, and lathers, who belonged to unions, would be employed on the project.[49]

Although some black laborers initially supported Wofford's analysis, union obstinacy caused most to shift their views. At first L. M. Gaillard, a black plumber who had negotiated the August agreement, found the problems no "fault of the union at all." Financial problems plagued black workers, and the initiation fee proved a formidable barrier. Between August and October, just six black carpenters had been able to raise the $25 down payment, and the Perusini Company hired four of the six at Elyton. Over time, however, the agreement tended to break down at the construction sites. In May 1940 the Sheet Metal Workers Local 48 informed housing officials that it had no black sheet metal workers, roofers, or waterproofers. After the

J. A. Jones Construction Company fired the several black carpenters it had hired to frame roofs, the company announced that it had exhausted all means of complying with the federal rules and would henceforth ignore them. Gaillard, who now looked askance at local unions, tendered a substantial list of grievances about job discrimination. Even though black painters, carpenters, and bricklayers could have met the federal requirements, the unions were "not giving the colored fellows a fair chance as far as work is concerned." The quotas went unheeded because the contractors and unions wanted to hire as many white workers as possible, Gaillard claimed, and hired blacks only when not enough whites were available.[50]

Even the labor quotas—with seemingly clearer regulations and more explicit social implications—could not ensure fair treatment for Birmingham's blacks. For one, moderate and conservative goals girded the program, despite its apparent radicalism. Weaver, who carried the programs to the USHA when he went there as a racial relations officer, explained that "their objective was to retain past occupational advances for Negroes; they were not designed to open new types of employment." Officials intended the hiring quotas to bring economic opportunity, not social change. The hiring goals remained guidelines, not ironclad rules. Also, Washington officials were overworked, and they lacked enforcement mechanisms. Observation and arm-twisting might bring white union leaders to the bargaining table, but those tactics could not assure compliance at the construction site.[51]

In addition to Washington's uncertain policy aims, other constraints blocked efforts at change. The black carpenters, unlike the NAACP, lacked the resources and knowledge to form effective coalitions with federal bureaucrats. The NAACP's conspicuous absence from the Elyton protest revealed the economic divisions separating professional and working-class blacks in Birmingham as well. And social divisions blocked any meaningful link between white and black workers. There was no solidarity cutting across race lines in working-class Birmingham. White workers supported federal spending because it provided jobs. In troubled times, working-class whites showed no interest in the welfare of blacks, especially if it threatened their economic position. Finally, national housing officials never backed up their empty threat to block future public housing in Birmingham. In 1939, for instance, the housing authority, after several months of debate, approved two new public housing developments, one for whites and one for blacks, on the fringes of the downtown business district.[52]

Birmingham's participation in Washington's slum clearance and public housing programs illustrated the certainty of New Deal action but the uncertainty of New Deal reform. Loose alliances emerged, however, between municipal groups in Birmingham (including labor, businessmen's groups, and blacks) and the federal government. The depths of the economic depression forced local government to accept federal relief and construction programs and the accompanying oversight. In Birmingham, municipal government moved reluctantly and haphazardly. Even that limited action hinted at the new relationship among the levels of government. As the city comptroller Charles Armstrong said, it "stands to reason that the more our cities accept donations from the superior government, the greater will be the latter's attempt to dominate the lower levels." Conversely, Washington generated scores of proposed remedies for the Depression but remained unsure how to meld its concern for economic relief with social fairness, particularly in regard to race relations in the South. Oversight of federal programs was tentative or weak. Still, public housing underscored Washington's growing role in the city, beginning trends that diluted the authority of local elected officials in certain policy areas. In Armstrong's words, local government "can't be dependent and independent at the same time."[53]

CHAPTER TWO

# Hill-Burton Supports Tradition

A *Time* correspondent roving the South in the spring of 1941 found war-related activity restoring the region's economic health—and even paving new avenues of growth. "The South was a-clatter with new building," the reporter wrote. Nowhere was hope greater than in Birmingham, whose economy at long last again showed vigor. Workers rushed back into steel and iron factories. Tennessee Coal and Iron began a $26 million plant expansion at its Fairfield location, initially planned a decade earlier. City leaders, echoing the confidence of the 1920s, talked boldly about developing the region's industrial promise, and the Chamber of Commerce began a drive to attract businesses and factories. They also bid to make the city a center of the state's education system. In 1944, two dozen local doctors, bankers, and lawyers formed the Birmingham Citizens' Committee, with the sole purpose of trying to lure the University of Alabama's new medical college. That action would eventually tie Birmingham into the postwar federal grant machine. Even as local leaders envisioned the TCI expansion as proof of the city's economic health, the medical college unwittingly would prove to be the city's industry of the future.[1]

The process of selecting a site for the medical college mixed political and academic intrigue. First announced as a vague campaign pledge during Governor Frank Dixon's 1938 gubernatorial race, the idea took shape when his successor, Chauncey Sparks, named a university-wide committee to pick a location. Tuscaloosa, Montgomery, and Mobile loomed as rivals to Birmingham for the university's seventh attempt, dating back more than fifty years, to start its own medical school. Advocates for each city pressed their advantages: Tuscaloosa was the site of the main campus; Montgomery was the state capital; Mobile's city fathers promised to open civic coffers to build a new campus; and Birmingham was the state's largest city. Oscar Wells, chairman of the First National Bank and the driving force behind Birmingham's recruitment committee, wanted to make sure his city offered the best bid. Birmingham's edge rested on an endowment of $160,000 donated by more than one hundred businessmen to defray the school's start-up costs, and Jefferson County officials agreed to convey to the school a block that contained Hillman and Jefferson Hospitals. Jefferson, built with New Deal funds, and Hillman, renovated with federal grants in the 1930s, served as the county's charity wards, and they could provide a source of patients for clinical training.[2]

Civic pride swelled in February 1944 after the University of Alabama's trustees picked Birmingham over its rivals. The *Birmingham News* highlighted the achievement of the Wells committee. The city had received another boost when the school's new dean, Roy Kracke, an Alabama native hired several months earlier, had lobbied for Birmingham. Kracke imagined a "center of medical activities" surrounding the college modeled on the Rush Medical Center in Chicago, where he had completed his medical education. No other place in Alabama could match Birmingham's resources, he believed. A lean, almost skeletal, intense man, Kracke, the author of several medical textbooks during his tenure in Emory University's pathology department, did not shy from the challenge of creating Alabama's medical school. At Emory, his research into blood disease had led to several prestigious research awards, earning him the respect of the Birmingham medical community. His drive won him the favor of its businessmen. Still, Kracke's most important audience lay outside Birmingham in Tuscaloosa, where he had to appease anxious administrators, and in Montgomery, where he had to wring funds from tightfisted politicians and bureaucrats. Kracke's energy would be tested as he tried to build a school in Alabama that matched his ambitions.[3]

The medical college's early efforts to achieve financial solvency, battling constantly with a niggardly legislature, threatened to thwart Kracke's goals. The college's outlook changed, however, thanks to the expanding postwar grant state fashioned in the nation's capital, in particular the Hospital Construction and Survey Act of 1946. Federal grants acted as catalysts for local funding sources, and a medical center began to emerge on Birmingham's Southside. Soon city leaders contemplated how to extend the economic aid to other areas in the city, especially in 1949, when civil rights pressures challenged southern segregation. A decade-long attempt to build a separate hospital for blacks, one in which black physicians could practice, previously had been met with a combination of opposition and indifference, but white businessmen and politicians now realized that federal grants could provide critical dollars to complete the project. In addition to meeting the ill-served health needs of Birmingham's African American community, the project, backers argued, would demonstrate that segregation was not incompatible with fairness for blacks. Most whites and blacks supported using the Hill-Burton Act (the common name of the hospital construction legislation after its two main Senate architects—Lister Hill, a Democrat from Alabama, and Harold Burton, an Ohio Republican) to assist the Sisters of Charity's effort to build Holy Family, the black hospital that was completed in 1954. Through its early implementation, Hill-Burton reinforced local customs but at the uncontemplated cost of a growing reliance on Washington. That dependence could be ignored in the late 1940s and early 1950s (as it had been for the most part in the 1930s) when economic and social policy remained discrete. Over time Birmingham's (and the medical college's) appetite for federal grant-in-aid funding increased—and Washington's policy aims would eventually shift.

In 1945, the Alabama Building Commission, the state government branch that funded capital projects, bought a handful of properties adjoining the hospitals, creating a three-and-a-half block site on the city's Southside for the new school. The school's earliest blueprints called for four additional hospitals, several medical clinics, and an educational center for returning veterans. (The university's existing Birmingham extension campus, established in 1936, was housed in a former residence on the northern edge of the city's downtown business district.) Kracke opened talks with local officials to bring the county's health department, a Veterans Administration hospital, and the university's new school of dentistry to the college's domain. The dean wanted to relocate the city's pediatric hospital and the state's psychiatric facility as well as build a "Negro Hospital." Other groups matched Kracke's enthusiasm. Administrators in Tuscaloosa announced their intentions to start a cancer foundation, and the Junior Chamber of Commerce promised to establish a mental hygiene clinic.[4]

State budgetary constraints tempered Kracke's expansive ambitions. Decades would pass before many of the dean's ideas reached fruition. A poor state with the second lowest per capita income in the nation in 1948, Alabama had a stingy legislature to match. Although voters in 1946 passed a $5 million bond issue that included $1.2 million to retire Jefferson Hospital's federal Reconstruction Finance Company loan, state money was tight, especially to fund the college's operations. The legislature, moreover, waited two years to fund the dental school it had created in 1945. Plans for another one and a half blocks for more medical buildings and a three-block park on the campus's western boundary went unfulfilled. The state government's penuriousness forced Kracke to use all his cleverness and savvy to fulfill his goals. In Alabama, where football was now king, the medical school dean found $350,000 in the university's athletic department budget to acquire residences for instructors and dormitories for students. With the money, the medical school bought an apartment building one block south of its hospitals. The fifty students in the school's first class had a place to live.[5]

A 1946 American Medical Association (AMA) report revealed the school's uncertain footing. The AMA accreditation team, led by Dr. Victor Johnson, found that the "school seems to have captured the imagination, loyalty and support of the people, government officials . . . as well as the medical profession." Yet Johnson frankly stated that most of its liabilities resulted from the inadequate state funding. AMA investigators also disparaged Jefferson County's unwillingness to pay the full daily cost of indigent patients, a deficit that sapped the college's operating budget. In this battle, the Birmingham-based school received lukewarm support from the administration in Tuscaloosa. University of Alabama president John Gallalee, for instance, agreed with the legislators who said the state should not pay for indigent care. Overall, the rural-dominated legislature did not want to subsidize "wealthy Jefferson County," a medical school administrator commented.[6] Overcrowding in the outpatient clinic buildings impaired proper instruction. Although Johnson ultimately recommended accreditation, he concluded that the Alabama school needed an "extensive building program" to facilitate future growth. The medical college, however, lacked a capital fund for those improvements.[7]

Because of the disputes over financing, Kracke constantly feuded with county politicians as well as his bosses in Tuscaloosa. At one point, relations between the medical dean and Gallalee became so strained—and the college's budget so tight—that the university president decided to countersign all medical school checks. In 1948, county officials and the *Birmingham Post* accused Kracke of mismanagement after a state audit revealed that the college had paid $3,121 to suppliers "for the disappearance of 90,000 milk bottles over a period of 18 months." In his defense, the dean said the school's budget shortfalls made it more economical to keep the bottles "for the serving of fruit juices, soft drinks, et cetera, to the patients" instead of returning them for refunds. "This is done," he said, "because at three cents the new bottle is the cheapest that we can obtain containers for such purposes." Two years later, the college's finances were so precarious that administrators worried that a recession would close the school. It already paid the lowest wage among area hospitals, resulting in heavy turnover in personnel. The constant monetary battles drained Kracke, and he knew that the public attacks against the school would hurt future funding efforts. "Of course, we cannot expect legislation to be enacted that will channel more money into an institution which the public believes to be mismanaged by its administrative officers," he told a reporter.[8]

Congressional legislation rejuvenated the Birmingham medical college's moribund expansion plans. Two weeks before the AMA's accreditation team visited the campus, Congress passed the Hospital Survey and Construction Act of 1946. The act, cosponsored by Alabama's Hill, sought to stimulate statewide health planning by subsidizing hospital construction. A Montgomery native and the son of a physician, Hill had been named after a famous British surgeon, Sir Joseph Lister, under whom Hill's father had studied in London. In addition to statewide grants for hospital surveys, the federal government would pay from one-third to two-thirds of approved hospital construction costs. First, the federal Public Health Service (PHS) had to accept each state's plan; then, the federal agency could begin to disperse grants according a formula that, because of its reliance on population and per capita income, favored poorer states with fewer hospital beds. Congressmen like Hill, a staunch economic New Dealer, wanted the government to subsidize the expansion of and improvements to the nation's infrastructure. The foray into health policy was similar to postwar efforts to build roads and houses. Historians of federal policy have noted that the legislators favored grants because they acted as a "device for projecting federal policy into new areas without raising troublesome questions about federal power."[9]

Hill-Burton had been created to favor hospital construction in rural areas; its implementation proved otherwise. Much of the bill was vague, typical of federal grant policy, and its loose language allowed states to manipulate the law. Many states targeted money for nonrural uses. As one scholar of medical history wrote, Hill-Burton, in time, provided for "strong urban medical centers on the one hand and rural community hospitals on the other." Moreover, in promoting the new legislation, the Alabama senator had wanted to limit federal oversight in its application. Hill continually referred to the bill as a "strong states' right law" that left the administration of hospitals in local hands. While that comment reflected the belief that local administrators and planners knew their communities best, it meant that southerners could continue to practice segregation in Hill-Burton facilities.[10]

Although Hill-Burton was not originally crafted to benefit them, American medical school officials, like Kracke, recognized the powerful possibilities in the new federal law. The bill could be the source of funding so difficult to come by from state legislatures and local governments. A *News* editorial reflected the community's anticipation of the law, noting that while Hill-Burton focused on rural hospitals, it hoped that a "sufficiently broad interpretation of meeting those needs will prevail so that certain portions of the Medical Center program in Birmingham may benefit." No doubt Birmingham needed improved health care facilities. With 2,049 hospital beds for the region's 640,000 people, Birmingham's facilities could be doubled before meeting Hill-Burton's minimum standards.[11]

Kracke exchanged letters with state and local health officials trying to fashion a strategy that would capture grant money. To do so, he readjusted the school's building program. Kracke declined federal assistance for a two-story addition to the Hillman outpatient clinic, allowing school officials to request a more ambitious Hill-Burton proposal for a new dental school building. The move carried risks because no one yet knew how state health planners and Washington bureaucrats would react to requests for research and educational facilities under the Hill-Burton law. Kracke knew the college's application would have to be creative. The medical school dean revealed his strategy, writing Gallalee that if the structure "could be construed as being an addition to the hospital, there might be a chance for such aid." The college's final building application included three dental beds so that it could qualify as a "hospital."[12]

Jefferson County health officer George Denison, an advocate of the medical center idea, also worked to ensure that Hill-Burton would help Birmingham. Since 1944 Denison had sought to link the health department to the medical college—and he enlisted the federal health bill to that end. In 1946, he pushed for a new public health building next to Jefferson Hospital. At the peak of wartime prosperity, Birmingham's commissioners had set aside $175,000 for the project, an amount matched by the county government. Hill-Burton enlarged Denison's plans. In 1947 Joseph Mountin, the PHS's southern region director, delivered $312,000 to Denison for construction on the $1 million building (the state also kicked in $300,000), which would house the health department, the county medical society, and other local health care agencies. The building, the first of its kind constructed under Hill-Burton, was a move toward the fulfillment of Kracke's vision of a medical center.[13]

Hill-Burton gave shape to a fledgling medical center on the city's Southside. In November 1949, state planners and the PHS's Mountin approved a $1.2 million seven-story building for the college's dentistry school and additional clinics, with federal grants providing one-third of the costs. The grant justified Kracke's earlier decision to wait for the bigger project. The PHS also paid one-third of the costs for the $1.5 million Crippled Children's

Hospital across the street from Jefferson Hospital and a part of Kracke's original master plan. The one-hundred-bed, privately run charity hospital was an autonomous unit within the Southside medical district; however, it functioned as an orthopedic observation and teaching adjunct for the college. When the hospital opened in 1951, the *Post* called it the "House that football built" because the lion's share of the $1 million local funding had been raised by the annual battle between the city's top high school teams. (Other area hospitals dipped into the federal coffers. Carraway Methodist Hospital received $200,000 to add a nursing wing. Moreover, the PHS approved St. Vincent Hospital's request for a new wing to house a maternity ward and ninety general use beds. St. Vincent's officials had been unable to raise enough money for the six-story addition until Washington contributed $500,000.)[14]

The grant-in-aid's influence at the Southside medical center could be measured in what was built there—and in what was not. Even though the PHS's program provided a minority share, the act's dollars stretched the ambition of health care planners and prodded local and state officials into action. Hill-Burton made "available funds for vastly more adequate buildings and equipment than heretofore had been contemplated," Kracke believed. When Congress cut funding for health facility construction in 1950 and again in 1951 it stymied the medical school dean's efforts to relocate the Children's Hospital to the Southside as well as plans to develop a 250-bed tuberculosis sanitarium.[15]

If not all developments in Birmingham's medical complex relied on Hill-Burton, they did involve federal aid of some fashion. The Veterans Administration (VA), for instance, helped stabilize the school's financial woes and it assisted the medical center concept. In 1946, the VA forged its relationship with the medical school when it purchased a city block from the cash-strapped college and began to build an eighty-bed hospital. The step represented a fundamental shift in agency policy, one that Kracke and other medical college deans had championed. In the postwar years, the VA began to locate its new hospitals in urban medical centers, reversing its previous practice of targeting rural areas for stand-alone facilities.[16]

The decision to sell the property to the VA affected one of Kracke's original ideas for the medical center: a hospital for blacks. The drive to build a black hospital predated Kracke's Birmingham tenure, beginning early in the decade as a result of the city's scarce medical facilities for blacks and growing demands during the war years for more equal treatment. Serious plans for a black hospital emerged in 1943 when local NAACP leaders, physicians, and prominent ministers formed the Birmingham and Jefferson County Negro Hospital Association (NHA). The group included NAACP attorney Arthur Shores, Bishop B. G. Shaw, Dr. H. H. Brewer, Dr. S. F. Harris, Rev. Preston Davis, Dr. E. W. Taggart, Oscar Adams, and H. D. Coke, editor of the biweekly *Birmingham World*. Several NHA members had been active in the Smithfield Court housing protests a decade earlier. Although ninety-seven businesses and twenty-seven hundred African Americans had donated at least $10 to become "lifetime" members of the NHA drive, the group had reached just 10 percent of its goal. NHA organizers needed to raise $300,000 to construct a one-hundred-bed hospital. When their efforts faltered, they approached white social welfare liberals to assist the project. White advisory board members included Denison; First National Bank of Birmingham trust officer Charles Zukoski; Erskine Ramsay, an octogenarian philanthropist who had made his fortune in coal mining; George Mattison Jr., president of the Woodstock Slag Corporation; and American Federation of Labor leader William Mitch. Later in 1943, after a second campaign, the pace of contributions increased, but the donations still fell far short of the target.[17]

The NHA effort represented the progressive edge of Birmingham's race relations. While some whites wanted to improve housing, education, and health care for blacks, this had to occur within the confines of Jim Crow. As Zukoski later reflected, before the Supreme Court's 1954 *Brown v. Board of Education* decision, few white liberals in Birmingham had become sufficiently "emboldened to face up to the necessity of desegregation." Before *Brown,* however, biracial committees could discuss how to improve the conditions for blacks without seeming to threaten the racial caste. Nonetheless, in the pre-*Brown* era, interracial dialogue often outweighed action. For the most part, the black middle class accepted these terms. The determination of whites to maintain racial supremacy cut across socioeconomic lines. White workers in the district's manufacturing plants and mines used union rules to keep blacks in subordinate positions. At the same time, social welfare organizations, led by white business leaders, maintained control over organizations dedicated to black uplift. Nothing better demonstrated the limitations of the social welfare activism than the failure to form a National Urban League branch in Birmingham, one of several examples of a swelling of race-conscious resistance during the war years that included challenges to segregated seating on city buses and to racial zoning laws. In fact, several of the whites who fought against a National Urban League office, viewed as a threat because of its links to organized labor, were key participants on interracial committees, whether through the local Community Chest or the NHA. In 1950, after blocking the Urban League office, white elites formed an interracial committee of the Jefferson County Coordinating Council of Social Forces, an umbrella group of charities. The interracial group discussed matters of concern to the city's African American community such as public health, housing, transportation, black police, and education but took few concrete steps in its six-year existence. It crumbled after the *Brown* ruling made even its moderation untenable.[18]

Kracke's idea to include a hospital for blacks in the medical center fit within the parameters of Birmingham's separate society. It also met a need; Alabama placed second to last in the nation in the number of general hospital beds at the end of World War II. Just two hundred beds, scattered through city hospitals and in facilities operated by major industrial employers like TCI, served the region's two hundred thousand blacks. The Community Chest also funded a twelve-bed clinic in a predominantly black community in north Birmingham. The medical school dean's plan was more tangible than past talk. The "demonstration of our concern for the health of our total population" set aside a specific half-block parcel for the NHA to purchase. Kracke attended several of the group's meetings to keep them informed of the medical school's building plan. Then the effort fell apart after the school cut a deal with the VA, disappointing the NHA's black members. The college's financial instability made it imperative to sell space to "allied institutions which are now ready to proceed with their building program," Kracke wrote Bishop Shaw in January 1946. Though the land was sold, Kracke continued to work to add medical facilities for blacks. In time, Hill-Burton provided a solution, although in the short run the legislation reinforced traditional racial relations.[19]

Still committed to "a separate hospital unit where Negro doctors can bring their private patients," Kracke forwarded several alternatives to the NHA's white advisory committee and medical school administrators. In one option, the fourteenth floor of segregated Jefferson Hospital would become a sixty-bed unit where black physicians could treat their patients. This could occur after the new dental building alleviated overcrowding in Jefferson. A second suggestion called for a separate black unit in Hillman Hospital, now emptied of patients and used for administrative offices, classrooms, and research laboratories. The ideas won a broad range of support: from Robert Durr, the African American who edited the *Birmingham Weekly Review* and chaired the Community Chest's Negro Advisory Council, to the *News,* whose editorial pages championed the establishment of a black hospital.[20]

Strict boundaries shaped Kracke's actions even though federal health officials found him to be "aggressive and not bound by tradition." In September 1946, Kracke closed down a training program for black nurses he had started several months earlier after space shortages caused white and black trainees occasionally to share equipment. The most vocal critic was University of Alabama trustee Hill Ferguson, a seventy-year-old Birmingham developer. Ferguson, a strident segregationist, would only become more reactionary during his remaining decade on the board. The university's board also included Gessner McCorvey, a Mobile businessman who would help lead the state's Dixiecrat revolt in 1948. Although Kracke wrote a local businessman that the training program would be halted until "facilities can be provided for proper segregation of students," he never restarted it.[21]

With Kracke's plans for a black hospital at a standstill, another group stepped into the breach. In July 1948, the Sisters of Charity, a Catholic order based in Nazareth, Kentucky, announced plans to build a sixty-bed hospital. The order had been active in Birmingham since 1943, when it opened a twelve-bed infirmary in Tuxedo by joining three shotgun shacks and borrowing equipment. It planned a new facility in the same section of Ensley. The Sisters, who had saved $60,000, kicked off a fund drive with white and "colored" divisions. The nuns sought another $450,000. Kracke backed the project, calling it "imperative that something be done to provide the Negro physician with adequate facilities to practice medicine." The Sisters' timing had been influenced by the county health department's decision to close a local maternity clinic that served blacks. The seven-year-old Slossfield Maternity Clinic had depended on annual grants of $46,000 from the federal Children's Bureau. Denison, the county health officer, said the clinic could not operate without the federal grants that had been cut. The Mineral District Medical Society, the organization representing the region's two dozen African American doctors, demanded replacement facilities, as did the local newspapers and the Young Men's Business Club. A *News* editorial noted: "We require segregation in Birmingham by city ordinance; yet we make it almost impossible for Negroes to be treated by members of their own race when they are ill, and we make it completely impossible for a Negro to enter a Birmingham hospital and be treated by a Negro doctor. As we have pointed out many times before, there is not one bed in a single accredited hospital in this county of half a million people, more than 40 percent of whom are colored, in which a sick Negro can be treated by a doctor of his race."[22]

As the Catholic charity's fund drive languished—raising just $87,000 of its $540,000 goal—a series of events jarred the local indifference. At the national level, President Harry Truman's election augured a changing racial climate. His successful campaign, which had included appeals to blacks in northern cities, along with the Dixiecrats' bolt from the convention, worried southerners who feared increased scrutiny over racial matters. Local issues heightened these concerns. Demands by Birmingham blacks for better housing initiated a protracted struggle over the racial composition of a city neighborhood. Beginning in the spring of 1949, several middle-class blacks tried to move into homes they had purchased on Center Street North in Smithfield. White vigilantes met the attempts with violence, bombing several homes throughout the summer. (In 1949, attorney Arthur Shores, who had fought the city commission's creation of a "buffer" residential district in Smithfield, would challenge the zoning ordinance in federal court, a case he won the next year.) While many white civic leaders fretted, John Newsome, Birmingham's congressional representative from 1945 to 1949, envisioned how federal grants could reinforce segregation. The former congressman urged local leaders to make Holy Family a Hill-Burton hospital. Federal aid, according to Newsome, could serve multiple purposes: it could reduce the need for local contributions, which had been hard to come by; it could remedy uneven medical care for blacks; and by providing better facilities it could "answer to those clamoring for civil rights legislation."[23]

Birmingham's white business class responded to the appeals. In the fall of 1949, Donald Comer, chairman of Avondale Mills, and Louis Pizitz, owner of an eponymous department store, took over the Holy Family fund-raising campaign. (The rechristened Negro Hospital Drive, operated out of the Junior Chamber of Commerce's offices, sought $150,000 to add to the nearly $100,000 held by the Sisters. The organizers also would request Hill-Burton funding equal to twice the local donation.) The son of former governor Braxton Bragg Comer, who had founded the successful textile mill, Comer was an active member of the Community Chest. His decision to champion the Holy Family campaign meshed easily with his core belief in segregation. To Comer, like Newsome, the community need (better health services for blacks) and the racial agenda intermingled. The textile magnate urged fellow white businessmen to contribute because "failure would be seized with glee by enemies of our way of life as a demonstration that they have been right and we have been wrong." Blacks and whites could coexist only in a segregated world, according to Comer, who believed that the Truman administration's and the Supreme Court's renewed attention to civil rights required improved separate-but-equal facilities. "This hospital matter is a real test," Comer wrote Mayor Cooper Green, "of whether we mean it when we say we can handle our own problems." Pizitz, an immigrant who had built his small retail shop into the city's second-largest department store, also contended that the Holy Family campaign could burnish an image tarnished by the recent spate of home bombings. Already Birmingham had a rough reputation dating back to labor violence in the 1930s. "I don't want Birmingham to be known as a place where people are flogged and their homes bombed," he wrote Green. "I want it to be known as a place where those who are financially successfully are glad to help our good public causes without regard to race or religion."[24]

Even with notables leading it and with extensive coverage from the three daily newspapers, the Holy Family drive took nearly a year. The leadership, including Green, the city's Episcopal bishop, and the president of the Chamber of Commerce, formed an auxiliary black division to solicit money in the African American community. Most black professionals supported it, and blacks contributed one-sixth of the $232,000 eventually raised in the drive. Birmingham's plan for a separate black facility was consistent with actions throughout the South. Atlanta's civic leaders, for instance, won federal grants totaling nearly $1.2 million to build a blacks-only wing for the city-operated Grady Memorial Hospital. The 116-bed wing would help to reverse the fact that in Atlanta "Negroes with moderate incomes had been taking a beating on hospital care." In Birmingham, construction workers broke ground for the sixty-two-bed hospital in September 1952 and finished it sixteen months later.[25]

In Birmingham, like Atlanta, some in the black middle class objected to the Hill-Burton hospital because they believed it solidified segregation. *Birmingham World* editor Emory Jackson was the most vocal critic against a project that came only "within the framework of southern tradition, meaning segregation." Whereas most members of Birmingham's black professional class accepted the efforts by white civic leaders to manage social change within the bounds of tradition, it was not unusual for Jackson, an editor at the biweekly since 1932, to be at odds with them. Active in the local and state NAACP branches, Jackson, known for his prickly manner, had an outlet in his column "The Tip-Off." In the early 1950s, he temporarily quit the civil rights organization because of a personal feud with the local chapter head, and his refusal to go along with the majority was evident in battles over Holy Family. In a typically caustic letter about the hospital, Jackson, a Morehouse College graduate, blasted fellow Omega Psi Phi fraternity members for sullying their names by supporting the fund drive's auxiliary committee. "The Brothers . . . should make up their minds, it seems to me," he wrote, "whether they intend to strive toward the realization of the program of the Fraternity's Social Action Objectives or undermine those noble goals through identification and services in those movements ingeniously designed to defeat the enlightened program of first-class citizenship and unsegregated opportunities for all American citizens." The local NAACP branch and the Mineral District Medical Society also attracted his ire for abandoning their principles. While Holy Family's patients would be black, the staff would be interracial and blacks would be denied policy-making power, the editor contended. "It would seem that the 'all-Negro' angle of the Holy Family Hospital is in a deliberate effort to set an unfortunate pattern in Alabama."[26]

Many of Jackson's testy remarks were unfair because they oversimplified the choices confronting other blacks such as members of the Mineral District Medical Society. The black physicians' group supported Holy Family because increased facilities met a real community health need, and they wanted open access at all local hospitals. Furthermore, the physicians did not abandon their interest in the medical center; they worked to build constructive professional relationships with their white colleagues. In June 1951, for instance, the Mineral District Medical Society used the college auditorium for its annual meeting and the labs for the clinical sessions. Nor did the NAACP ignore the medical center. In the early 1950s, the civil rights group monitored the treatment of staff at the VA hospital, investigated rumors that the hospital had a gentleman's agreement not to accept black patients, and asked Governor Gordon Persons to open the medical college to all qualified students regardless of race. Throughout the 1950s black students sought admission to various units in the college.[27] Yet Jackson was right when he noted that whites would not integrate facilities if they could avoid it. Acting Medical School dean Tinsley Harrison summarized the basic question in a 1951 letter to a university trustee:

> A physician who has charge of a private patient in any hospital must necessarily assume authority over all who participate in the care of the patient. We have some negro nurses but we do not have negro technicians, dietitians, interns, residents. . . . If we assign our people in these various positions to responsibilities which involve taking orders from negro physicians they would probably leave us and seek positions elsewhere. If we did not assign such responsibilities to these individuals, the negro doctor would be unable to give proper service to his patient and both patient and physician could justifiably accuse us of unfair discrimination.[28]

Yet at the beginning of the 1950s, the more striking and everyday concern to the medical school's administrators and supporters was its financial health. The agreement with Jefferson County for care of indigent patients remained the college's principal fiscal drain, and the state's stinginess exacerbated those problems. School administrators fought continuously with county officials to increase the county government's daily patient payment. County commissioners balked, saying that they already spent $700,000 annually on University Hospital (the renamed Jefferson Hospital). College officials openly worried that if they raised rates they would lose patients needed to train doctors but if they did not raise the rates revenue would be drained from other purposes.[29]

At the same time, the school faced a leadership crisis. Kracke, the school's first dean, died suddenly in June 1950 while on the road to Sylacauga to visit a patient. Birmingham native Tinsley Harrison, who received his medical training at Johns Hopkins University, returned to his hometown from Dallas, where he had helped to organize the Southwest Medical School, to serve as interim dean until a search committee found a permanent replacement. A heart surgeon, Harrison became chairman of the school's department of medicine after serving for a year as acting dean. Kracke's replacement, James J. Durrett, a former federal Food and Drug Administration official, was a bureaucrat, not a visionary. The University of Alabama's trustees picked Durrett in 1951 because after a long career in federal public health agencies, he seemed to be a technocrat, able and willing to manage a complex organization. Moreover, he had spent much of his career in Washington. Yet Durrett lacked the personal dynamism and leadership skills needed to guide the school, and, in many people's eyes, the school languished. Never a practicing physician, Durrett failed to win the confidence of the faculty, even though the Tuscaloosa native had graduated from Harvard Medical School. Also, he struggled to persuade key businessmen about the school's prospects. In 1952, for instance, the Committee of 100, a civic group focused on industrial recruitment, refused to lobby the state legislature on the school's behalf for more funding, even though the committee featured the medical college in its promotional literature. Worse, Alabama Power executive Thomas Martin donated money to the fledgling Southern Research Institute rather than to the medical school.[30]

During Durrett's tenure, a pervasive unease permeated the medical center. The college "suffered from an insufficiency of financial support and of physical facilities, from mediocre teaching in some departments and from a lack of research activity in most," the school's top clinical faculty member wrote a university trustee. Kracke's goals remained unachieved. Earlier plans for a cancer institute, a pediatric hospital, an expanded general education campus, and a mental health facility never left the drawing boards. More recent additions to that blueprint—improvements for the medical school such as expanded outpatient clinics, an X-ray department, a rehabilitation center, a new library and office building, and dormitories—floundered because of federal and state funding cutbacks. In April 1951, a finance subcommittee of the state legislature reported that the medical college needed a stronger administration, more patients, and better planning. Despite its criticism, the report did not significantly increase state funding. Medical college administrators would have to look outside Alabama to build the school's future.[31]

CHAPTER THREE

# Federal Urban Renewal in an Era of Decline

A postwar *Saturday Evening Post* series of profiles of American cities pointed up contrasts between Birmingham and Atlanta. Harold Martin's essay about the Alabama city contended that "Birmingham has been the South's No. 1 industrial promise for nearly 70 years." The magazine's report about Atlanta, however, focused not on potential but on action and results. By 1945, Atlanta had three thousand branch offices of national firms, and over the next two years the Chamber of Commerce's Industrial Bureau, the city's two-decades old recruitment arm, helped lure more than three hundred new facilities and several thousand jobs to the metropolitan region. Even as Birmingham leaders spoke of a rivalry with Atlanta, the Georgia capital had consolidated its edge during the war years, notably by solidifying its position as the federal government's southeastern nerve center. Moreover, at the end of World War II, the value of products manufactured in Atlanta, the *Saturday Evening Post* alerted its readers, outstripped "those of her huffing, puffing industrial sister, Birmingham" 130 miles to the east.[1]

The end of the Depression nevertheless brought a return of optimism to Birmingham's leaders that in time would yield to a sense of foreboding, an underlying gloom, about the city's future. Results rarely matched ambition in the Magic City. Even wartime growth had circumscribed effects, as revealed in a Chamber of Commerce campaign to lure federal agencies and new businesses to Birmingham, a battle that had begun during the 1930s. Local "transportation systems are not bogged down with war workers or new plants, since Birmingham industries merely converted from peace time production to war goods. Here, there was no great influx of war workers," a Chamber report explained. After the war, with the industrial economy at full production, when "the retail business [was] unbelievably good, the stores . . . crowded, and the streets full of people," the city seemed poised to resume its battle against Atlanta. This is "Birmingham's golden opportunity to cash in on its wealth of natural resources," said Ervin Jackson, an insurance and banking executive who chaired the Chamber. To diversify the city's manufacturing base and build its white-collar workforce, Jackson helped to establish the Birmingham District Industrial Development Corporation. Recruitment committees formed, failed, and disbanded throughout the late 1940s. The insurance executive and his colleagues watched with alarm as Atlanta and other southern cities christened new branch offices and plants.[2]

Dissatisfaction over the inability to build on wartime prosperity occasionally boiled over into acrimony. Charges flew in late 1946 after both the Ford Motor Company and the General Motors Corporation (GM) announced plans for assembly plants in suburban Atlanta. (In addition, Jackson and others observed the opening of GM and Borg-Warner auto parts plants and two steel-based construction materials plants in Chattanooga, Tennessee's own gritty iron-and-steel town.) A veterans' group falsely charged that Ford—and also GM and Chrysler—had intended to locate in Bessemer, Birmingham's industrial suburb, until TCI refused to sell it steel. "They were all very enthusiastic over the prospects of coming here—but, as I say, something very strange happened. That strange thing that happened was a lot of interference thrown in the way by [TCI]," George Banks wrote Mayor Cooper Green. Birmingham recruiters had not sought the Ford plant, nor had the automakers come calling; the corporations picked Atlanta for the advantages of its distribution network, and "no other locations were given serious consideration." Birmingham's iron and steel economy did not prove a viable foundation for postwar greatness. Record orders at existing plants, for one, shut off the possibility of manufacturing diversification as firms continued the same production lines to meet backlogged orders. The city's industrial history—that left it with a highly unionized labor force earning a higher wage than its counterparts in the region and a rough-and-tumble reputation for labor violence—caused business agents touring the South for new plant sites to bypass Birmingham. Finally, local business leaders divided (generally industrialists against emerging commercial interests) over whether to pursue manufacturing or white-collar jobs more aggressively.[3]

Switching tactics, Green pushed suburban annexation as the key to Birmingham's postwar development. In 1948 the mayor, a former Tarrant City real estate and insurance agent who had been the city postmaster for nine years before his electoral victory in 1940, organized the Greater Birmingham Citizens Committee. The group pressed to annex outlying residential and industrial suburbs to enlarge the city's tax base, in part so the city commission could fulfill a $29 million capital campaign to improve city services that had been deferred during the war. A year later, with a merger vote upcoming, an optimistic Green even lectured Atlanta Civitan Club members that his city was "pushing ahead" of theirs, a prediction premised on a successful merger that would boost Birmingham's population ahead of Atlanta's. To be sure, growth in Birmingham fueled Green's boast, but the mayor's myopic focus on the center city caused him to misinterpret the relative positions of the two southeastern metropolises. In truth, during the 1940s, the population in metropolitan Atlanta boomed and its job base diversified (especially in outlying regions), while the Birmingham area remained stagnant in comparison.[4]

The merger drive ultimately failed, and it exposed divisions within the city's white economic elite. The commissioners also split, with Eugene "Bull" Connor opposing his colleagues Green and James Morgan. Downtown business groups and the city's three daily newspapers supported Green. Birmingham's manufacturing interests, who had long fought to keep their largest plants outside the city's boundaries and away from its taxes, opposed the merger. Indeed, in 1948 officials at TCI, Woodward Iron and Steel, Republic Steel, and Sloss-Sheffield had blocked a statewide ballot initiative to change Alabama's annexation laws to favor cities over outlying areas. The "Big Mules" had their own editorial support in *Alabama: The News Magazine of the Deep South,* which was funded by manufacturers, and the local Congress of Industrial Organizations (CIO) union bosses backed their employers. Green tried to make the industrialists' intransigence a centerpiece of the campaign, briefly reviving the rumor that TCI blocked Ford's and GM's plans to locate near Birmingham in order to tie the merger effort to business recruitment goals. TCI treated the city "like a company town" and had "posed as our benefactor in times of need. Now is the time to call their [*sic*] hand and look at the FACTS," read a Greater Birmingham Committee advertisement. Industrialists dismissed such appeals. Donald Comer, chairman of Avondale Mills, contended that TCI paid about one-fifth of the total wages in the Birmingham district. "Those of us who have lived many years in Birmingham recognize that TCI has perhaps made the greatest single contribution of any enterprise or individual to the building of Birmingham," he reasoned. A CIO pamphlet noted that industry would be harmed if it were "subjected to heavy municipal taxes and regulations."[5]

Green later targeted a second scapegoat to explain Atlanta's relative advantage over Birmingham and the need for annexation. This time, he directed his ire toward the federal government, in particular the Census Bureau for overcounting Atlanta's population in 1940, giving the Georgia capital an unfair recruiting advantage. Ford and "other commercial agencies chose Atlanta for the same reason," Green charged, adding that he had the "correspondence to prove it." Though false, the mayor's conspiracy theory resonated with the widespread belief in Washington's essential role in the postwar urban economy. As postwar optimism faded in Birmingham, hopes for growth once again became attached to pro-development, Washington-based grants—the Housing Act of 1949, in this case—that provided the seed money and the initiative to contemplate projects not possible with local resources alone. Politicians and Birmingham's increasingly powerful real estate interests first focused slum clearance and renewal efforts on the area surrounding the University of Alabama Medical College. Organizing the project revealed growing divisions among the city's business class; executing the plans again illustrated that Birmingham's African Americans gained leverage through federal intervention. Black protests in 1953 caused slight alterations to the city's renewal proposal, an activism that became more threatening following the Supreme Court's 1954 *Brown v. Board of Education* ruling. Just as the pro-growth, moderating leadership seemed ready to take root in the Alabama city, race—specifically, the preservation of segregation—became the number one issue for many of Birmingham's middle- and working-class residents. A second redevelopment effort in Avondale in 1955 and Connor's return to power in 1957 highlighted the widening political and social fissures in the city. With signs of economic decline abounding in the 1950s, the city's commercial interests tried to forward a pro-growth agenda (reliant on federal aid) increasingly at odds with the views of the majority of Birmingham's voters.[6]

The Housing Act of 1949 offered new opportunities to rebuild cities throughout the nation. Local elites took advantage of the bill's commercial slant. Initiated as a wartime measure to revitalize the moribund government-subsidized housing program, the act, which gained bipartisan support when it became clear that returning veterans would swamp the nation's existing residential market, ended up as an economic development bill. The purpose changed as Congress made it more palatable to conservative politicians and tried to mollify powerful real estate lobbies who had opposed it. The law differed from its predecessor, the United States Housing Act of 1937, because the number of new homes built no longer needed to match the number of dilapidated houses razed by a city. A Housing and Home Finance Agency (HHFA) report for local governments heralded the bill's potential for urban rejuvenation and underscored the federal government's capacity to bankroll local enterprise. Under the main terms of the housing bill, the HHFA would pay two-thirds of the acquisition and clearance costs of locally initiated projects, and the agency's report, titled "Slum Clearance Under the Housing Act of 1949," emphasized that new housing—whether public or private—need not replace cleared slums. The law supported the clearance of areas that were either residential before clearance or would be redeveloped for housing. The act's requirement that cities ensure "decent, safe, and sanitary" permanent housing options for displaced slum dwellers received scant attention in the agency's bulletin. The grant-in-aid law attached few specific conditions beyond requiring the HHFA's approval of locally conceived redevelopment plans, but applicants did have to "comply with such other conditions as the [HHFA] Administrator finds" before receiving funding.[7]

The grant program helped usher a new era in Birmingham. Harold Harper, the director of the Housing Authority of the Birmingham District the local agency that would implement the federal law, moved to build a consensus around it. The bill arrived at an opportune time because the medical college's opening in 1945 had revived the debate about slum clearance, in part because mixed-income African American neighborhoods surrounded the school. The Jefferson County Health Department began a long-range property survey that year that officials expected to use as the basis of an antislum drive. Those plans remained stalled because of strong opposition to government-subsidized housing for the displaced and meager local funding. The Housing Act altered the terms of the debate. While some officials, such as county health officer George Denison, championed building replacement homes with the new subsidies, Harper recognized that the new bill had a diluted emphasis on housing. The current legislation, unlike its 1937 predecessor, favored downtown redevelopment projects, which would prove an easier sell in Birmingham. Even though the housing authority supervised more than fifteen hundred units for whites and one thousand units for blacks, public housing brought objections from real estate interests. To push for projects consistent with the altered intent of the legislation, Harper sought allies among the city's commercial elite.[8]

Harper first approached real estate executive Hill Ferguson, an 1896 graduate of the University of Alabama and the school's Birmingham-area trustee since 1919. An ardent city booster who had served terms as head of the Jefferson County Planning Commission and the county's Board of Equalization, Ferguson envisioned how the medical college might benefit from the law. In October 1949, he wrote University of Alabama president John Gallalee that "we are overlooking a golden opportunity if we do not get in on Title I, which permits the University to acquire property from which slums and old houses are to be removed for purposes other than new housing." The cautious Gallalee's response, which reflected the school's perpetual financial worries, indicated that the university might be interested in one block for the medical college.[9]

While Ferguson worked to persuade university officials and to rope other real estate developers into the proposal, Harper pushed the idea to Commissioners Green, Morgan, and Connor, who ultimately would need to approve any application the HABD made to the HHFA. Morgan called the bill "the biggest bargain ever offered Birmingham. We would be foolish not to get our share of this money while the getting is good." The city moved to meet the requirements to pursue Title I funding, the redevelopment portion of the legislation. Harper hired a New York City planning firm to assist the local housing authority. In a February 1950 resolution, the commissioners permitted the HABD to seek $2.5 million in capital grant funds for slum clearance and redevelopment in Birmingham.[10]

A series of planning meetings in the spring of 1950 further solidified city leaders' intentions to use federal grants to try to remake the downtown. Denison attended the discussions along with Harper, Ferguson, Roy Kracke, dean of the medical school, James F. Sulzby Jr., the chairman of the city's planning board and an owner of large tracts of downtown real estate, and George Byrum, head of the zoning board. The Health Department report cited squalid conditions in eight white and twelve black neighborhoods. (It noted that nearly all of the city's black areas could be considered as blighted according to the county's criteria for substandard housing.) The study favored clearance of several downtown residential neighborhoods surrounding the medical center. "The fringe area must eventually be cleared of all slum and most standard dwellings to provide expansion for business and industry," it emphasized. The group did not completely abandon government-subsidized housing. The document called for fifteen hundred units for whites and one thousand homes for blacks, but it did contend that no new housing should go downtown. Later in the year, the HABD contracted for two five-hundred-unit housing projects, one for each race. They would not interfere with downtown development, however. Each was built on vacant land, away from the central business district.[11]

The ad hoc committee proposed three projects, and the plan calling for the acquisition of four and a half blocks surrounding the medical center quickly moved to the forefront. Proposals for Avondale and Tuxedo Junction, more economically depressed black neighborhoods than the Southside areas near the college, called for commercial and light industrial uses and limited replacement of demolished homes. In December 1951, the city commission moved to cement civic unity for the redevelopment proposals by establishing the Citizens Advisory Group (CAG). The CAG, dominated by local real estate interests, was, in essence, a macrocosm of the city's planning board. The city's seven-member planning board, chaired by Sulzby, was an advisory group begun in 1943 through National Resources Planning Board funding. The board had no staff and concentrated on zoning, road construction, and public parks. Birmingham was one of just three cities larger than 250,000 people without a master plan to guide its growth. Sulzby, past president of the influential Birmingham Real Estate Board, chaired the CAG meetings. The most active members included fifteen local real estate executives (including ten previous presidents of the city's real estate board), seven banking or insurance executives, seven college or health officials, five downtown merchants, and three industrialists.[12]

The leadership of the redevelopment drive represented a significant shift from New Deal–era efforts that relied on federal housing dollars and highlighted the splits among the city's white leadership. Commercial leaders, in particular real estate interests and downtown merchants and professionals, dominated the CAG. In contrast, during the 1930s social welfare and labor activists had championed the federal grant programs. This time, labor leaders were nowhere to be found and manufacturing executives had a minimal role in shaping the development agenda. Manufacturers and industrialists, for example, were active in the city's Committee of 100, a two-year-old organization dedicated to diversifying the city's industrial base. While seven men served on both the CAG and the Committee of 100, only William Engel, head of an eponymous commercial real estate and development firm, took an active role on both. Commercial and industrial interests pursued their different agendas—a divergence among business leaders that would influence the city's future. TCI, for instance, moved its headquarters from downtown Birmingham to Fairfield near its largest mill.

Understanding how the Housing Act could spark the city's economic development, CAG members embraced the medical center proposal. Concerns about the future of the medical college inspired some members, but most wanted the opportunity to clear slums for nonresidential purposes, and they perceived an economic advantage in the new law. Jefferson Steiner, a past leader of the Birmingham Real Estate Board, encapsulated these views in a CAG meeting when he asked, "What is a finer product of private enterprise than the fruits of medical progress?" The land, he continued, "is located so conveniently that it can be utilized more profitably than for the Negro rental business." The CAG, buoyed by visions of growth, pushed for a bigger program. Ferguson wrote HABD chief Harper that the proposed area "would make as near an ideal campus for the Medical Center as can be acquired." Developer Robert Jemison headed a subcommittee that reported that the "need for additional land for expansion of the medical and health facilities is paramount." It proposed a twenty-two-block site.[13]

Heeding the CAG's advice, Birmingham housing officials enlarged the project's scope, tripling the original Site A (as it was called in planning documents) proposal to twelve and a half blocks. Site A also became the HABD's sole focus, a change that mixed financial considerations and the advice of Hale Walker, an HHFA bureaucrat based in Atlanta, who noted that a single proposal stood a better chance of winning approval. Nevertheless, HABD officials took a more restrained look at the undertaking than the CAG. They knew that the notoriously thin municipal budget made it difficult to increase the city's $400,000 share (for planning work and one-third of acquisition and clearance costs) of the project. Also, the HABD's Harper knew his agency would have problems showing federal bureaucrats how it would relocate the three thousand additional residents displaced in a twenty-two-block project.[14]

By January 1953, the HABD, with the assistance of Harland Bartholomew's nationally renowned urban planning firm, completed its proposal for the twelve-and-a-half block renewal project. The planners did not use poverty to justify the program; rather, economic promise recommended Site A. The Southside neighborhoods slated for demolition had a population of 2,750, including 2,000 African American residents. More than three-fourths of the area's 756 homes were dilapidated or lacked a private bath, and their population density was five times that of the rest of the city. Health department investigators reported higher than average rates for infant mortality, syphilis, and crime. The Southside communities were not the city's most depressed areas. Both Tuxedo Junction and Avondale, for instance, had more squalid neighborhoods; one study estimated that almost 90 percent of blacks' homes there were substandard. The medical center expansion, limited commercial development, and residential housing would replace the residences in Site A. The original 1953 plans called for five and a half blocks for the college's educational and health facilities, two blocks for the Veterans Administration hospital, one block for a park and pay parking, and three blocks for private, whites-only housing.[15]

City planners now eyed the regulatory hurdles they needed to leap in order to capture $4.5 million in federal grants and loans for the project. On March 30, more than three hundred residents debated the proposal's future at a federally mandated public hearing. A cross section of the city attended: whites and blacks (about one-third of the audience), white collar and working class, government representatives and plain folk came to the city auditorium. Engel, past president of the Chamber, called the meeting critical to the city's economic health. Mayor Green, about to leave government to go into economic development work for Alabama Power, referred to the project as the city's number one priority. Recalling his involvement as an intermediary between Washington bureaucrats and college officials during the medical school's brief history, the mayor emphasized one aspect of the project all but ignored in the other panelists' booster speeches: the central role of the federal government.

The CAG's script for the event lacked one feature: African American backing. Jemison, the developer of the affluent suburb of Mountain Brook, offered that the plan "will provide better living conditions, better health conditions, better educational facilities . . . for our colored population of Birmingham." Few blacks in the audience accepted his reasoning, and black support mattered. The HHFA required a plan to relocate displaced blacks; however, the housing authority did not have one, and because of the restricted black housing market, relocation posed a formidable problem. Sulzby's advisory group had sought the endorsement of Rev. John W. Goodgame Jr., pastor of the city's largest church, to offset the absence of suitable relocation. Goodgame demurred. Instead, the pastor of Sixth Avenue Baptist, located in the project area, opposed the Site A proposal. At the meeting, he spoke against the city's neglect of its black residents and criticized the segregated facilities called for in the redevelopment blueprint. Vague relocation plans would release blacks into the discriminatory housing market. "We find ourselves," Goodgame said, "hemmed in Birmingham unable to move right or left because of certain regulations and laws." Oscar Adams Jr., one of several black lawyers in Birmingham, also objected. He represented twenty-four black homeowners, who, he told the HABD's panel, would be hard-pressed to find equivalent homes elsewhere.[16]

The CAG and housing officials had expected quick approval of their redevelopment project, but their expectation foundered because they could not show a "sincere attitude on the part of the community in helping the

Negroes find building sites for relocation." White civic leaders intended to manage black opposition to the project through the traditional discussion-and-delay tactics of the Jefferson County Council on Social Forces' Interracial Committee. They neglected to consider how federal participation altered customary racial bargaining. Problems surfaced after HABD chairman J. Orlando Ogle, an insurance executive, made what he expected to be a favorable presentation to the HHFA's program review committee and its regional director of slum clearance, Bruce Wedge, in Atlanta in May 1953. The existence of the whites-only housing provision in the city's program gave local blacks an opening to challenge the plan. They used the leverage inherent in the federal role and bypassed Birmingham officials, making their case in Washington instead.[17]

The Birmingham branch of the NAACP took the lead in the protest, an unsurprising role given that the protest began with a core group of middle-class professional blacks who would lose their homes and have trouble finding suitable property elsewhere. The twenty-four original protesters grew into the sixty-three-member Home Owners Protective League, whose lawyer, the twenty-eight-year old Howard University–trained Adams, filed suit in county court to block the project. The court dismissed the case brought by Adams, son of a prominent newspaper publisher, whose independent streak showed through in his decisions to leave the office of Arthur Shores, Birmingham's preeminent black lawyer, and also to form a branch of the Abraham Lincoln Republican Club even as black voters moved toward the Democratic Party. Nevertheless, like other professional class blacks he belonged to the NAACP, having joined when a student at Industrial High School. Adams asked for the NAACP's assistance after the court ruled against him. Despite fading popularity and internecine bickering, the NAACP remained equipped to fight a middle-class battle that mixed housing and federal policy issues. The opposition to the Southside project recalled the Smithfield Court controversy in the 1930s. The resolve of local black leaders had only been strengthened on May 26, when the three city commissioners deleted the project's nondiscrimination clause as they approved the overall plan.[18]

A small cadre of black professionals dominated the local NAACP's leadership. Its president in 1953, W. C. Patton, was a former schoolteacher who had become a salesman for the American Woodmen Insurance Company, a typical line of work among that year's officers. The vice-president, E. B. Colvin, was a supervisor at the Pilgrim Health and Life Insurance Company, the treasurer, B. A. Carter, was a district manager for the North Carolina Insurance Company, and H. S. Norris, the secretary, served the Productive Industrial Insurance Company as district manager. All had offices in the Masonic Temple on Fourth Avenue North, the heart of the Birmingham's black business community and also the home of the NAACP branch. Also, the national office had opened the southeastern regional office there in 1952 to counter waning membership numbers, bringing Ruby Hurley from her position as head of the national office's youth activities. Hurley and her bosses hoped to reverse declining local membership, which dropped from 8,500 to 1,508 in 1951, roughly the 1940 level. Even though the NAACP had taken the lead on voter registration drives and the city's racial zoning case, it offered few tangible benefits to the city's struggling working-class blacks. Moreover, intramural battles, often pitting mercurial Emory Jackson, editor of the *Birmingham World,* against other NAACP leaders, also hurt the group. In 1952 Jackson, a member of the Omega Psi Phi fraternity, resigned as secretary of the NAACP, contending that Alpha Phi Alpha members dominated the membership drive. He also used his bully pulpit as editor of the twice-weekly newspaper to charge that W. E. Shortridge, a local dentist who chaired the branch's membership committee, had tried to weaken the civil rights group by joining the Jefferson County Coordinating Council's interracial division.[19]

The whites-only housing and the lack of suitable relocation properties in the Site A planning inflamed the NAACP leaders because it indicated backsliding toward the city's racial zoning laws declared unconstitutional by a federal appeals court in 1950. The NAACP did not want to allow the city "to take a backward step" in racial zoning "under the guise" of medical progress. Patton viewed the medical center protest as a fight against segregation, even though the NAACP historically supported slum clearance and low-cost housing. Still, the organization opposed "the elimination of Negroes from good areas and the extension and perpetuation of racial segregation." Blacks deserved full citizenship, Hurley noted as she readied for the 1953 southeastern region meeting, adding that the NAACP's main battles would be to "eliminate segregation and discrimination in housing, recreation facilities, and places of accommodation" as well as in jobs and voting rights. "We understand the conditions [on the Southside] are horrible and need to be cleared, but not so people will have to move to similar conditions in other areas." Hurley simply called the plan "Negro clearance."[20]

The NAACP had organizational strengths from which to fight its case against the city's redevelopment plan. The local leaders' determination to protect hard-fought gains on housing melded with the commitment from national and regional officials to end segregation. The NAACP's local and national structure allowed it to develop a two-pronged strategy. Attorney Adams chaired a six-member study committee—including Hurley, Patton, Jackson, and Rev. Hiram Scruggs, the leader of the original homeowners group—to coordinate the protest in Birmingham. Hurley organized a letter-writing campaign directed at the HHFA; hundreds of residents of the project area, NAACP officials, ministers, and other prominent blacks sent letters and telegrams to HHFA bureaucrats in the nation's capital. The NAACP also sent a petition, signed by more than seven hundred people, to Albert Cole, the former Kansas congressman whom President Dwight D. Eisenhower had appointed to head the HHFA, outlining their objections to the plan. In time, Cole sent Birmingham officials a list of the twelve major complaints repeated in the letters.[21]

The NAACP's national office, which had been pushing desegregation in public housing for more than a year, also unleashed Clarence Mitchell, its chief Washington strategist. Mitchell's extensive connections took the Birmingham case into the hallways of the HHFA bureaucracy. In June, for example, he lobbied Cole and Nathaniel Keith, Cole's top deputy and chief of the agency's slum clearance division, pressing the unfairness of the white-only housing especially as it was combined with no specific plans for black housing. After telling Mitchell that he would personally review the Birmingham file, Cole wrote the HABD's Ogle that the agency would delay approval beyond the June 30 target date if the housing issues had not been solved.[22]

In the words of Bruce Wedge, the HHFA regional administrator in Atlanta, the NAACP protest had "seriously jeopardized compliance with federal standards." Cole's eventual decision to delay the project touched off a series of meetings throughout the summer between Birmingham and NAACP leaders, city officials and HHFA bureaucrats, and NAACP leaders and federal housing officials. Meanwhile, Birmingham's white civic elite watched as other cities received approval on their projects. The delay frustrated newly elected mayor James Morgan, who wrote Jemison, after an August 14 meeting with Cole, that the administrator had put off a decision because he "had been bombarded for some time by the NAACP in opposition to the project." In those talks, however, federal officials counseled their Birmingham colleagues on how to win approval. They recommended dropping the whites-only housing, adding black housing, or finding open land for black developments.[23]

Local negotiations in July and August produced a breakthrough of sorts. Adams and Hugh Denman, a former real estate broker who had become the top aide to the HABD's Harper, hammered out a deal. Adams found Denman easier to bargain with than Harper or the city's politicians because he did not try to appeal to a public constituency. The two men compromised on several fronts, each trying to find a pragmatic solution to a fight over principle. The African American lawyer wanted to cut a deal because his original clients, the Southside homeowners, had become antsy. They had not wanted to block the medical center project but to get better relocation terms. First, Denman indicated an opening on the housing front, assuring Adams that Republic Steel had agreed to sell fifty acres on Jasper Road in north Birmingham to black investors. Next, Denman said the housing agency would ensure that job opportunities in the medical center project were open "to all persons who qualified for them and to make a special effort to incorporate" black tradesmen such as brick masons and carpenters. The local housing authority also agreed to hire a black realty firm to assist in relocation and to use black law firms (Adams's among them) to do title searches. Moreover, Denman agreed to drop the whites-only housing from the plan. The deletion of the segregated housing and the promise of a new black residential neighborhood seemed to offer the best deal within the parameters available to Adams.[24]

In tandem with the local bargain, a letter to Cole's top legal deputy at the HHFA from Maxwell Rabb, an Eisenhower administration domestic affairs counselor who served as the president's unofficial racial policy adviser, sealed the project's approval. The medical center proposal could not be delayed because of the NAACP's objections about possible future discrimination at the medical college. Federal legislation, including the Hill-Burton Act, did not prohibit the existence of separate-but-equal medical facilities,

Rabb wrote. Days after receiving Rabb's letter, Cole gave the $4.9 million Birmingham project the green light. In his November 1953 missive to the city's housing authority, Cole, noting the recent NAACP protest and summer negotiations, reminded Harper that the current plans (with no whites-only housing) could not be amended without his agency's approval, and he urged the city to establish a functional relocation plan. The NAACP continued to fight, unsuccessfully in federal court in Birmingham, to open public housing designated for whites to displaced black residents.[25]

The medical center renewal project marked a step toward a more ambitious and activist agenda for Birmingham's municipal government. The commissioners appeared ready to embrace the economic strategies of Birmingham's real estate and downtown business elites. Not coincidentally, for the first time in more than a decade, new commissioners infused local government with fresh ideas. The trio of Green, Morgan, and Connor had served together since 1940, sweeping elections in 1941, 1945, and 1949, when they defeated challengers in a field swelled by World War II veterans. Despite their long tenure, the three had never run as a bloc or acted as a cohesive unit; instead, frequent and vocal disagreements marked their terms. The commissioners fought over annexation, public housing, and urban redevelopment. Several factors—including an internecine battle in the sheriff's department that led to Connor's downfall and Mayor Green's decision to head Alabama Power's economic development efforts—conspired to make 1953 a year of political change.[26]

While Green voluntarily left politics, scandal dissuaded Connor, fresh from a gubernatorial bid in 1950, from seeking reelection. Connor's iron rule over the city's police department, one of his responsibilities as commissioner for public safety, had bred factionalism within the police force, and a disgruntled detective sought to topple Connor. Henry Darnell seized an opportunity when he raided the downtown Tutwiler Hotel on December 21, 1951, finding Connor in a room with a woman who was not his wife, which violated a city ordinance. The ensuing scandal touched off a flurry of charges and countercharges between his supporters and those like organized labor that had tired of the erstwhile baseball announcer. The *News* also called for Connor's resignation. The commission held an inquiry, which led to an impeachment trial that Connor survived. Still, to quiet his opponents, Connor retired from politics.[27]

Without the old guard, Birmingham's 1953 elections mimicked earlier municipal elections throughout the postwar South, where candidates ran and won on platforms that focused on economic development and increased municipal services. Morgan, a longtime favorite of the downtown business class, won a convincing majority to replace Green as mayor. In winning his fifth campaign, the onetime shopkeeper had emphasized the need for urban planning, and he had retained the Chamber's backing by calling for the annexation of outlying suburbs, a key growth issue. Robert Lindbergh, a former clerk in the Jefferson County sheriff's department, handily defeated his opponents. Only thirty-eight votes separated Sheriff's Deputy Wade Bradley, a Korean War veteran, from James "Jabo" Waggoner, an employee of the city's streets and sanitation department, for the third seat.[28]

One element of the new commission's pro-growth message was a more restrained position on race. In January 1954, in one of its earliest steps, the commission expunged the part of the municipal code that prohibited blacks and whites from playing together in sports events. Self-interest more than racial liberalism motivated the action. They feared that the city's Southern Association baseball team, the Birmingham Barons, would lose its standing in the minor league if rival teams integrated and the Barons did not. Lindbergh reassured voters that Birmingham did not want to abandon segregation, just eliminate its burdensome aspects. Still, he harbored few doubts about the southern racial code's long-term status. "Doing away with segregation is slowly, but surely coming to pass," he told the Ensley Chamber of Commerce days after the election.[29]

*Brown v. Board of Education* shattered hopes of advancing Birmingham-style moderation. Anticipating an adverse Supreme Court ruling in the case, groups like the American States Rights Association jockeyed to provide an appropriate response. The association, formed in Birmingham although it sought members statewide, mixed traditional white supremacy appeals with newer Cold War–era warnings equating desegregation with communism. One of the association's leaflets called for "aid to fight against the F.E.P.C. [Fair Employment Practices Committee], to maintain segregation, to further good race relations, to keep communist propaganda out of our schools, [and] to preserve states' rights." While the group had varied backing (the historian Robert Corley claims that Sidney Smyer, president of the Birmingham Realty Company, and Hugh Morrow, chairman of the U.S. Pipe and Foundry Company, held behind-the-scenes power), second-tier financial and insurance executives took public roles. The association's board of governors included such men as William Hoover, president of the Employers Insurance Company, and Frank B. Yeilding, president of Jefferson Federal Savings and Loan. Both companies served the city's working- and lower-middle-class white residents.[30]

The association organized a petition drive that eventually put the sports segregation issue before the electorate. In the balloting, which followed the Supreme Court's ruling by two weeks, Birmingham residents reversed the commissioners' action. Despite the endorsement of the commission's position by the city's two daily newspapers, the voters passed by a three-to-one margin a stricter sports segregation ordinance that banned interaction between the races at any game "with cards, dice, dominoes, or checkers [or] a softball, basketball, baseball, football, golf, track, and swimming pool." Heavy turnout—larger than for the 1953 Democratic primary in the commission races—underscored the measure's importance. The landslide obscured emerging fissures among residents, in this case the intensity of support for the law differed by economic status. To be sure, all sections of Birmingham backed the bill, but it received strongest backing (more than 83 percent) in white working-class communities such as West End, Ensley, and East Lake. In white-collar, upper-income communities such as Forest Park and along Highland Avenue, voters also advocated sports segregation, although by a two-to-one margin.[31]

Editors at the *News* and the *Post-Herald* wrung their hands over the vote, calling it a regrettable act that shamed the city. The *Montgomery Advertiser*'s assessment highlighted working-class support for the measure. An *Advertiser* editorial charged that Birmingham's unions had opposed sports desegregation and that union members had supplied much of the vote to overrule the commission. "It would be rash to shove a town such as Birmingham toward de-segregation," the editorial commented. "Birmingham is plainly not one of the South's many soft underbellies. Birmingham is often a raw industrial town given to arson and dynamite incidents. It is scarcely to be doubted that there are sections of Birmingham where, if mingling were forcibly attempted, brutishness and violence would be the attendants." The *Advertiser*'s analysis, however incomplete, highlighted an elemental truth in

Birmingham: segregation mattered more to lower-income and working-class whites, especially those who lived near blacks and competed against them for jobs. These cracks would reappear in white Birmingham with upcoming urban renewal efforts. Eventually stresses over race and economic development, exacerbated by suburbanization and the city's declining industrial economy, hardened Birmingham's political arteries, making compromise difficult.[32]

Chastened by the voters over moderating segregation, the commissioners moved ahead on their economic development agenda, which depended on congressional legislation. In 1954, Congress amended its blueprint for cities, changing the original 1949 law to favor downtown renewal over public housing and shifting the remaining housing focus to rehabilitation, not massive projects. Another revision required comprehensive planning; essentially no city could receive federal aid without a "Workable Program for Urban Renewal" that surveyed a city's housing stock and outlined an improvement plan. Thus November 1954 found Birmingham health officials—and soon a revamped planning commission—reviewing the city's housing conditions to comply with the congressional mandate. Mayor Morgan reorganized Sulzby's planning board, turning it into the Birmingham Planning Commission, a municipal department, a move that solidified real estate and downtown business interests' control over metropolitan planning efforts. The commission's twelve-member advisory board included five real estate developers, four executives in central city concerns, two public officials, and one representative from a craft union but no industrialists.[33]

Birmingham's first "Workable Plan" called for a project in Avondale, modifying the proposal drafted four years earlier when leaders had selected the medical center redevelopment. To replace the more than two thousand homes slated for demolition in the African American section of the neighborhood, the HABD called for mixed commercial and industrial development along with housing for blacks. Also, the school board wanted to build an elementary school and a vocational high school for blacks on a portion of the seventy-eight-acre site. A Chamber study claimed that private interests would not develop the area on their own but would become involved if Washington subsidized the $3 million clearance and acquisition costs.[34]

The still controversial issue of government-subsidized housing initially dominated the Avondale debate. Real estate interests now divided on public housing, essentially pitting landlords, even prosperous ones like Joseph Meade, who owned and managed hundreds of rental units occupied by black tenants in Ensley, against those committed to using the downtown property, now filled with black housing, for other purposes. In this case the commissioners rallied around men such as Hill Ferguson who saw an opportunity to rebuild the city's sluggish economy and shape the neighborhoods where blacks lived. Morgan railed against those who rented "joints not fit for people or rats to live in. There are filthy slums spreading out in all directions from City Hall [and] you've had twenty years to do something about them." The commissioners approved a 750-unit project as part of the Avondale plan.[35]

Birmingham needed more and better housing, especially for blacks, because city hall aggressively sought to move blacks from areas targeted for redevelopment to other parts of the city. One popular tactic was code enforcement, which had been encouraged by Congress's 1954 amendments to the housing bill. In areas like the Southside medical center, Birmingham officials hoped to encourage commercial development, not new housing. Within three years, the various renewal efforts could be expected to uproot about twenty-seven hundred black families, about half of whom would not have decent alternatives. Strict code enforcement of dilapidated housing was especially popular on the Southside, in areas surrounding the medical center and the headquarters of Liberty National Insurance, whose executives played a key role in supporting the city's projects. The massive relocation that followed the enforcement on the Southside produced a further dependence on federal housing programs. Developers like Ferguson, along with the increasingly marginalized social welfare activists, argued that the federal programs bolstered standards for black homes. (The percentage of substandard black homes, measured by the federal housing census, dropped from about 90 percent in 1930 to half that in the mid-1950s.)[36]

Development efforts redefined Birmingham, ultimately affecting race relations and political alliances. As the city's economy sagged in the 1950s, however, the resulting battles played out differently than in more prosperous areas, like Atlanta. By uprooting black families, city leaders set in motion powerful social forces. Yet at the same time, they hoped to defy change by using federal housing subsidies such as Section 221 loans to protect white neighborhoods against black encroachment. Section 221 loans, a mortgage guarantee to aid existing home rehabilitation in the 1954 federal law, allowed planners to separate the races even after federal judges declared racial zoning laws unconstitutional. Governments in Atlanta and Chicago, among others, adopted the tactic. In Birmingham, Morgan especially advocated the subsidies for the white community surrounding Birmingham Southern College, the liberal arts school that had educated many of the city's economic leaders. The area near the college had long been a racial battleground. It was contiguous to the Smithfield neighborhoods where whites had bombed the homes of blacks in the late 1940s. In all, Morgan requested more than two thousand Section 221 loans.[37]

Birmingham's growth and migration patterns differed markedly from those of Atlanta. During the 1940s and 1950s blacks who came to Birmingham or were pushed out of their homes mostly crowded into historically black areas. In Atlanta, in contrast, uprooted black families faced a less restrictive housing market; they moved into neighborhoods abandoned by whites racing into suburban areas following jobs. From 1940 to 1960, Atlanta's black population grew 15 percent, while its white population decreased by a similar percentage. Conversely, Birmingham's black and white populations both increased, by 9 and 7 percent, during the decades. Overcrowding in Birmingham's black neighborhoods became most pronounced in the 1950s. Blacks did not move into new areas because, for the most part, working-class and middle-class whites remained in Birmingham. In the 1950s, the biggest suburban growth came in the upper-income suburbs of Mountain Brook, where the population increased from 8,400 to 12,600, and Homewood, which grew from 12,800 to 20,300. Birmingham's and Atlanta's opposed demographic trends, among other factors, likely eased racial tensions in Atlanta and exacerbated them in the Alabama city, where displaced blacks (as well as in-migrants) looked for homes on the periphery of white neighborhoods. It was a combustible situation, as the earlier Dynamite Hill bombings indicated.[38]

Beginning in the 1930s, the population and economic base in metropolitan Atlanta grew as a whole, while the Birmingham area remained stagnant by comparison. The divergent patterns quickened during the war years and afterward. The populations of Atlanta and Birmingham proper differed by less than 5,000 people in the late 1940s, but Atlanta's metropolitan region had 150,000 more residents than Birmingham's. Moreover, in contrast to

TABLE I BIRMINGHAM POPULATION, 1910–1980

| YEAR | CITY | % OF ATLANTA | METRO REGION | % OF ATLANTA |
|---|---|---|---|---|
| 1910 | 133,000 | 85 | 226,000 | 83 |
| 1920 | 179,000 | 89 | 310,000 | 89 |
| 1930 | 260,000 | 96 | 431,000 | 93 |
| 1940 | 268,000 | 89 | 460,000 | 82 |
| 1950 | 326,000 | 98 | 559,000 | 77 |
| 1960 | 341,000 | 70 | 635,000 | 62 |
| 1970 | 301,000 | 61 | 739,000 | 53 |
| 1980 | 284,000 | 67 | 815,000 | 37 |

national trends, Birmingham's population grew faster in the center city than in outlying areas during the decade. Overall, the Atlanta metropolitan region increased by half while Birmingham's grew by about one-fifth. While the Birmingham region was 93 percent the size of Atlanta in 1930, that percentage fell to 75 percent in 1940 and to 63 percent in 1950. In 1950, Atlanta's suburban regions were more populous than the city for the first time, while Birmingham was 50 percent larger than its outlying areas. Suburbanization redefined Atlanta, creating a sprawling metropolitan complex where residential dispersion went hand in hand with job growth. The Atlanta economy diversified as well. In 1950 a smaller percentage of employees worked in manufacturing and a larger percentage worked in communications, finance, insurance and real estate, professional services, and government than a decade earlier. Moreover, the economy in its surrounding counties was even more varied than in the center city. This transformation stood in sharp contrast to Birmingham, where outlying communities and the city were heavily blue collar. TCI's Fairfield factory and industrialized Bessemer (a violent town in the 1950s) meant that rustbelt suburbs surrounded Birmingham to the northwest and the southwest. Finally, Atlanta's suburbs were wealthier than the city, unlike Birmingham and its environs.

Residential dispersion had political consequences too. Middle-class white flight in Atlanta served to unite that city's white and black businessmen into a formidable political coalition. As blacks became a significant percentage of the city's population, the politicians who represented Atlanta's white civic elite made the city's African Americans a key part of its electoral bloc. In 1949, Mayor William Hartsfield, who cleverly called his city "too busy to hate," started to campaign for the growing black vote. The population shifts throughout the 1950s were so pronounced that in ten years, Atlanta changed from having the smallest concentration of nonwhite residents among major southern cities to the biggest, just larger than the 40 percent in Birmingham, a number that had held steady throughout the century. Atlanta's black business class mimicked its white counterpart. Thanks to its "numerous black colleges and universities, Atlanta also had many black white-collar workers" and a "vibrant economy," according to one historian of the period, which Birmingham lacked. Although blacks in the Alabama city had a higher median income than Atlanta's—most likely because of the city's industrial wages—Birmingham had a far smaller professional class. In 1950 more than 11 percent of Atlanta's African American workers held white-collar occupations, compared to 5 percent in Birmingham—a disparity that continued to widen. In fact, low growth during the 1950s (and then decline in the 1960s) indicated that Birmingham, in contrast to Atlanta, lost many of its ambitious blacks. Owing in part to the absence of a powerful black middle class and in large part to the growing political strength of the remaining blue-collar whites, Birmingham did not develop a governing coalition like Atlanta's moderating leadership.[39]

Growing racial tensions in the post-*Brown* era complicated renewal efforts that depended on grants from Washington. In June 1955, the three commissioners backed away from the Avondale plan that they once had endorsed. The business class had to battle for its position. Morgan attacked the creeping federal control over local affairs, and Bradley noted a "gradual relinquishing by local government of authority and jurisdiction" to Washington. The housing program had "gone too far, there are too many regulations now," Morgan said at one commission meeting. At the same time, he admitted that federal "Workable Program" mandates strained the budget, making it difficult for the city to fund its share of the project. HHFA requirements would add $200,000 in expenditures to a city already facing a $1.3 million deficit. Nevertheless, determined Birmingham elites, eager to use federal grants to rebuild their city, did not allow the project to languish. The Chamber, led by James A. Head, owner of the state's largest office supply company, urged the commissioners to reverse course again. Businessmen focused their lobbying on Lindbergh, the city's police commissioner, who finally recommended a $1.2 million bond issue to finance the project.[40]

The commissioners knew that, given the electorate's economic conservatism, the bond issue, scheduled for September, would be a tough fight. Eight months earlier, voters had rejected, by a three-to-one margin, two proposals to raise $3.5 million for the city's financially strapped schools. The Chamber, the city's two daily newspapers, and the Birmingham Trades Council, which knew the project meant jobs, lined up behind the Avondale bond issue, one of several proposals on the ballot. The Birmingham Real Estate Board, controlled by Meade, opposed the initiative because it would lead to public housing. The $1.2 million Avondale bond issue, which included about $100,000 to assist the medical center clearance, passed by a thin margin: 5,952 to 5,365.[41]

The September 1955 election revealed economic and social divisions in Birmingham over federally sponsored urban renewal. The city's white-collar middle class favored the Avondale project, while working-class voters cooled to the plan. Residents of north Birmingham, Wylam, Pratt City, and Ensley, heavily populated by less-skilled operatives and with black areas nearby, also balked at the project. The measure lost by a two-to-one margin in Wylam and by three to two in Ensley. Residents of West End, home to skilled industrial workers, craftsmen, and white-collar lower middle class (such as clerks, insurance and real estate agents, and bookkeepers) split on it. In contrast, residents of middle-class neighborhoods in south Birmingham, like Forest Park and along the Highland Avenue corridor, where many of the city's remaining white-collar professionals and managers lived, voted two to one for the bond issue. The project passed because of lukewarm support for it in the nearby communities of Avondale, Woodlawn, and East Lake. Skilled workers may have voted along with W. M. McDuffie, business agent for the bricklayer's union and chairman of the city's Trades Council, who backed the proposal. Moreover, these working- and lower-middle-class voters might have split with demographically similar residents from other areas of the city because of their proximity to the project. Nearby residents, who would gain tangible benefits from the slum clearance, such as a new multilane highway eliminating bottlenecks between East Lake and downtown, slightly favored the plan. Their key role can be underscored by contrasting the successful Avondale vote with the failed civic center bond vote, another issue favored by the city's downtown business interests. In the September balloting, the civic center land acquisition returns mirrored the Avondale vote in all communities except Woodlawn, Avondale, and East Lake, which were narrowly against it. The $300,000 bond issue for land adjacent to city hall lost by five hundred votes.[42]

The competitive Avondale bond vote revealed fractures in Birmingham's white electorate that continued into the 1960s. Blue-collar and lower-middle-class whites in Ensley, West End, and East Lake, for example, voted differently than affluent and middle-class whites in Forest Park and Southside neighborhoods. Working-class voters—as municipal elections in the 1950s and 1960s underscored—found the economic development issues favored by local commercial leaders less compelling than cases involving bedrock social values. The Avondale bond turnout was far lower in the working-class communities than it had been for the sports segregation vote, for example. Economic development emerged as a wedge issue in local elections, especially because it carried the taint of federal intervention. Still, as development matters moved to the top of the economic leadership's agenda, the group's political base waned owing to suburbanization and the failure of annexation. While suburbanites might dominate the city's executive offices and powerful government boards, lower-middle-class and blue-collar residents of the city had the electoral majority and thus held a measure of political power, especially on election day.

In 1957, "Bull" Connor's return to city government further revealed the power of the working-class vote in Birmingham—and the open clash between blue-collar interests and the policies of the economic elite. After leaving the commission in 1953, Connor ran his Avondale gas station, sold radio advertisements, and attempted political comebacks. His bids for county sheriff in 1955 and for commissioner of public improvements in 1956 failed. Commentators noted that he lost the special 1956 election—for the commission seat Wade Bradley abandoned when he moved from Birmingham—because his opponent, Waggoner, had the backing of organized labor. A year later, the candidate one newspaper called "Mr. Segregation" ran hard on racial issues. For the first time in his political career, Connor, the darling of the local gentry in the 1930s, received labor's endorsement. He defeated the incumbent commissioner for public safety, Robert Lindbergh, because of union support. The 103-vote victory (15,891 to 15,788) came because of high turnout in the populous working-class communities of East Lake and Ensley, which Connor won by three-to-one and two-to-one margins. The winner also defeated Lindbergh in Huffman, Woodlawn, Inglenook, and Wylam, although the incumbent claimed Southside and Avondale. As further evidence of his segregationist appeal, Connor secured the votes of those supporting the most rabid racial candidates who had been eliminated in the primary. Connor actually ran second in the Democratic primary by more than 2,500 votes, but in the runoff he gained more of the 4,500 votes that had gone to other candidates, including the 1,675 votes garnered by Asa Carter, a Ku Klux Klan activist.[43]

In the late 1950s white supremacy played well to many Birmingham voters, especially to the working class and union members. Local and national civil rights protests by blacks had increased since the *Brown* ruling. The manner and pace of that local protest had increased, the historian Glenn Eskew explains, after the state attorney general banned the NAACP in 1956. The NAACP's replacement, the Alabama Christian Movement for Human Rights (ACMHR), founded by a Baptist minister, Fred Shuttlesworth, accelerated direct action protest in the state's largest city. Racial violence followed each of the campaigns led by the minister at the Bethel Baptist Church, which led *Time* to refer to Birmingham as "integration's hottest crucible." At the same time, industrial workers tried to weather the effects of a local economic decline. Area unions had a long history of institutionalizing the power of white workers through job classifications and other means. This practice would become even more important as the region's economy stalled.[44]

Evidence of Birmingham's economic stagnation abounded in the mid-1950s. In the business district, one needed only to look at old photographs. "The skyline has remained virtually unchanged since the late 20s," went a *News* editorial that harked back to an era when the city's economy grew faster than Atlanta's. Empty lots littered the downtown landscape. More buildings had been torn down in the 1950s than had been built, and the inner core held less office space than it did a decade earlier. Another *News* editorial complained that instead of being used for new construction, valuable downtown real estate had been turned into parking lots. Birmingham's business district suffered a net loss of more than three hundred businesses between

1954 and 1960. Local merchants felt the pinch as retail sales dropped, and wholesale sales suffered too. While downtown merchants had accounted for 37 percent of the metropolitan region's retail trade in 1948, their share had fallen to 27 percent in 1958.[45]

The city's industrial prospects turned bleaker too. Although barely evident at the time, a decades-long expansionary period in the local steel economy halted in the mid-1950s. Predominantly unionized manufacturing jobs had given Birmingham labor the highest wage level in the South, and skilled workers in the city earned a wage above the national norm. In 1957, the average factory worker in Birmingham earned $4,676 as compared to $4,224 in Atlanta. Yet the highest-paying industries were hit hardest. Pig iron production, the dominant industry in the Birmingham district, stagnated and employment fell. While the metropolitan region netted 13,300 new positions between 1950 and 1964, it lost 12,650 manufacturing jobs, 3,300 of them in the metal industries. The number of coal miners in the region plunged from 17,100 to 4,300 in a similar period. Republic Steel suspended its ore production in 1956 and TCI closed all its mines by 1962, when it started to substitute Venezuelan ore for Red Mountain ore. Moreover, the region witnessed a decline in construction and transportation employment (primarily on the railroads) in the 1950s. Instead of classifying Birmingham with other southern cities, economists tended to consider it with northern rustbelt communities such as Detroit, Chicago, Pittsburgh, and Philadelphia. Conditions only worsened as the decade progressed, for the Alabama city's employment base contracted 10 percent between 1958 and 1963. In 1962, the federal Department of Commerce listed Birmingham as a "depressed" area. The city "suffers from some of the worst aspects of both industrialization and segregation," *New York Times* columnist James Reston noted.[46]

While the amount of office space and the number of retail establishments in the city fell, the suburban economy grew. In Mountain Brook, Ervin Jackson, who had championed the city's growth after World War II, built Office Park on an empty lot near the village's shopping district. The three-story building was among the first suburban office buildings in the United States. Several years later, Mountain Brook's city manager extolled the "atmosphere of shady lawns, quiet streets and plenty of parking space" in his town's new five-building office complex. This bucolic calm stood in contrast to the "hubbub of downtown Birmingham—commuting, parking and waiting for elevators to reach upper floors," city manager Asa Green noted.[47]

Throughout the 1950s, the municipal government teetered on the edge of bankruptcy. Declining tax receipts from downtown property made local residents feel the pinch of that decade's recessions. Birmingham already had the lowest tax rate among the nation's ninety-four largest cities and smaller than expected revenues failed to match even the city's thin budgets. Birmingham, which had not added any new taxes since 1940, had the lowest per capita revenue rate of any southern city. The city government, for instance, averaged $45 in revenue for each resident compared to $80 per resident in Memphis and $63 in Atlanta. Besides its low tax rate, Birmingham historically had a low assessment rate that undervalued the taxable property.[48]

City leaders, who a decade earlier had crowed about becoming the Southeast's dominant city, now worried as they lost ground to the region's major metropolitan areas. Birmingham grew more slowly in the 1950s than New Orleans, Atlanta, Memphis, and Louisville. The relative growth numbers surprised the economic leadership, who had not expected the "relatively heavy outmigration experienced in the city." Birmingham, according to a Chamber report, needed better balance among manufacturing, trade, and business services. Birmingham still remained "a long way from having a thoroughly diversified economy and trade to cushion a shock in any single industry," commented developer William Engel, adding that "downtown is on the defensive."[49]

Searching for answers, some businessmen believed that a renewed commitment to urban planning and redevelopment, with a focus on regionwide cooperation, could reverse Birmingham's economic woes. In 1956 real estate magnate Sidney Smyer, who lived in suburban Vestavia Hills, worked to organize the Metropolitan Planning Commission to lead the rebuilding. Born into a prominent Birmingham family, Smyer had won two terms in the state legislature in 1934 and 1938 under the banner of civil service reform and conservative, minimalist government. In the 1930s, he also fought government-subsidized housing. His political connections led to his appointment as general counsel to the Birmingham Realty Company, which owned vast tracts of property downtown and throughout Jefferson County.

In 1953, Smyer became the company's president. As his stake in property development grew, so did his promotion of regional planning. A charter member of the Jefferson County Planning Commission in 1947, Smyer now hoped to form a comprehensive group that would chart the region's future transportation and land use needs and coordinate industrial development and public works projects. Smyer's agenda matched that of the Chamber and other businessmen's groups. Also, the HABD proposed a third redevelopment project, an ambitious $32 million plan for code enforcement, slum clearance, public housing, and commercial building in Ensley and Pratt City (Site C from the original 1950 plan). Because of a combination of municipal austerity and shifting federal goals, it was nearly a decade before work began on a smaller project there.[50]

Smyer, Head, Lewis Jeffers, the president of Hayes Aircraft, and attorney Joseph Johnston sponsored a study to parallel other efforts to reverse Birmingham's decline. The four men hired the Southern Institute of Management to provide an economic and psychological profile of the city. In June 1958, the Louisville-based firm began its "audit," relying on questionnaires, interviews, government statistics, and newspaper reports, to attempt to discover and explain Birmingham's "personality." The consultants sought to create composites of the city's economy, its leadership, and its quality of life. If Smyer's circle had initiated the audit to reassure residents about their city's future, answers to the preliminary questionnaires—distributed to several hundred civic leaders—proved otherwise. The consultants reported that Birmingham's leaders had fundamental doubts about their city. The city suffered from uncertainty, inferiority, and defensiveness, the investigators wrote. The report, with its imprecise psychological jargon, noted the city's hesitancy in its fear of failure and change, self-doubt, and absence of trust. Thankful for their present prosperity, business leaders worried about what lay ahead. In the words of one anonymous executive, many "were disturbed about their future in Birmingham as it related to Birmingham's opportunity for growth and, therefore, their own continued expansion." Smyer and his colleagues canceled the rest of the survey.[51]

CHAPTER FOUR

# The Medical Center Turns to Grant Funding

In 1954 S. Richardson Hill Jr. faced what at first glance seemed an obvious choice between remaining at Harvard University Medical College or accepting a position as assistant professor of endocrinology and metabolism at the University of Alabama Medical College. A 1943 graduate of Duke University and later the Bowman Gray School of Medicine at Wake Forest University, both in his native North Carolina, Hill had completed his residency at Harvard's Peter Bent Bingham Hospital. Hill seemed destined for a distinguished career at Harvard, or so Tinsley Harrison, dean of the Birmingham-based school's department of medicine, wrote him. Harrison knew Hill because the younger physician had contributed two chapters to Harrison's textbook *Principles of Internal Medicine.* Forget convention, Harrison also told Hill. Harrison urged Hill to take a risk and move to Birmingham to help build a medical school on which he could leave his own mark. Harrison's ego-probing logic swayed Hill, who would later use it himself to lure key faculty members to Birmingham. Hill became the fifth doctor in the school's department of medicine—and two decades later he would run the entire school. Nonetheless, when he arrived in Birmingham, Hill found the school's facilities "primitive" and the atmosphere "family-like" when compared to his Boston environment. Charles A. "Scotty" McCallum had a similar reaction two years earlier after following several of his Tufts Dental School professors south. McCallum, trained as a navy pilot, considered the small four-block medical center "a real frontier," yet he too sensed the opportunities for growth and development in Birmingham.[1]

Several factors pointed toward a new era for Birmingham's cash-strapped medical school, which had failed to establish a national or even regional reputation at the eve of Hill's arrival. For one, the medical college had new leadership, the result of simmering feuds among school administrators, who long had chafed at the college's secondary status within the university's hierarchy, and its tenuous position in the state's funding scheme that "threatened [its] financial stability." Harrison even urged Dean James Durrett to find a way to gain independence from Tuscaloosa. By the summer of 1953, discontent at the Birmingham campus finally captured the attention of university administrators in Tuscaloosa. President Oliver C. Carmichael, who recently had returned to his home state from the Carnegie Foundation, realized that the school was at a crossroads.[2]

Carmichael decided to appoint an outside three-doctor panel to evaluate the institution and to chart its future. The committee reflected both Carmichael's ambitions for the school and the influences that would shape the postwar growth of health care. To chair the committee, the university president recruited a friend from New York philanthropy circles, Dr. T. Duckett Jones, vice-president and medical director of the Helen Whitney Hay Foundation. The panel also included Dr. Maxwell Lapham, dean of the Tulane University School of Medicine, and Dr. Jack Masur, an assistant surgeon general in the federal Public Health Service. Issued in 1954, the Jones Survey (as it came to be known) energized the campus. It called for real administrative independence, pointed out opportunities for growth, and provided a rationale for action not stasis. The committee also foreshadowed the future impetus for change from outside the city.[3]

The Jones Survey, which formalized the medical center concept in Birmingham, marked a turning point, administrators later noted, that allowed the college to begin to fulfill its promise. A new generation of leadership, both in the college and among its local business backers, strengthened a relationship with the city once marked by bickering. At the urging of federal bureaucrats in 1956, Birmingham planners now sought to use the entire Southside slum clearance tract for the college, and an ingenious solution a year later helped make that possible. Concurrently, the deepening congressional commitment to health sciences and medicine, seen primarily in the explosion of National Institutes of Health (NIH) funding, allowed Birmingham-based doctors and administrators to expand both their physical campus and the college's teaching and research programs. In the early 1960s long-range planning began to bear dividends and a building boom commenced. In 1962, moreover, federal and state operating sources pulled near even (and moving in opposite directions), underscoring the influences on the Southside school, which soon came under even stricter scrutiny from Washington.

The Jones Survey sparked an administrative overhaul at the college. The report recommended that to ensure better representation within the University of Alabama system, the school needed a Birmingham-based vice-president for health affairs as well as a separate board. Carmichael, who would quit his post in 1955 because of public pressure after a controversial attempt to desegregate the university, requested Durrett's resignation. The board of trustees replaced Durrett, a diffident and unpopular administrator, with Robert C. Berson. The doctors at the college, especially Harrison and Champ Lyons, the school's chief of surgery, had never fully embraced Durrett, a career bureaucrat. The college's senior medical staff as well as the university's administrators believed that the school needed a builder with a vision for the future, not a mere manager to husband its meager resources. In 1955, Berson, a Vanderbilt Medical College graduate and World War II veteran, became the university's new vice-president for health affairs. The trustees expected the forty-two-year-old Berson, coauthor of *Medical Schools in the United States at Mid-Century,* to provide dynamic, farsighted leadership. The publication of *Medical Schools* capped his tenure as the executive director of the American Association of Medical Colleges. Previously he had taught medicine at Vanderbilt and the University of Illinois. He was just one of several men who arrived in the early 1950s who would transform the college and lead it for the next four decades.[4]

Berson proved determined to follow the survey's key operational recommendations. Scolding the previous administration for allowing haphazard expansion, Jones had contended that the school required a coherent master plan to guide growth. Moreover, to establish its academic reputation, the school needed to pursue research grants and expand its facilities, which would require a larger operating budget or significant outside capital investment. Fortunately for the school, its internal reorganization coincided with the city's slum clearance project surrounding the school. These overlapping events pushed the school's new ambitious agenda in line with the goals of a faction of the city's economic elite.[5]

The creation of the Medical Center Advisory Board (MCAB) in April 1955 gave the school a measure of independence from Tuscaloosa. The seventeen-member panel, appointed from districts statewide but dominated by Birmingham businessmen, gave the campus a powerful set of advocates. It also tied the city's professional leadership to the school. Among the first MCAB appointees were Birmingham stalwarts Hill Ferguson and Frank Spain. Longtime University of Alabama trustee Ferguson had been one of the first champions of the urban renewal project for the land surrounding the school earlier in the decade. Spain, a lawyer and a former chairman of the city's housing authority, was familiar with federal development legislation. During a 1953 public hearing for the medical center clearance, Spain had called the college the city's top priority, noting that it had brought "more people to Birmingham than any other industry." In time, Spain would back those thoughts by donating more than $2 million to the school.[6] The MCAB's executive committee also included a generation of Birmingham businessmen with few ties to the city's traditional industrial economy. Ehney Camp, an insurance executive and a 1928 Alabama graduate whose firm, the Liberty National Insurance Company, had its headquarters on the Southside near the medical college, became the committee's vice-chairman. Liberty's assets had more than doubled during the Depression, and for three decades after 1952 its dividend and earnings increases outpaced those of all companies listed on the New York Stock Exchange. Camp's aggressiveness matched Liberty's culture.[7]

The new leadership focused on the medical college's future. In the summer of 1955 Berson started an in-house planning committee to develop specific expansion options. The committee consisted of academic department heads, the college's top administrators, the Birmingham members of the MCAB, and the college's architects. Berson outlined a general proposal for the development of the medical center that included the modernization of the Jefferson-Hillman Hospital, a new student center, a library, a second hospital, an outpatient center, a nurses' residence, and a reorganization of the clinical departments. A year earlier, the university's trustees moved the college's Birmingham extension center from its downtown location to Tidwell Hall, the new academic wing of the general sciences–dental school building.[8]

Despite grand expectations, the planning committee's early urban renewal efforts were tentative. The members sought to determine how much land the college should request from Birmingham's ongoing Southside project, a decision framed by how to finance any acquisition. In public, they expected that the college could use four blocks of the overall land clearance project. In private, they did not know what they wanted because previously "there had been so little concentrated, detailed study of the total needs of the Medical Center so future developments could only be visualized in vague outlines." All calculations depended on generous federal (and state) assistance because Berson's proposed building program would cost about $10 million, of which the university could provide less than one-tenth. Alabama Building Commission officials, moreover, told Berson that the state did not have the money to purchase even the land, which was estimated to cost $2 million.[9]

Berson's committee bickered with city planning officials over the particular parcels the college selected for its use, further endangering any long-range strategy. Its request did not match the five and a half blocks the Housing Authority of the Birmingham District, responsible for the Southside renewal project, had reserved for the college in its 1953 grant application. The discrepancy threatened subsequent federal grant payments, and Harold Harper, the HABD's executive director, complained that redrafting the project proposal would strain his agency's budget and resources. Harper did not want to change the plans to accommodate the medical college because earlier Dean Durrett had made an ambiguous pledge to purchase the land in the clearance site. The college committee also sparred with city planners over its requests to close some of the streets in the project area.[10]

Doubt still plagued the ambitions of the college administrators. At several meetings Berson wondered if the college was overreaching by seeking a development that outstripped its current resources. Local businessmen on the MCAB demurred. The college needed to widen its public relations campaign, not narrow its expectations, Camp contended. The opportunity to use federal grants to expand might end. Camp, understanding the importance of forming a consensus in the business community in support of the college's growth, took charge. Local businessmen, he believed, could influence Mayor James Morgan, who in turn would lobby the HABD for the college. The Liberty executive arranged a series of conferences among Morgan, the HABD's executive board, and college administrators to settle their differences. The meetings, held at the authority's offices, centered around the disputed parcels, the college's future plans, its inability to finance the land designated for it, and the problems involved with changing the HABD's redevelopment plan.[11]

The college's advocates mobilized an effective array of supporters. Morgan, fulfilling his expected role as catalyst, informed the HABD board that it must "understand that the city's efforts are in the sole interest of the medical school [and] that nothing should come between the medical college [and] other projects that will go in there." Camp intimated that disagreements and consequent space limitations might force the university to build an auxiliary campus in another city, possibly Mobile. Furthermore, Joseph Volker, the dental school dean, opined that the Eisenhower administration appeared ready "to out-democrat the Democrats" on public health construction policy. If the school could finance the land acquisition, he maintained, it might expect federal aid to balance an ambitious construction and research budget.[12]

In the face of this formidable consensus, HABD officials relented. They agreed to explore various financing options for the college's purchase of its five blocks and to give the school first choice of the available land even though this would invite further red tape and delay. To smooth the planning, Camp, Berson, Hugh Denman, the HABD's urban renewal chief, and Orlando Ogle, the authority chairman, decided to discuss their options with federal Housing and Home Finance Agency officers in Atlanta in

April 1956. As with most significant issues regarding urban renewal the ultimate solutions would be made in conference with federal officials, who controlled the project's purse strings.[13]

The Atlanta meeting reoriented the entire medical center project. Bruce Wedge, the HHFA's regional administrator, preempted the anticipated talk about shifting the particular parcels for the medical college by asking if five blocks were enough for the school. The HABD's plan called for a motel, offices, and commercial development to surround the college. A former National Resources Planning Board regional administrator, Wedge long had worked to push civic leaders in the South to embrace federal urban development programs. In 1941, for instance, he wrote Atlanta's mayor that "since our regional office is located here, we are particularly interested in seeing a capital improvement program made." A visit to Birmingham in 1955 convinced the HHFA bureaucrat that it would be shortsighted for the college to obtain a fraction of the redevelopment of the area. Rather, the medical school should acquire all the land. Berson countered Wedge's question by noting that the college's request merely fulfilled its "urgent needs" because administrators were uncertain how to finance the proposed acquisition, let alone a larger one. "This was too limited an objective, that the future was a long time and that there was little doubt but that the future would bring even greater needs," Wedge responded. A change, however, would require the local housing agency to resubmit site and financial plans and offer proof that the college could buy the property.[14]

The primary motivation behind the Southside project in 1953, Morgan claimed, had been slum clearance, not the expansion of the medical center. After Wedge's bold suggestion the focus clearly shifted. College and city officials embraced the new direction, unifying a planning process that earlier had been marked by squabbles over specific parcels and street closings. Despite the new consensus, redevelopment hurdles remained. Both the Medical Center Advisory Board and the university's trustees approved the new development idea, as did Birmingham's housing authority. College officials, however, remained uncertain about how to finance the purchase, which the housing agency estimated at $2.7 million.[15]

Money worries led to an impasse with the Atlanta-based HHFA planners. Wedge and his staff spurned the school's plan, suggested by Governor James Folsom, to make a $100,000 down payment and acquire options for the property because it placed an undue financial burden on the HABD. Next, the college planned to resell some of the parcels to private hospitals. The Housing Act of 1954 had no provisions for development by a non-profit institution and forbade resale of urban renewal property by its developer. HABD lawyers tried to persuade HHFA bureaucrats that they need not hold Birmingham to all the statutory requirements. College administrators, meanwhile, worried about how to plan for the land they coveted, while continuing to face HHFA disapproval because they did not yet have a specific framework for the entire ten-block site. The HABD continued to own the land and pay the interest on federal development loans until the college bought the property. Moreover, the contract included no guarantee that the college would buy the land, which made Harper uncomfortable given the school's historical financial weakness.[16]

Berson's staff knew that their plans depended more on statewide and national politics than on local decisions. Camp and the planning committee plotted accordingly, setting their sights toward Washington. The dynamism and unpredictability of medical research made it pointless as well as impossible for the college to commit itself to an exact scheme. Camp wrote the HHFA's Urban Renewal Administration director, Richard Steiner, that "by the time we might wish to construct a tuberculosis hospital, it may be evident that this dread killer is on the run and it would not be wise to build a tuberculosis hospital." "Let us suppose that earth-shaking developments in the cancer field are discovered this might require the construction of special facilities for cancer treatment," he continued. The medical center redevelopment, Camp argued, was unique and thus should not be bound to rules that governed residential or commercial construction.[17] To highlight the college's importance to the entire state of Alabama, Camp organized a meeting in Washington with HHFA administrator Albert Cole, Wedge, the entire Alabama congressional delegation, the HABD's Denman, college deans, and Birmingham businessmen. The July 1957 meeting did not solve the remaining bureaucratic tangles but it did evidence a common goal: completion of the project. "We're going to find out how to do this thing," remarked Steiner, "and get it done."[18]

Closing the deal required original thinking, however. Denman, head of the HABD's redevelopment division, proposed a creative solution to the impasse. Born in 1897 in Jacksonville, Alabama, and nicknamed "Flash" in high school, Denman had come to Birmingham in 1923 and worked in real estate and life insurance. In 1952, the veteran of the Office of Price Administration signed on as the housing authority's urban renewal chief, eventually succeeding Harper as its director. Denman advanced the idea that the college would use the land as a campus, a word that "embodied the whole redevelopment plan [and] satisfied the authorities." The novel "campus" solution gave federal HHFA bureaucrats the escape they needed from agency regulations that prevented vague plans and the resale of property in order to eliminate development dreamers and speculators. HHFA's Cole later told Spain that Denman's idea pioneered the college renewal concept and sparked the 1959 amendments to the Housing Act.[19]

The HHFA also accepted the campus concept in September 1957 because funding seemed more secure. A $4.5 million bond issue would go before the state's voters in December, fulfilling an idea that Camp had suggested to Berson's planning committee a year earlier. Appointed chairman of Governor Folsom's steering committee to work out details for the site purchase, Camp convinced the state legislature to back his proposal. Camp and Spain persuaded Camp's boss, Frank Samford, Liberty's president since 1931 and an Auburn trustee, to lead the campaign to ensure that the in-state rivalry between the University of Alabama and Auburn University would not derail the bond issue. Spain and Samford had been boyhood friends in Troy, a relationship that strengthened as they advanced in their careers in Birmingham and served on local boards together. Spain's law firm, in fact, represented Liberty. The Committee for the Adoption of Amendment No. 4, consisting of businessmen, professionals, and educators from all areas of the state, pursued an active public relations campaign. Voters statewide approved the $4.5 million bond issue, which provided $2.7 million for the land purchase, $1 million to match a National Institutes of Health grant for a new research building, and $750,000 to match a Hill-Burton grant for a nurses' residence in the medical center. The bond issues, with state money to match federal grants for two additional buildings to demonstrate a renewed commitment to expansion at the medical center, meant that college officials needed a plan to fill the new space.[20]

Despite the state's generosity, the school could not rely on local contributions or the Alabama legislature for its institutional needs. In his final report as leader of the medical college two years earlier, former dean Durrett had concluded that the funding problem "is too complex and beyond our own means. We must play our part in the established national policies and cooperative programs."[21] The dean had based his assessment on the college's day-to-day finances and the typically bleak outlook for local financing. Alabama-based funding shortcomings were especially evident in the college's operating budget. The indigent patient agreement with Jefferson County remained the college's principal financial drain, and officials from the college and the county government constantly bickered over the terms of the 1945 deal that transferred Hillman and Jefferson Hospitals to the medical school. The medical school had agreed to accept city and county indigent patients at Jefferson in return for a fixed fee from the local government, and administrators constantly wanted more money to match the actual patient costs. In 1956, for example, the county government paid the hospital just $11 per day for each patient but the true cost was $18. University Hospital lost more than $1 million in 1956 thanks to indigent patient costs as well as its emergency room and clinical operations (to which the county contributed no money).[22]

The ongoing cost differential sapped the college's operating budget—and created a problem that seemed to defy solutions. If the hospital raised the cost of private beds, paying patients might go elsewhere, thus reducing both the patient load, critical for the establishment of clinics and for teaching, and the college's income. So the college could not increase the number of indigent patients to meet its clinical teaching needs without jeopardizing its own financial stability. In fact, hospital administrators reduced the number of indigent beds in the hospital from 240 to 200, although they wanted double that number for adequate clinical instruction. (The next year, they announced plans to cut another 50-plus beds.) The operating losses drained resources that might have been used to increase salaries or modernize the school. A 1958 Chamber of Commerce study, for instance, recommended that Jefferson County should have 600 beds for indigent care; however, this would cost $5.8 million, while the county's annual appropriation for indigent care totaled $1.02 million. Birmingham compared poorly to other southern cities in its public health funding. Per capita appropriations for hospital operating funds reached $1.14 in the Alabama city, the report noted, compared to $3.14 in Louisville, $4.07 in Atlanta, and $4.58 in Memphis. Each of these cities had at least twice as many indigent beds as Birmingham.[23]

At first, college officials had looked toward Montgomery. "As we have pointed out frequently in the past," the *Birmingham News* editors wrote in January 1955, "support of the Medical College is clearly a state responsibility." The rural-dominated legislature, nonetheless, declined to pay any portion of the indigent patient services in the state's most urban county. Lawmakers even refused two years later to adopt the necessary legislation to receive federal matching funds for indigent care, an action that may have cost the state $6 million in federal aid. Overall, state assistance remained weak. Throughout the 1950s the legislature's contributions to operating costs and capital construction were the lowest in the South. Comparable medical centers in Kentucky, Florida, Mississippi, and North Carolina had received five times more in state capital aid than the Birmingham campus in that period. Taken together, the isolated decisions by legislators had ripple effects in other areas of the college. The college might have had a $4 million cache to match Hill-Burton funds if not for annual losses on indigent and outpatient services, dental school dean Volker estimated.[24] University of Alabama president Frank A. Rose worried about the cumulative effect of Alabama's niggardliness. The medical college needed better equipment, more resources, and a larger staff, and its employees deserved higher salaries. Medical staff blamed the university when they had to turn away patients because of a lack of beds in the teaching hospital. "The Medical Center problems are critical and morale is low," he explained to the university's trustees. "How much longer can we beg the services of those outstanding people?"[25]

Once again medical school administrators found the answers to their to local problems in Washington, this time through the burgeoning role of the National Institutes of Health. Federal grants began to meet operational and programmatic needs in addition to infrastructure and capital requests. In the 1950s congressional support for medical research mushroomed. The total federal budget for medical research grew from $3 million to $76 million in the 1940s, but from 1955 to 1960 solid congressional backing pushed the NIH budget from $81 million to $400 million. In medical policy—as in housing, transportation, and other areas—the postwar Congresses underwrote infrastructure expansion that states could not or would not do on their own. The growth of the NIH mattered to the medical college because Alabama communities battled for the state's Hill-Burton awards. Even though Alabama ranked seventh in 1959 in total Hill-Burton grants, trailing only New York, California, Ohio, Illinois, North Carolina, and Texas, just a small fraction of the $42 million the state received had gone to Birmingham's medical center. Several factors frustrated medical center advocates. The rural-friendly legislature pressured the state health department to distribute the funds to all areas of the state. Alabama's school construction fund also was small, restricting the college's ability to match Hill-Burton grants. Eventually Berson and Volker suggested that the state form a separate category, distinct from requests by hospitals in Jefferson County or other sections of the state, to consider medical center applications. It did not.[26]

Although Hill-Burton grants proved difficult to win in the 1950s, medical administrators pursued NIH funding to bolster the school's research program. The school received less than $80,000 in outside research grants in 1951, but five years later that total had multiplied more than six times, with the majority of dollars from the NIH. In 1955 the college's research operations were placed under Joseph Volker, the first dean of the dental school. A New Jersey native, Volker had a Ph.D. in chemistry as well as an M.D., and he had come to Birmingham in 1949 from Tufts University to build a program from scratch. The assignment suited Volker's temperament—his broad planning vision, his pragmatism, and his relentless pursuit of goals. The new responsibility was also a consolation prize from Berson, whom the trustees had picked over Volker for the school's top job. Volker had the credentials for his post. In the early 1950s, the dental school had won more federal grant money than the medical college, and the dental school dean knew that the college's reputation depended on its ability to improve its research capabilities. Despite the appointment, Volker chafed under Berson's leadership, but, for the most part, he suppressed his frustration. Frequent consulting work at other universities (which brought several job offers) won his colleagues' respect, and he showed his value to the college through his industrious fund-raising. He served on various NIH committees to hone his Washington credentials. He became such an able grant-winner that his colleagues would joke that every time Volker stopped to pick a quarter off the ground, the federal government matched it.[27]

In 1956 Volker lobbied NIH officials for a new research building knowing that the school's research budget could increase only if its facilities improved. The promise of a significant infusion of federal funds, Berson noted, loosened local purse strings. The NIH approved Volker's request and offered $1 million for a six-story facility. In March 1958, groundbreaking began on the 100,000-square-foot building with 180 labs. The next year the college received $1 million in funding for research, a total that placed the Birmingham school in the top quarter of the nation's eighty medical colleges. Completion of the Health Sciences Research Building prompted an explosion of outside grants. The NIH awarded $500,000 in March 1960 to the Birmingham school for care and study of clinical patients, making it one of six institutions to win the coveted prize. In 1961, the college received $2.5 million in research and training grants, a $1 million increase from the previous year. A year later, the medical center's research budget totaled $3 million on 152 grants. Twenty-two different agencies and foundations provided the aid, with the federal Public Health Service (including the NIH) responsible for three-fourths of the support.[28]

Dean Berson's long-range planning also began to reap dividends by the end of the decade, thanks in large measure to the flood of federal research funding for the health sciences. The medical center of 1958—University Hospital, the county health building, the Basic Sciences building, the VA hospital, and the Crippled Children's Hospital—had changed little since the early 1950s. A transformation began after the urban renewal land acquisition and the NIH-sponsored health sciences building, which ended a long construction drought. Birmingham's private Children's Hospital gained a $1 million Hill-Burton grant (1958), allowing it to relocate to the medical center. The next year the nursing school received $1.25 million in federal construction money and the National Guard decided to build an evacuation hospital armory in the medical center. The scope and variety of federal aid widened in the 1960s. In 1961 federal hospital construction grants tripled the $600,000 donated by Frank Spain for a forty-six-bed rehabilitation hospital, which included physical, occupational, speech, and hearing therapy. A Hill-Burton grant contributed $130,000 toward the Eye Foundation's hospital, another project first proposed in the mid-1950s. Soon after, University Hospital received $800,000 for renovations and a mental health wing and the NIH gave $220,000 to renovate the hospital's third floor for cardiovascular study. In 1962, the HHFA's Community Facility Administration made a $1.5 million low-interest loan to the college for the construction of 128 apartments for students and faculty.[29]

Even as medical school administrators and trustees complained about inadequate local and state funding, the school took great strides after 1958 and continued to cast a significant shadow over the city. By 1962 it had become Birmingham's second largest employer. To be sure, the Southside medical complex had grown separate and distinct from much of the rest of the New South iron and steel town, but its development revealed, particularly to the city's commercial leaders, the promise of federal aid. In the 1960s, however, the federal role deepened as the school increasingly depended on Washington-based agencies for operational as well as construction funding. This shift occurred both because the state legislature consistently failed to give the school its full budget request and because congressional spending for health issues increased. The state's strict budgets made it "imperative that support through research and teaching grants and through any new pattern of Federal financial support be eagerly and successfully sought," a 1960 Medical College Advisory Board memo stated.[30]

Tinsley Harrison, chairman of the school's department of medicine, contended that the increases in NIH assistance allowed the college to escape its doldrums of the early 1950s. Income sources for the medical center changed between 1955 and 1962. Thanks especially to the proliferation of NIH research and training grants, Washington's role was ascendant. The percentage of federal research grants to total income increased to 19 percent in 1962 from 8 percent in 1956. During the same period, the proportion of state money declined from 40 to 22 percent. Unlike the university's arts and sciences campus in Tuscaloosa, the Birmingham school did not have a student-based state formula for budgeting. The legislature consistently fell about 40 percent short of the college's requested budget amounts throughout the 1950s and early 1960s. State appropriations increased marginally during this period, but they did not keep pace with the overall growth of the medical school's budget. (Revenue from patient care and tuition remained constant at about 60 percent of the school's budget.) In 1960, an

American Medical Association accreditation team found that Washington-based capital funding had sparked greater long-range planning and campus development. The investigators lauded the school's improved research program, which had been extended under Volker and depended almost entirely on federal aid.[31]

In 1962, the year that federal research and training grants nearly matched the operating funds provided by the Alabama legislature, another significant transition shaped the medical center. Berson left Birmingham for San Antonio to start the University of Texas's new medical school. In July, the restless Volker, interviewing for the presidency of the University of Rochester's medical school, became the college's top official. He promoted thirty-nine-year-old S. Richardson Hill to dean of the medical college (a position Berson also had held) and Scotty McCallum, his former student at Tufts, to dean of the dental school. The personnel moves brought policy changes. Volker organized twice-monthly summit meetings, in which the new leadership team plotted an aggressive strategy to pursue federal dollars. They sought new facilities, planned administrative and programmatic changes, and outlined ways to upgrade and expand the school's academic program. In particular, the Volker administration would seek new buildings for its basic sciences department, outpatient and dental clinics, a library for basic research needs, a student union, and a second hospital. Hill and McCallum also drafted plans to boost student enrollment in all areas, part of an ambitious plan to augment the school's educational mission.[32]

The new team understood that reliance on federal aid benefited the medical center but also complicated its operations. As the administrators drafted the 1963 fiscal year budget, Volker noted to his staff that for the first time federal sources would exceed state appropriations at the college. With the federal government again upping its health-related spending for capital projects, the administration hoped to match its recent research grant–winning prowess with construction awards. As the federal government took firmer stands on matters of racial justice, for instance, planning at the medical center became entwined with local and national civil rights issues. In June 1963, President John Kennedy's Executive Order 11114 forbade job discrimination in federal grant programs. Moreover, the federal Civil Rights Commission had recommended a year earlier that the president deny Hill-Burton funds to segregated facilities. College officials could not ignore federal standards attached to health grants—not with pending applications for $2 million in federal construction loans, the cornerstone of its growth plans, and its $4 million research budget. College officials quietly took action. University Hospital, for instance, established equal-pay-for-equal-work guidelines, and officials decided to hire "the most competent applicant" in nursing and technical support positions. By 1964, the hospital employed 37 black nurses and 181 licensed practical nurses and had hired black electrocardiogram technicians. Nonetheless, administrators tried to act outside the public eye because they had to appeal both to state officials fiercely hostile to change and to federal bureaucrats. In 1963, the college employed 843 blacks, one-third its workforce, though most of them were relegated to menial service positions. "Our dilemma is a simple one," Volker wrote Oliver Carmichael, Alabama's former chancellor. "On the one hand we are increasingly dependent upon federal support for construction, and the financing of research and instruction [and] such grants forbid discrimination in job employment. On the other the elected officials have what they believe to be a mandate from the population to maintain the local custom of segregation of the races." In a decade, the college had moved from an economic crossroads to a social one.[33]

CHAPTER FIVE

# Birmingham Changes Its Government

A series of *New York Times* articles in 1960 riled Birmingham's political and economic leaders. One story, written by Pulitzer Prize–winner Harrison Salisbury ran under the headline "Fear and Hatred Grip Birmingham." Writing in often overheated and molten prose, Salisbury charged that "more than a few citizens, both white and Negro, harbor growing fear the hour will strike when the smoke of civil strife will mingle with that of the hearths and forges." Incensed local officials threatened to sue the reporter and the newspaper for libel. At the core of their anger, however, was the fear that the stories would undermine businessmen's efforts to recruit new companies to restore a stagnating economy. Salisbury drew a picture of violence and lawlessness certain to dissuade outsiders who might consider putting a branch office or a plant in Birmingham. He wrote of a tense, uneasy place where "every reasoned approach, every inch of middle ground has been fragmented by the emotional dynamite of racism, reinforced by the whip, the razor, the gun, the bomb, the torch, the club, the knife, the mob, [and] the police."[1]

Because of the pointed protests from the business community, the *Times*'s editors went to the extraordinary length of allowing city leaders to write a front-page letter challenging Salisbury's contentions. Signed by William Engel and Mortimer Jordan, president of the Chamber of Commerce, it called Salisbury's reporting "biased, warped, and misleading." Even as they defended their city and argued that "Birmingham people do not see themselves in the image of Harrison Salisbury," members of the local economic elite would come to recognize that they had lost the middle ground. Boosters long had sought to minimize the appearance of racial and political tension in the city, and they fretted that they could no longer influence events there. The twin pressures of economic decline and civil rights protests had undermined their position. Salisbury had recognized that, even if he overdramatized it.[2]

At the time Salisbury's articles appeared, Birmingham business elites already had made two unsuccessful attempts to reassert their control. The Birmingham Downtown Improvement Association (BDIA), formed in 1957 and further proof of the diverging interests of commercial and manufacturing interests, had not sparked significant change in the center city. The next year, a suburban-led merger campaign failed primarily because of fears of integrated schools. The events perpetuated the feuding between business leaders and city politicians and helped derail several redevelopment proposals. In 1961, desperate elites resurrected the idea of changing the form of city government as a way to reestablish their political influence. Momentum for the idea built in some quarters as the city's violent reactions to civil rights demonstrators—the Freedom Riders, for example—and that year's municipal elections reinforced the primacy of the "Bull" Connor–led segregation-first commission. As the Martin Luther King Jr. movement eyed the city as the location for its next round of protests, Chamber chairman Sidney Smyer pushed even harder for the governance change. In a close 1962 vote, city residents voted for a mayor-council, in effect tossing out the three commissioners, who refused to vacate their offices, leaving Birmingham with two governments in the spring of 1963 when King's campaign began. The new mayor, political veteran Albert Boutwell, moved quickly to align the city's interests with those of the medical center, then planning what would become a second forty-two-block renewal project. Although the city would continue to struggle to address its racial and economic fissures, the new political leadership clearly embraced the medical center and its related economy as the city's top priority and as its engine of future growth.

At the Chamber of Commerce's annual dinner in September 1958, its members had listened to a planner from their northern industrial counterpart, Pittsburgh, tell how that city rebuilt its economy. The lesson, which focused on how comprehensive planning and federal urban renewal had sparked an economic rally in Pittsburgh, resonated with businessmen in the audience, many of whom recently had joined the Birmingham Downtown Improvement Association, a group composed mostly of retailers, real estate executives, and bankers. They too had pinned their development hopes on Washington-based grants. Organized in April 1957 the BDIA, sought, as the *Post-Herald* reported, to "pump new blood into Birmingham's ailing downtown business section." Its fourteen-point agenda called for better roads connecting the city and outlying areas, improved traffic and parking patterns, and slum clearance, urban renewal, and cultural development in the central business district. Clarence Hanson, publisher of the *Birmingham News* and the driving force behind the group, supported it because he felt other organizations, such as the Committee of 100, did not sufficiently address local economic concerns. Hanson, in fact, had started the BDIA after the Committee of 100's leadership blocked his attempts to redirect its mission. Already feuding with some of the industrialists about his newspaper's editorial positions, he believed the committee concentrated too much on blue-collar manufacturing recruitment and not enough on white-collar service sector jobs.[3]

Launched with fanfare and a $500,000 budget in late 1949, the Committee of 100 could claim only mixed results in its first decade. TCI president Art Wiebel, who chaired the group, could boast that by 1958 it had lured more than 130 new plants to Jefferson County and had helped convince 90 more companies to expand existing plants, leading to twenty-five thousand jobs. Nearly half of these positions, however, could be attributed to the Hayes Aircraft modification plant (1950), which the committee had lured to a former World War II airplane modification plant next to the municipal airport. The committee's efforts paled before those of Atlanta's industrial recruiters, who claimed to have secured 454 manufacturing plants and more than forty thousand jobs between 1946 and 1954.[4]

The commercial service elite imagined a different future than did the industrialists, the famed Big Mules who supposedly held sway over the city. While personal animosity had played a pivotal role in the formation of the BDIA, so had economic factionalism. Birmingham's leadership class could not find a unified position. The BDIA members—including old-line developers like Robert Jemison Jr., self-made entrepreneurs like Elton B. Stephens, and retailers like Louis Pizitz—defined a mission for the new group distinct from that of the committee. Just thirteen men, for example, belonged to both the Committee of 100 and the BDIA, which had 150 founding members. The committee had a broad representation in banking, retailing, real estate, and manufacturing, but men from the last field dominated its leadership and shaped its policy. The BDIA called for a more clear-cut planning agenda, one that focused on downtown growth to offset fears of declining revenues and business stagnation. Generally unimpressed with the committee's intermittent industrial recruitment, the BDIA sought to energize the city's urban core in hopes of counteracting the centrifugal tug on business that accompanied residential suburbanization (of which, paradoxically, they were the vanguard).[5]

The BDIA prodded the split commission into taking several limited steps. First, a $10,000 contribution from the BDIA led to the hiring of Harland Bartholomew's planning firm to draft a master plan. Despite the donation, Commissioner Eugene "Bull" Connor voted against the effort. Next, the group worked with the city's planning department to find a downtown renewal project. More than ever, such a plan would rely on Washington's assistance because, Mayor James Morgan noted, the city's weak balance sheet limited its assistance to code enforcement and condemnation. To anchor the project the businessmen's group proposed a downtown merchandise mart. BDIA president Elton B. Stephens pointed to New Orleans's retail center and Atlanta's own newly built $5.5 million facility as reasons why those cities' growth rates surpassed Birmingham's. "Other cities are acting," the *News* editorialized, "and if we do not we will surely be left far behind." A second proposal included downtown Morris Avenue, once the city's wholesale hub, and decaying city blocks on the eastern edge of the central business district. In May 1959, the Housing Authority of the Birmingham

District requested federal planning money to make a more detailed study of those plans. Commissioners Morgan and James Waggoner supported those efforts; Connor opposed them.[6]

Besides pushing for greater attention to the urban core, the BDIA, with the help of the Chamber, formed the Greater Birmingham Committee to renew talks about regionalism, specifically a merger between city and suburbs. Committee members cited Atlanta's annexation of Buckhead as the spark to that city's dynamism. The Greater Birmingham Committee imagined the potential in joining prosperous residential suburbs—home to many of the city's business leaders—and the ailing central business district. The Birmingham Realty Company's Sidney Smyer, like other committee members, linked economic development and politics. Voters in a greater Birmingham would be more likely to push politicians to embrace downtown renewal, they thought. Stephens, a self-made magazine subscription magnate from rural Clio, warned that without steps such as annexation "there is an omnipresent danger that Birmingham may become an 'absentee ownership city,'" by which he meant not so much control by northern-based firms as the abandonment of the city by the local economic elite.[7]

Curiously, Stephens's solution as to how locals could exert more control over their own affairs called for the inclusion of outside influences—namely, federal grant programs. Even as racial issues clouded the political agenda in 1959, Stephens could still argue that Washington's money came without social strings. By his logic, annexation could lead to an infusion of federal development dollars that, in turn, would generate the prosperity that would allow Birmingham to avoid future aid or directives from Washington. A budding economy would then forestall mounting civil rights pressures. Stephens, like Frank Spain and Liberty National's Frank Samford, rural-born men who came to dominate the city's business class, cared about good roads and economic development. No racial moderate, he moved to Mountain Brook in part to avoid race issues and pushed for a better connector road between his suburban home and downtown office. Despite his natural political conservatism, Stephens believed local government should take a more active role in turning around the regional economy.[8]

Merger talk advanced in the fall of 1958 when advocates put the measure on the next year's ballot and formed the Citizens for Merger Committee (CMC) to run the campaign. Octogenarian Jemison, the developer of

Mountain Brook, chaired the CMC. Reflecting the tortured logic behind the idea, he noted that with "our traditional southern way of life, only bold action will enable Birmingham to remain a vital force in the nation." The pro-merger group trotted out political stalwarts such as former state senator and corporate attorney James A. Simpson, whose client list included TCI and Frank Dixon, Alabama's governor from 1939 to 1943. Nevertheless, a younger generation, including Stephens and Newman Waters, a Vestavia Hills resident who owned downtown and suburban offices and theaters, set the committee's policy. The drive differed from the effort led by former mayor Cooper Green in 1949. Now businessmen advocated the inclusion of Shades Valley suburban communities such as Mountain Brook and Homewood, but they ignored the industrial suburbs bordering the city to the north and west. The change reflected the political goals of annexation.[9]

The merger proposal won a broad range of endorsements, but it failed to gain a clear consensus in the city's business community. Backers included the two daily newspapers, local trade unions, and Mayor Morgan. The powerful Birmingham Real Estate Board, with 650 members in the city and suburbs, and the Chamber of Commerce also supported the proposal. The Committee of 100 remained silent, however. Although it never publicly endorsed or disavowed the idea, many of its members worked in public or private against the merger. Industrialists such as Richard Stockham, president of a family-owned pipe-making plant, feared the future annexation of manufacturing areas. Higher taxes would result, opponents claimed, hindering business recruitment efforts. Stockham's stance further revealed the opposing outlooks of the manufacturing elite (the Big Mules) and leaders in the city's emerging service economy. The inability of the factions to join forces weakened the proposal. A *News* editorial charged that Red Mountain, a natural geological boundary, should not serve as an artificial economic divide for the region: "If Birmingham, strangled as it is by smaller municipalities on all sides, deteriorates into a second class city every suburb will suffer with it."[10]

Leaders favoring merger resurrected the dusty Birmingham-Atlanta rivalry concept to further their cause. The Atlanta analogy clarified the theme of the CMC's lobbying efforts: the need for businessmen to hold political control of Birmingham. "BIRMINGHAM Needs Us and We Need BIRMINGHAM," shouted one pamphlet. The CMC also circulated a letter from

Atlanta mayor William Hartsfield extolling suburban annexation and explaining how the 1952 Buckhead annexation had energized his city. "When the limits of a city remain static for too long a time," Hartsfield wrote, "there is a tremendous migration of new and youthful, active, child-raising citizens into the suburbs. These constitute the 'cream of the crop.' Unless some way is found to reach out and include these people in the active, voting management of the city, it will have a disastrous effect on the future management of the town." CMC leaders seconded the Buckhead theme. In contrast, continued economic decline and stagnation threatened their own city. Houston, Dallas, New Orleans, and Memphis also had witnessed population and land gains during the 1950s while Birmingham had not, the CMC argued in a series of newspaper advertisements. Nonetheless, even merger advocates found the Atlanta links overdone. "Atlanta has left us so far behind, that it is silly to compare the two cities," Waters said.[11]

Annexation backers disagreed about the underlying need for political control over the suburbs. Some believed it necessary to offset a growing black electorate; others wanted to counteract decisions made by working-class whites. Mountain Brook resident Walter J. Hanna, a Hayes Aircraft executive, and Simpson, a lawyer who had supported "Bull" Connor's return to politics in 1957, envisioned a greater Birmingham to fight civil rights agitation and to preserve white political supremacy. Simpson feared blacks would become the critical swing bloc in local elections as they had been in some recent national and regional contests. By 1958, a decade and a half after *Smith v. Allwright* (1944), about eleven thousand blacks in Jefferson County could vote, doubling the 1954 figures. Those numbers meant that blacks constituted about 10 percent of the city electorate, and with just one in ten African Americans registered to vote, Simpson viewed the future with trepidation. While whites worried that blacks might overwhelm the rolls, black activists fretted about apathy and complacency among their race. *Birmingham World* editor Emory Jackson urged African American residents outside the city's professional class to register.[12]

The CMC leaders more often than not focused on white politics, ignoring racial issues whenever possible. Speaking in Homewood, attorney George "Peach" Taylor argued that a merger would add conservative votes on election days, delivering the leadership needed to reverse Birmingham's woes. Well-to-do suburbanites had long since split with working-class voters in

Birmingham on national and statewide issues. In the 1946 Democratic senatorial primary, Simpson himself had won more than 65 percent of the vote in Jefferson County's wealthiest white-collar suburbs; however, John Sparkman won more than two-thirds of the vote in working-class neighborhoods in east and west Birmingham. While Dwight Eisenhower won 46 percent of the countywide vote in the 1952 presidential election, 80 percent of the ballots in Mountain Brook went for the retired general. George Wallace, moreover, failed to carry Birmingham's suburbs in either his 1958 or 1962 gubernatorial campaigns.[13]

Merger advocates recognized the political bind they had created by becoming "daytime" citizens of the city. One proponent estimated that three-fourths of the city's business and industrial leaders lived in either suburban Mountain Brook or Homewood, whose median incomes were triple and double, respectively, the city's figure of $5,000. Moreover, two-thirds of the population in the two towns either worked for or owned firms located in Birmingham's central business district, according to city planners. Mayor Morgan guessed that Mountain Brook residents filled one-third of city board positions. As a consequence of suburban abandonment, "other groups less interested in long-range community advancement and integrity have moved in," the CMC's "Peach" Taylor said in a speech in Homewood. Several thousand united suburban voters actually could control citywide elections, which had often been decided by just a handful of votes, Taylor noted. In 1953, for instance, Wade Bradley had defeated "Jabo" Waggoner by less than fifty votes, and in 1957 "Bull" Connor had returned as public safety commissioner by a 103-vote margin. For his part, Connor feared consolidation because it would dilute his new power base. As he told Mountain Brook mayor Charles Zukoski, "You talk like Birmingham is going to get something when we take in Homewood and Mountain Brook. I think it's just the other way around."[14]

The over-the-mountain elite feared that working-class political control would make strict segregation, not economic development, the central issue of Birmingham politics. Yet the social issue could not be avoided, and even though the CMC tried to bury it, race was on the minds of suburban voters. The antimerger forces turned to school desegregation as the antidote to the CMC's pitch. Opponents knew they could not rely only on arguments about political efficiency (taxation, municipal services, and the city manager government). School integration became a principal issue, one that had emerged several years earlier when the Alabama Christian Movement for Human Rights (ACMHR), the direct action protest group led by the Reverend Fred Shuttlesworth, filed a lawsuit in an effort to integrate Birmingham's schools. As the matter worked its way through the court system, the Citizens Information Committee (CIC), the antiannexation faction chaired by Stockham, president of his family's Stockham Valve and Fittings, seized the case as its own, quick to exploit the fears of suburban parents who equated annexation with mixed-race schools. The CIC kept the matter before residents of Mountain Brook and Homewood with mailings and advertisements. The parent-teacher association at Mountain Brook's Crestline Elementary School proposed that the town form its own school system. Because no blacks owned homes there, the community could avoid school integration if its schools (part of the county system) were independent. "The schooling of more than 2,000 Mountain Brook children hangs in the balance," and annexation would surely tie its schools into the city's integration battles, suggested one CIC pamphlet. The Mountain Brook City Council talked about a referendum for separation, and just two weeks before the May merger vote, a town government committee reported in favor of independent schools.[15]

Suburbanites, who turned out in droves, rejected annexation. In Mountain Brook, where three-fourths of registered voters went to the polls, residents defeated the measure by 2,350 to 1,492. Homewood residents also turned thumbs down, although by a narrower margin. The potential merger benefits articulated by advocates, including economic growth and conservative political leadership, turned out to be no match for the pressing matter of school integration. According to the voters, the best way to retain white control and local social customs—Simpson's stated goals—was to avoid Birmingham, not to join it. "We fear the sharp possibility that an entire city's future welfare was at stake and was all but tossed down the drain for a variety of small reasons," the *News* observed.[16]

Far from linking the city and suburbs on a common platform defending segregation, the antimerger vote heightened tensions between suburban business leaders and Birmingham politicians. Connor and Waggoner had considered the movement a slap at the city. Their latent hostility emerged during a campaign several months later to build an urban-suburban roadway, on the drawing board in some fashion since the 1940s, a project touted by merger advocates and at the top of the BDIA agenda. The suburban spur would relieve two clogged local roads that fed all Mountain Brook and Homewood traffic over Red Mountain into Birmingham.[17] BDIA president Stephens asked the city commissioners to fund a feasibility study (which would release federal matching money). They said no to the $50,000 request. Shades Valley residents had spurned Birmingham, so the city commissioners decided to tweak the suburbanites. Mayor Morgan, long a proponent of regional growth, felt burned and said the city would not help to pay for a road to assist inconvenienced suburban drivers. In response to Stephens's comment that the lack of a new road would cause stagnation in Birmingham, Morgan asserted that it was the antiannexation suburbanites who had inflicted the most harm on the city. A new road, Morgan charged, would just make the exodus easier and allow Shades Valley residents "to make faces at us." Waggoner said the city would focus its efforts on people who lived, paid taxes, and voted in the city. A frustrated Stephens accused the city of "building a dam between Birmingham and Shades Valley and thus deterring the growth of downtown Birmingham." He might have been talking about his neighbors as well. The peevishness both sides exhibited about the expressway funding did not put an end to future planning or road-building projects, but it manifested the divisions in metropolitan Birmingham.[18]

Ever wary of the city's economic decline, the BDIA pushed ahead on its other objectives: better roads and downtown renewal. The snail's pace of change further frustrated Birmingham's business class and darkened their outlook about the future. While the testy relations between the city's economic and political leadership contributed to the crisis atmosphere in Birmingham, the city's awkward relationship with the state legislature along with the narrow, self-interested actions of business leaders exacerbated the problem. Six months after the annexation fiasco, the BDIA, having obtained partial funding from the state and surrounding local governments, negotiated a compromise about the suburban spur over Red Mountain with the city commissioners, who agreed to fund a reduced share of the feasibility plan. The study initiated a slow, decade-long building schedule for the expressway. Birmingham's poor relationship with the state government, which dispensed federal highway funds, added to the constant delays. Governor George Wallace, mindful of his losses in the Birmingham suburbs, kept a tight lid on the highway money targeted for the state's largest county. Jefferson County did not receive funding proportionate to its population, and Birmingham had received no state dollars for major highway construction since 1952 because of the choices of Montgomery-based policymakers and the city's own decision not to fund basic road studies as did other municipalities. The absence of adequate studies put Birmingham at a disadvantage as it battled with other cities for federal renewal grants, said city planning director John Steinichen, who rated his department's work "incomplete" and "ineffective." Partly that was by the design of the three-member commission, which now wanted to limit Washington's role in the city and refused to allow Steinichen to join a regionwide planning group that would have doubled the department's budget and brought more grants to the city.[19]

Meanwhile, the BDIA's downtown renewal efforts sputtered, disappointments that stood in sharp contrast to the gathering momentum at the Southside medical center. In early 1960, businessmen and planners managed to win the support of Morgan and Waggoner—but not Connor—to study a twenty-two-block site on the eastern edge of the central business district. But a special urban renewal committee that included Morgan, Senator John Sparkman, Hugh Denman of the HABD, Stephens, and Roper Dial, who ran Sears's Birmingham operations, failed to adopt a plan. The group's consultant, Arthur D. Little, offered a bleak assessment, reporting that the economic dispersion to the suburbs would continue and that embattled downtown retailers (when faced with a specific project) did not want more competition. In March 1961, Stephens told the committee that, while the special advisory group he chaired favored urban renewal in principle, it recommended the committee disband because "a suitable land use was not found." Rather than spend $1.5 million of scarce municipal funds, Stephens said the city should continue ongoing efforts to locate a U.S. Postal Service mail handling facility in the area. When challenged, the BDIA had proven to be self-focused and cautious.[20]

Members of Birmingham's business class, seeking to restore economic vitality and a sense of order to the community, found themselves in an untenable position because in their rush to the suburbs they had abandoned their direct role in electoral politics. Their redevelopment agenda, which included a reliance on federal grant programs, ignored the threat of intervention that accompanied such projects. The medical center and past public housing projects had shown how African Americans could gain leverage from the presence of federal bureaucrats, and the racial stakes had risen by the late 1950s. Insulated from racial issues in their suburban residential neighborhoods, the business class ignored those concerns, further evidence of their tin ears toward city politics. Meanwhile, Birmingham politicians, threatened by the possibility of rising opportunities for local blacks, increasingly embraced the working-class and lower-middle-class constituencies that dominated the electorate. The stance adopted by Birmingham's elite mimicked that of business moderates in other southern cities; nonetheless, without a political base, they failed to implement a plan. In January 1961, the Birmingham Realty Company's Sidney Smyer, now head of the Chamber of Commerce, forwarded a plan that he hoped would alter the balance of political power. Along with typical proposals—urban-suburban consolidation, downtown redevelopment, more persistent business recruitment, and cooperation among business factions in the city—the senior executive of the city's largest downtown property owner suggested that the city reconsider its system of government.[21]

Changing the form of government resurrected an idea debated during the early 1950s, when the commission first had come under attack. Smyer called the three-man commission (in which each commissioner was responsible for several areas of governance) inefficient, outdated, and riven by personal conflict. He also thought structural reform might aid consolidation. In 1955, for instance, Jefferson County's legislative delegation had approved a statute allowing Birmingham's voters to decide among a commission, mayor-council, or manager-council form of government. A petition signed by 10 percent of the electorate could force a special referendum. The proposal, however, had been buried under the reaction to *Brown* and subsequent civil rights protests. Connor, who as a pro–civil service reform state legislator in the 1930s had favored abolishing of the commission and who had supported the state delegation's action when he was out of office in the mid-1950s, now opposed any change. He cited civil rights issues as paramount. In 1959, Connor told the Committee for Better Government that after Nashville had adopted a mayor-council government, blacks won election to that city's council.[22]

With Birmingham's 1961 primary elections just weeks away, Smyer coyly insisted that his proposal lacked political motivation and should not be interpreted as a direct attack against any sitting commissioner. While the developer insisted publicly that the plan was apolitical, he privately told colleagues that he did not want the idea linked too closely with merger talk. If the effort appeared to be suburban bullying, it might lose support in the city, for bad blood remained from the 1959 annexation attempt. Businessmen continued to view consolidation as the easiest way to jump-start Birmingham's economy. One month after first proposing the idea, the Chamber president moved ahead on it, although, as a political cover, he commissioned the Birmingham Bar Association to study various forms of municipal government. Any opinion could be cloaked as the view of disinterested experts, and Smyer said the Chamber would not lobby for a particular conclusion. In April 1961, the Bar Association's working committee began meeting. Smyer's public stance would shift as civil rights demonstrations and local elections altered Birmingham's landscape.[23]

Direct civil rights protest squeezed Birmingham like a vise, adding tension to and then splintering the complex and uneasy relationship among racial and socioeconomic groups in the metropolitan region. Glenn Eskew has demonstrated that the state's banishment of the NAACP and the rise of Shuttlesworth's ACMHR moved race leadership from Birmingham's cautious black professional elite to more aggressive ministers. The religious leaders fought harder than black businessmen against segregation. Each Shuttlesworth-led civil rights campaign raised racial tensions in the city. White counterviolence then led to several unfavorable profiles in the national media. The subsequent decision by leaders of national civil rights organizations to target Birmingham further raised the racial and political stakes.

Always known as a tough town—"integration's hottest crucible," in *Time*'s phrase—Birmingham soon became seared into the national consciousness as an epithet for southern backwardness and racism. The arrival of the Freedom Riders on May 14, 1961, fresh from violence in nearby Anniston, helped to secure that reputation. When a bus filled with civil rights protesters upholding desegregation in interstate travel pulled into Birmingham's Trailways station a gang of white rowdies met it. With no police on hand to guard the riders, a short, vicious, and one-sided brawl followed as the waiting crowd pummeled the activists. In the fifteen minutes before the police arrived, *Post-Herald* photographer Tommy Langston documented the beatings; his pictures were transmitted worldwide. Smyer, for instance, saw them while attending a Rotary conference in Japan. Rumors of Ku Klux Klan violence had swirled about the city before the Freedom Riders reached Birmingham, and writers contend that Connor, the public safety commissioner, had negotiated a deal with leaders of the hate group, giving them a quarter-hour alone with the riders before he would send in the police.[24]

No fans of the Freedom Riders or their motives, Birmingham's commercial leaders worried about how outsiders would interpret the bloody spectacle. The violence dramatized long-standing differences between the business elite, whose paramount concern was the city's economic stagnation, and the city's political leaders, who were more fierce in their defense of segregation. Developer William Engel, who lived in Mountain Brook, blamed the racial unrest on working-class whites, Connor's political base. "Unfortunately, it's just those people for whom we're spending time and money to bring in industry to provide work who are causing all the trouble," said the former chairman of the Committee of 100. Following the Freedom Riders episode, Engel, chairman of the local United Jewish Alliance, stated that Birmingham faced a crisis and needed to move forward or "eat the dust of other cities." Otherwise, "Birmingham will be a city of infamy known for violence." Engel, Smyer, and the commercial elite maintained that lawlessness jeopardized their business recruitment. Smyer told the *Wall Street Journal* that several companies decided against moving to Alabama after the Freedom Riders incident. They were among the civic leaders who considered the commissioners culpable, writing Senator Lister Hill that "some authorities seemed deliberately to have evaded their responsibilities." The *News* repeated this view in an editorial a week after the violence. One month earlier the newspaper had endorsed Connor's reelection bid, but now it asked, echoing the headline of Salisbury's controversial article, "when will the people demand that fear and hatred be driven from the streets?" One answer depended on support for the ideas of Smyer's Chamber advisory committee.[25]

The Freedom Riders incident palpably affected city elections, although in a way that alarmed the business moderates. Race became the defining issue in the Democratic runoff for the president of the city commission (in common parlance, the mayor). Two weeks earlier, Connor and Waggoner had breezed to reelection to their commission posts. Connor had won with his highest count ever, 61 percent of the vote, carrying forty-two of the city's fifty-one precincts. His widest margins came in the city's lower-middle-class and blue-collar neighborhoods. Two University of Alabama Law School graduates battled in the runoff to replace Morgan as mayor. After twenty-four years on the commission, Morgan had stepped down. Publicly, he cited fatigue, but he told friends that he had no stomach for the city's divisive racial and class politics. Entering the runoff, former Federal Bureau of Investigation (FBI) agent Arthur Hanes, who had been head of security at Hayes Aircraft since 1951, trailed Tom King. During the primary both men generally had avoided overt racial politics. King, a former United States district attorney and senior aide to Representative George Huddleston, had centered his campaign on the economic issues favored by the city's commercial elite, in particular airport expansion and a merger with outlying suburbs. In the final two weeks before the vote, Hanes torched King on the race issue and reversed the earlier polls. To emphasize King's black support in the primary, Hanes circulated a picture of King shaking hands with an African American. Hanes also tarred the former congressional aide as "Washington's candidate," code for integrationist sentiment. On May 30, 1961 Hanes beat King by nearly 4,000 votes, 21,133 to 17,364.[26]

The *News* wondered if Hanes could unite the city. An editorial cited three blocs that the new mayor would need to unite: his backers, King supporters, and the forty thousand eligible voters, half the electorate, who had not voted. Promoting the message of the business moderates (publisher Clarence Hanson was a founding member of the BDIA), the newspaper's post-election editorial urged Hanes to focus on economic development, to improve local government services, especially for schools and parks, and to show moderation on racial issues. Nonetheless, from the time of the Democratic primary to when the new commission took office the relationship between politicians and the city's business leadership again shifted. In October, the Bar Association had issued its report, recommending the mayor-council as the best form of government for the city, expressing its dissatisfaction, however obliquely, with the commission.[27]

The Hanes-led commission wasted little time in rejecting the advice of the city's business class. Rather than deliberative calm, it favored racial brinksmanship. The first clash centered on the commissioners' reaction to a federal court order barring segregation of the city's recreational facilities. After January 1962 the commission could no longer enforce City Ordinance No. 859, Federal District Court judge Hobart Grooms ruled in October. Grooms's decision responded to a lawsuit filed two years earlier by the ACMHR. Rather than comply with the judge's order, the commissioners closed the city's recreation facilities, shutting down four golf courses, sixty-seven parks, and thirty-eight playgrounds. Their action affected whites and blacks alike and unleashed a groundswell of emotion that made consensus impossible.[28]

The decision dismayed business moderates, but a newspaper poll showed that public opinion split on the matter. Forest Park resident Travis Wolfe accused the commissioners of shortsightedly following the rowdies, noting metaphorically that they "were cutting off their noses to spite their faces." The closing of the parks hurt attempts to restore the city's economy, the Chamber charged. Chief city planner John Steinichen, who announced his resignation (to go to Atlanta), asserted that the controversy not only would hurt promotional efforts but would complicate and possibly curtail the use of federal grants. "Let me warn you that federal aid is going to increase and not decrease. I don't see how you can ignore the possibilities of federal aid, at least be in a position to obtain it. Remember, we are already up to our ears in federal aid," he informed the commissioners.[29]

Still, it was meddling by outsiders that angered many residents. A swarm of letters to the commissioners backed Connor, Hanes, and Waggoner. In many letters, Birmingham residents included the city's commercial elite among the outsiders. Thanking Hanes for defending segregation, T. W. Aitken, treasurer of the local Brotherhood of Railroad Trainmen, wrote that "for as you know, nearly all of them live outside of our city limits and should not have a say-so as to how our city should be run."[30] The commissioners concurred. In response to the Chamber and to celebrate their defiance of court-ordered desegregation, they called on residents to reject the court's usurpation of local authority, and they attacked the business class for caving in on the race issue. Their January declaration urged citizens to resist "those ready, for fear or for favors, or through indifference to their public duty, to bend their necks to the yoke and to kiss the hand of the tyrant. If there are those among us who, for another dollar in the till, or for another industry in our city, or for fear of the printed or broadcast tongue-lashings of those who, contrary to Biblical injunction, set themselves up as our judges, would yield in this cacophony of intimidation, bribery, cajolery, economic compulsion, political pressure, clerical suasion and outright threats of fine and imprisonment, let them answer to their consciences."[31]

Desperate business moderates, their political base weakened, attempted to reach out to the black professional class. Failing to lessen the extremism on one side, they hoped to defuse the pressures on the other flank. In spring 1962, at the urging of James Head, owner of the state's largest office supply store, Smyer and A. G. Gaston, a black millionaire with substantial stakes in real estate and insurance, began to meet. They enlarged their talks to include other business leaders, including members of the Smyers-led Senior Citizens Committee, an advisory group of Chamber members influential in the financial, commercial, and manufacturing communities. For the most part, however, Smyer and Gaston met alone. In the meetings, the two sought to remove the most offensive elements of segregation. The commission refused overtures to meet with the Smyer-Gaston group. At the same time, the conferences could have little measurable impact because Gaston did not represent the African American civil rights activists. Birmingham's black community had its own socioeconomic splinters, and the professional middle class no longer set the civil rights agenda for direct action activists led by Shuttlesworth and the ACMHR. Moreover, students from Miles College in Fairfield would make their own demands, for instance, for integration at the city's department stores.[32]

Homegrown civil rights demonstrations, like those of the Miles College students, only underscored the business moderates' impotence. Furthermore, they could not convince the commission to accept even the smallest compromises on the color line to head off those protests. Starting in March, Miles students had organized boycotts against Birmingham's two biggest downtown department stores, Loveman's and Pizitz's, which in the short term had tremendous success. In addition to seeking the desegregation of lunch counters and rest rooms, the protesters wanted the stores to hire black sales workers. African Americans, 40 percent of the city's population, accounted for about one-third of the business at those stores. The boycott dried up nearly all of those sales, pushing bottom lines of the struggling downtown retailers into the red. Although the boycott faltered after several months, Martin Luther King Jr.'s Southern Christian Leadership Conference (SCLC) now eyed the Alabama city as the site for its next direct action campaign. To head off those possible demonstrations, Smyer's Senior Citizens Committee sought to broker an agreement with local groups. The committee urged the stores to remove the "colored" signs from above water fountains and rest rooms. The city commission refused any compromise, in contrast to Atlanta, where Mayor Ivan Allen ordered the removal of racial signs in city hall in his first day in office. When the commissioners became aware that the stores had made those small changes, the police, under Connor's direction, increased inspections and threatened substantial fines for violations of local segregation ordinances. The stores capitulated, reinstalling the signs.[33]

As civil rights protests deepened the political stalemate in Birmingham, business moderates returned to the idea of changing the form of city government. Not only had the intractable city commission—as its response to the Freedom Riders, the park desegregation lawsuit, and the department store negotiations had shown—given the city a public relations black eye, but it also blocked businessmen's participation in government, according to a 1962 Chamber working paper. A poor image, a stagnant economy, and integration squabbles hindered the city, the draft noted. The Senior Citizens Committee remained committed to federally funded urban renewal and business recruitment, but it offered few concrete solutions (beyond avoiding protests and violence) about how to ease the racial impasse. The commercial elite did not view the civil rights demonstrations as part of a struggle for social justice but as a hurdle in their efforts to rebuild the city. Smyer adopted a pragmatic outlook. "You might say it was a dollar-and-cents thing. If we're going to have good business in Birmingham we better change our way of living," he later said. More often than not, the committee debated cosmetic solutions to redefine Birmingham's image. At one point, the *News*'s Hanson, mindful of the press's power to influence opinion, suggested that the Chamber organize receptions for out-of-state reporters who came to Birmingham to cover civil rights protests. Hanson hoped that a dose of "southern hospitality" would give journalists a favorable impression of the city and its potential.[34]

Several young lawyers, eager reformers who had cut their teeth working in government and Democratic campaigns, devised a strategy to put the change-in-government idea before the voters. David Vann, an attorney who later served as the city's mayor from 1975 to 1979, was the chief tactician. A former law clerk for Justice Hugo Black during the Supreme Court's 1954 term and the Birmingham-area captain of John Kennedy's 1960 presidential campaign, Vann studied political trends and was an astute vote counter. The results of the 1962 Democratic gubernatorial primary and runoff revealed to Vann that the area's white-collar elite and growing black electorate could form a majority if they both supported the same candidate or issue. In the 1962 votes, the two factions had backed the same candidate, Tuscaloosa attorney Ryan deGraffenried. The trend was especially apparent in the May runoff election. (In the Democratic primary, Connor ran fifth among seven candidates statewide.) While George Wallace whipped the pro-business moderate in the statewide race, deGraffenried had carried Jefferson County by cobbling together a coalition of wealthy suburban and urban whites as well as black voters. Vann believed that a similar combination—minus the suburban voters—could dethrone the commission. Vann, working with fellow attorneys Tom King and Charles Morgan, also found a way to overcome the difficulty in getting a petition with 10 percent of the city's registered voters, an expected stumbling block, and the matter before the electorate. In the wake of the Supreme Court's *Baker v. Carr* (1962) ruling, a Federal District Court judge ordered that Alabama hold a special election for a reapportioned state legislature. The mayor-council advocates could put petitions outside the polling places on the August election day. As voters cast ballots they could also sign the petitions.

Smyer, buoyed by Vann's strategy, took charge of the campaign, assembling an eclectic group that eventually named itself Citizens for Progress. He enlisted the support of the Birmingham Real Estate Board. Vann, drawing on his work on the Kennedy campaign, brought in the Birmingham Labor Council. But the coalition was not easy to sustain, and leading businessmen proved reluctant to step forward and publicly disavow the commission. In July 1962—one month before the petitions would be placed outside the polls—Smyer and Vann asked twenty-five senior business executives to help lead the campaign; all refused. Frustrated by his colleagues' political timidity, Smyer suggested a grassroots move. Instead of a campaign led by "notables," the Citizens for Progress agenda would be pushed by a team of "anybodies." Citizens for Progress would demonstrate a groundswell of public support for the change. A core of activists gathered signatures from several hundred residents in mid-July, which the group then published in a series of newspaper advertisements. One of the so-called anybodies was a housepainter named William Jenkins, a member of the political action committee of the Birmingham Labor Council, who had the same name as a prominent judge in town. Vann remembered later that it helped the organization because many residents assumed that the judge backed the change-in-government plan.[35]

The anybody movement, along with the relative ease in gathering signatures, created enough momentum to place the issue on the ballot. At first, the editorial pages remained silent; then the *Post-Herald,* led by its editor Duard LeGrand, began to criticize the commissioners as ineffective. The *Post-Herald*'s editorial board scolded Connor for taking a month's vacation after his unsuccessful run for governor. "Not since the dark depression days of the early 1930s have the citizens of Birmingham faced so many problems and never has the leadership at City Hall been so lacking," a July editorial commented. After Citizens for Progress collected eleven thousand signatures on the August special election day, the two newspapers more actively supported the campaign. Smyer's group protected its petitions in a safety deposit box at the First National Bank, fearful that commission allies would seek to destroy the valuable list. The petition would give Birmingham voters the opportunity to choose among three forms of government: commission, mayor-council, and manager-council.[36]

The campaign unfolded relatively quietly, as if each side was uncertain about how best to frame its case. Both groups appealed for racial solidarity, although Citizens for Progress tended to couch its support for reform in dry, apolitical arguments about efficient government. The commissioners talked about political loyalty, occasionally charging that Citizens for Progress sought to abolish segregation or that half of its petition signatures were from blacks. Chamber leaders worked behind the scenes, according to businessman Newman Waters, to undermine the commission. "It is my sincere opinion that the officials of the Chamber have not for the past several years made an honest and sincere attempt to co-operate with the City Commissioners," Waters wrote the Chamber's executive director several months after the campaign. Connor, Waggoner, and Hanes appeared to be saving the race card for the runoff election (a staple of almost every local vote), following a strategy similar to that of Hanes's successful mayoral race in 1961. Citizens for Progress leaders did not agree that the mayor-council system would lead to the election of blacks, and they willingly made the point when necessary. Vann said that it would stop white flight. "Unless we adopt the mayor-council form of government this is exactly what is going to happen. The white people are moving out, the Negroes are moving in."[37]

The commissioners' bungling responses to the political challenges in the campaign reinforced their opponents' claims that they were obstructionists not leaders and that commission government was subject to personal abuse. After vainly challenging the signatures on the petition, for example, the commissioners refused to schedule a special referendum as state law dictated. A county judge intervened and set a November vote. Next, the commissioners threatened to dismiss any city employee who had signed the petition. Connor alternately called Vann a "communist" or an agent of "Bobby Soxer Kennedy" and charged that Supreme Court Justice (and Birmingham native) Hugo Black had sent Vann, his former law clerk, to the city "to brainwash us." The reformers painted the politicians as corrupt and willing to retain office by any means. A week before the vote the *News* published a verbatim copy of notes from a secret meeting between the commissioners and city firefighters in which Hanes offered a pay raise in exchange for votes for the commission. Citizens for Progress seized on the exchange. "Why do you care where the money is coming from, we are here to talk about raises not taxes," an advertisement quoted Hanes as saying in the October meeting, before ending with the group's tag line, "Let's end this kind of corruption in City Hall—vote mayor-council."[38]

The November balloting was close, but the mayor-council model won an outright majority of 52 percent, avoiding the need for a second ballot. The mayor-council defeated the commission option by 2,401 votes—19,317 to 16,916—in an election in which more eligible voters stayed home than participated. Less than 3 percent picked the manager-council form (which had had no visible advocacy during the campaign). Voting followed the patterns predicted by Vann that summer. A coalition of white-collar middle-class whites and blacks gave the mayor-council option its 800-vote majority over the other two choices combined. Voters in Forest Park, Roebuck, Southside neighborhoods along Highland Avenue, and black communities in Smithfield and Ensley supported the change. Blacks voted more than three to one for the mayor-council option. Conversely, residents of Ensley, West End, and East Lake backed the commission. The winning coalition was the kind of union that Hanes had exploited in his 1961 runoff election victory against Tom King. This time, however, the commissioners could not tar the mayor-council movement with black support because the slim majority meant there would be no runoff election.[39]

When voters next went to the polls in a series of critical elections that would shape Birmingham's future, the city had become the focus of the national civil rights campaign. In March and April 1963, when residents twice voted for a mayor and a nine-member city council elected in citywide districts, the Southern Christian Leadership Conference protested against segregation. Beginning in the fall of 1962 and continuing through early 1963, the King-led organization devised Project X, a program of sit-ins against unequal facilities in Birmingham's downtown department stores. The SCLC leadership, smarting from setbacks elsewhere, wanted to find the right battleground for its cause. Besides its reputation as a segregationist stronghold, Birmingham's confused political climate offered an inviting target. To SCLC leaders, it was a "city that combined the plantation attitudes of the surrounding Alabama counties with the bare-knuckled politics of its steel mill economy, personified in both aspects by its local police commissioner." Nevertheless, the elections caused the SCLC to delay Project X, originally scheduled to begin in March. The civil rights group did not want to aid "Bull" Connor's run for mayor. Also, the campaign encountered disarray in Birmingham's African American community. Prominent businessmen and some ministers, including Gaston and newspaper editor Emory Jackson, counseled caution because they did not favor direct action protest. The *Birmingham World* even went so far as to call the early marches "wasteful and worthless." Indeed, at one point more than three-fourths of the city's four hundred black ministers voted against a showdown in their city. The wider community seemed disinterested as well.[40]

In the March mayoral primary, Albert Boutwell, a former Jefferson County state senator (1947–59) and lieutenant governor under John Patterson (1959–63), led the three other candidates for mayor: Connor, King, and Waggoner. Boutwell's platform targeted economic growth, annexation, and the need for new ideas and leadership to solve the city's high unemployment rate and fiscal problems (including an end to the deficit spending of the previous three years). The runoff pitted Boutwell against Connor. Residents, understanding the stakes, turned out in record numbers for the April 2 vote. Boutwell defeated Connor, 29,630 votes to 21,648. The results featured similar patterns as in the November 1962 change-in-government election. Boutwell, who received 58 percent of the final tally, ran strongest in the affluent and middle-class white communities and black precincts, while Connor did best in Ensley and East Lake. African Americans, one-eighth of the city's nearly eighty thousand registered voters, supplied crucial margins to the "moderate" candidate. The fifty-eight-year-old lawyer's victory kept intact his untarnished election record. Known more for his caution and indecisiveness than for any strong ideas (he "never took a position on any issue," Elton Stephens remembered), Boutwell knew how to bend with the winds of popular opinion. Indeed, the Montgomery press corps had rated him an effective legislator for those very skills. Having chaired Governor Gordon Persons's Interim Committee on Segregation in the Public Schools, his name had been attached to the state's 1955 pupil-placement law, which had maintained school segregation. Although that fact solidified Boutwell's segregationist credentials, in 1963 he ran as a moderate and as a candidate for change. A *New York Times* reporter claimed that the election signaled the demise of the Connor regime and "the beginning of a new era for Alabama's largest city." That prediction proved premature.[41]

King's forces capitalized on Birmingham's tense and uncertain atmosphere. Demonstrations restarted on April 3, the day after the mayoral election, and as the protests unfolded, a new strategy emerged. When Boutwell and the new eight-man, one-woman council took their oaths of office on April 15, King languished in a Birmingham prison cell, where he wrote his eloquent "Letter from a Birmingham Jail." King and other SCLC leaders had sought jail in order to jump-start the languishing movement. The campaign received an unexpected boost when the commissioners refused to vacate their offices to the newly elected government; it would take the state supreme court a month to resolve the dispute. Thus when SCLC marchers intensified their actions, Birmingham had either two governments or no government at all. In the meantime, Connor still held sway over the police force, and his bid to retain power gave SCLC leaders cause for optimism in a dispiriting campaign. Wyatt Tee Walker, King's chief strategist, wanted to continue the marches, which the city deemed illegal, so as to fill the jails and dramatize the confrontation. Moreover, Walker saw that Connor had brought out the police dogs to meet one march. Officers had not unleashed the dogs, but their presence indicated to Walker that the stakes might soon be raised. In mid-April, Project X became Project C, which stood for confrontation.[42]

At the core of the revised strategy was the decision to have the city's schoolchildren march on May 2, a shift that eventually galvanized a nation. Connor's orders the following day to untether the fire hoses and unleash the police dogs to stop the marchers have since defined Birmingham. Those actions, captured by the media and broadcast nationwide, brought public scorn upon the city and convinced the Kennedy administration to put its authority behind a local solution. The events—and the political vacuum in the city—allowed businessmen to compromise. Talks between commercial leaders, with Vann as their negotiator, and the SCLC resumed on May 5. A sense of urgency permeated the discussions. Five days later the two sides reached a tentative agreement, calling for merchants to desegregate lunch counters, rest rooms, and fitting rooms and to hire black workers. It also mandated continued interracial meetings.

After civil rights protesters and business leaders negotiated a truce, Birmingham's numbing pattern of protest and retaliatory violence resumed. Someone bombed the black-owned Gaston Motel, host to visiting civil rights leaders during the protests. This senseless reprisal prompted *New York Times* columnist Russell Baker to comment that "nothing makes much sense in Birmingham." Instead of observing a city full of potential, as journalists had over the years, Baker saw its contradictions, calling it "a place of bizarre non-sequiturs." In his "Observer" column, Baker noted a fundamental dissonance underlying the economic and political unrest: resistance to Washington's social intervention but acceptance of federal aid for economic development. He contrasted the contempt that some residents held for Washington's civil rights mediators with the five miles of interstate highway under construction in Birmingham's southeastern corner for which the federal government footed 90 percent of the bill. This conundrum was acute in Alabama. Despite Governor George Wallace's posturing, Alabama received more federal dollars as a percentage of its general revenue, 22 percent, than all but Mississippi and four western states.[43]

On the same day that Baker's column appeared, the Alabama Supreme Court ruled that the mayor-council system was Birmingham's legal government. Following the April and May demonstrations, the new mayor contended in a speech to several hundred residents at the city's civic auditorium that past and future problems "can all be solved by local people at the local level." Boutwell's assertion embodied the contradiction that Baker had noted. Not only did the mayor ignore established patterns between Birmingham and Washington, which were certain to intensify as the federal government strengthened its oversight of racial and urban matters, but it disingenuously overlooked his own agenda too. Throughout the mayoral campaign, the former lieutenant governor had called for urban renewal and had promoted the further expansion at the medical center, Birmingham's shining example of a federally funded development program. Moreover, Boutwell backed the creation of a four-year liberal arts college at the Southside campus, lauding the school's role as an employer and as a magnet for the city's industrial recruiters. Indeed, the veteran of Montgomery's legislative hallways had cited his insider's experience as building the crucial skills needed to win funding for the college's future growth.[44]

In his first days at the helm of the city's government, Boutwell moved to align Birmingham's future with the medical center, an action that echoed the goals of many change-in-government advocates. The medical center "was the city's hope," according to Charles Morgan, a leader of Citizens for Progress. It was "an enterprise other than steel and coal and railroads" that had brought "new people and research and the twentieth century to the city." Any expansion of the medical center meant a greater role for Washington in local affairs. The funding trends at the college continued to skew toward federal sources and away from state provision. By 1966, the school had a $25 million budget, of which federal grants provided one-third and state contributions less than one-quarter.[45]

Other observers found evidence of a different Birmingham at the Southside medical complex. A month after the King-led civil rights campaign ended, the *Wall Street Journal* published a front-page story under the headline "A Birmingham Story: Amid Race Problems, Medical School Offers a Contrast." The reporter overplayed the medical center as an "enlightened community," but he rightly called it an engine for change in Birmingham. The *Journal*'s account detailed the professional relationship between

Dr. Sterling Edwards, a leading cardiologist and researcher, and Clarence Forrest, his black technician. Edwards allowed Forrest to teach medical students how to sew artificial arteries into dogs because Forrest was so skilled at the task. While the story showed how expertise and talent could cut across typical racial boundaries, for the most part a clear economic hierarchy separated the races at the medical center. Although the college employed more than eight hundred blacks in 1963, its African American workers held more than 80 percent of the menial service positions and less than 3 percent of office or clerical jobs. This situation previewed how whites and blacks would be positioned in the postindustrial, commercial-services economy that would develop in Birmingham and other cities.[46]

Medical college administrators, for the most part, avoided racial politics; instead, they focused on building their campus. The medical college did face its own version of civil rights reform in 1963, when citywide events intruded at the school, leading to limited steps to end discrimination there. (On September 10, the day after several students desegregated two of Birmingham's public schools, the Medical College Faculty Council voted to support the petition's principle. The other items on that day's council agenda noted an upcoming visit from a National Institutes of Health official about a possible demonstration grant. The two points, side by side on the agenda, highlighted the links between two of the most pressing matters—federal funding and questions of racial equity—facing the medical college.) While Birmingham and its two rival governments floundered amid civil rights demonstrations in the first five months of 1963, college officials initiated a series of long-range studies. Joseph Volker, the college's senior administrator, and S. Richardson Hill, dean of the medical college, prepared presentations for the Medical Center Advisory Board, the special committee of University of Alabama trustees that oversaw the Birmingham school, and the school's internal planning committee. The campus needed to expand because Volker expected that within five years the fifteen-acre site would be filled. In April 1963, administrators gathered state health and public works construction officials and MCAB members, including local executives Ehney Camp, Frank Spain, and Hill Ferguson, to discuss expansion. The group debated the acquisition of nine blocks through federal urban renewal. This time, Volker, normally expansion-minded, preached moderation. He worried that the historically tight University of Alabama budget and the stingy legislature would make a larger plan impossible. We need "to plan the minimum expansion necessary to achieve the maximum matching funds," he told the MCAB.[47]

In the summer of 1963, the Boutwell government, searching for a way to move Birmingham beyond the politics of race and into the politics of development, latched onto the medical complex's ongoing effort. The convergence of the goals of city politicians and the college administrators served to boost each group's objectives. The school's planning committee invited the new mayor and council members to a July meeting at the medical center to discuss expansion. Federal urban renewal required approval from city hall, further encouraging the union between the doctors and the politicians. (This Washington-bolstered relationship also marginalized the role of the state legislature.) Although distracted by the municipality's debt and budgetary shortfalls left by the commissioners, Boutwell and the council cast an attentive glance toward the Southside. The mayor hoped the medical center could present a positive and progressive image for Birmingham. Development might also serve as a unifying cry for the 212-member, biracial Community Affairs Committee (CAC), which included twenty-seven African Americans and had been created by Boutwell to study community-wide racial and economic problems.[48]

In the CAC, Boutwell had copied the blueprint used by business moderates in other southern cities such as Atlanta and Dallas to gain political control. Indeed, the Chamber's Senior Citizens Committee had cited Dallas's efforts as it tried to steer city government beyond acrimonious and violent demonstrations when school integration arrived. But the CAC, which also held its first meeting in July 1963, proved ineffective as a policy-making body. To many in Birmingham, especially whites in the city's eastern and western neighborhoods that had backed both the commission government and Connor's bid for mayor, the CAC represented a further political usurpation by over-the-mountain businessmen. Lou Harper's "Lay of the Land" column in the weekly *Eastern Sun* seethed with class resentment as he noted that "plush Mountain Brook" had more members on the CAC than the larger white enclaves in the city. Mountain Brook, with roughly 17,000 residents, had sixty-seven CAC members, while the 250,000 people in West End, Woodlawn, and similar neighborhoods had sixty-four representatives. Harper feared that the Chamber and BDIA dictated the appointments, which would mean that the wealthy suburbanites would remain aloof from the city's toughest problems and avoid the economic consequences of consolidation. In its present role "Mountain Brook will be able to have her cake and eat it too."[49]

Internal criticism dogged the CAC, highlighting the business moderates' recalcitrance toward social change when not pushed by outside forces. Many leading white businessmen, most prominently Frank Samford, president of Liberty National Insurance, and Stephens, refused to join, citing busy workloads but seemingly more put off about compromising on racial matters. Stephens urged Boutwell to push for highway construction, annexation, and black policemen for black areas, but he also counseled the mayor to fight desegregation with all means short of violence. Key Foster, an attorney who had served on interracial committees before *Brown*, said he would participate in the CAC but not in its "group relations" committee: "I am a dedicated segregationist and I am convinced that integration will never work in the South." In part to allay such sentiments, the mayor first appointed no African Americans to the group's executive committee, but then, feeling the pressure from black protesters, added civil rights attorney Arthur Shores to the group. After a fitful year, the CAC disbanded.[50]

Meanwhile, Boutwell met throughout the summer of 1963 with Volker and other senior health officials about medical center matters that had "specific implications regarding the prosperity and growth of Birmingham." The leaders discussed expansion plans as well as the continuing indigent care deficit at University Hospital. Volker underscored the wisdom of attaching the city's future to the burgeoning health care industry. More than four thousand people worked in the medical center, which pumped $40 million annually into the local economy. Through these meetings, which also included the HABD's Denman, the parties agreed to enlarge the renewal proposal, with the politicians, in a reversal of past practice, pushing for a bigger project. The mayor-council government, trying to place economic development at the top of its agenda, wanted to solidify its standing with the city's commercial elite, many of whom were longtime advocates of the medical center. By early 1964, college officials, in tune with Boutwell's ambitions, hoped to acquire forty-five blocks of land to the south and west of the campus, a fivefold increase over Volker's original goal. "There probably is no facet of urban renewal," Smyer wrote Volker, "which would be more profitable to this community than the continued use of land in the expansion of the medical center," for the health complex had "proved to be one of the greatest industrial assets to Birmingham." To ensure that the city's business class and residents at large embraced the idea, MCAB member and University of Alabama trustee Camp, now executive vice-president at Liberty National, suggested that the mayor organize a citywide committee backing the project.[51]

Boutwell introduced his 140-member community planning committee on Christmas Eve 1964, and it affirmed the new direction the city would take. The announcement of the Mayor's Committee for the Medical Center coincided with a time of hope and faith, for the health complex could resurrect the city's slumping economy, which had lost 10 percent of its jobs in the past five years. Health care could be an engine for job creation, Boutwell emphasized. The *News* agreed: the city's potential rested in medicine, not iron or steel. Its editorial urged residents to imagine the changes in the city's Southside since World War II. "This newspaper sees the Center as one of the most important factors, possibly the major factor in this city's future." Former mayor James Morgan, now a real estate executive, suggested that the expansion would be the economic equivalent in jobs and salaries of adding fifty industrial plants.[52]

Just as Birmingham's largest daily had ceased to link the city's fortunes to the iron and steel industry, Boutwell's advisory committee reflected a shift in local leadership. The commercial and medical elite, the vanguard of Birmingham's more moderate pro-growth politics, dominated the committee. Jack McSpadden, a Liberty executive, chaired the group. Insurance, legal, and financial professionals held twenty-seven spots, whereas real estate interests and developers had another fifteen places. Boutwell did include eight union representatives, two more than given to executives of the city's manufacturing firms. Twenty-three health care or education officials, as well as ten downtown merchants, also served on the committee.

This planning effort contrasted with the one a decade earlier in a significant way. The committee included twelve blacks—including lawyers Arthur Shores and Orzell Billingsley, Wilbur Hollins, a prominent black real estate broker, Dr. Herschell Hamilton, and insurance executive Paul Harris—along with the white professionals. The HABD's Denman had insisted on black participation. The federal Housing and Home Finance Agency's

"Workable Program" rules, toughened in 1961 and more vigorously enforced in 1965, required real interracial participation from planning through construction. The need to placate federal rulemakers amid a major renewal effort also provoked changes in local government. In December 1964, the city council, by a five-to-four vote, placed Hollins, a founder of the Progressive Democratic Council in 1937, on the planning commission. Hollins was the first African American appointed to a city agency or independent board. City leaders had begun to understand the politics of moderation. Besides trying to meet the HHFA's programmatic requirements, Boutwell also thought that the participation of African Americans on the panel could simplify relocation planning, given that the majority of Southside residents to be displaced by the project were black.[53]

The mayor's committee served its purpose, guiding the proposal over the political and public relations hurdles and providing "a second wind" for the mayor-council government. The pursuit of federal development grants, along with the pressures of race, continued to shape the local agenda. In November 1965, Bruce Wedge, the HHFA's regional manager, approved advanced planning money and reserved $5.8 million in grants and loans for land acquisition, beginning a twelve-year odyssey to complete the project. Other municipal initiatives dovetailed with long-standing goals of Birmingham's professional elite, including better suburban links, highway construction, and a civic center with adjoining space for trade shows. The planning commission made the central business district its top priority. In December, HHFA regional administrator William Slayton set aside $2.15 million for a sixty-one-acre civic center and arena to the north of the business district, culminating a decade of work, and construction began on the Red Mountain Expressway. City planners estimated that in the next decade urban renewal and highway building would displace nearly eleven thousand (disproportionately black) families, affecting 10 percent of the city's residents and nearly 20 percent of its black residents. Each project deepened the city's dependence on Washington and quickened the social and demographic changes in the metropolitan region. Birmingham, a full participant in the federal grant economy, like other American cities, would witness stricter federal regulation, a suburban explosion, and the effects of the postindustrial economy.[54]

CHAPTER SIX

# Change and Its Limits in Birmingham

In the mid-1960s, when northern cities erupted like urban tinderboxes into flames of protest and riot, their southern counterparts remained peaceful by comparison. The relative quiet in landmarks of the civil rights era—Atlanta, Birmingham, Montgomery, and Jackson—intrigued observers, like the reporter who cited the "national tendency—perhaps even a need—to equate quiet with racial progress." Visiting Alabama's largest city two and a half years after the dramatic confrontations between black demonstrators and Eugene "Bull" Connor's police force, Paul Good found "some disquieting truths about the effect of the civil-rights movement in the urban South." He contrasted the integration of most public facilities with the abundant and grinding poverty among inner-city African Americans that robbed those residents of the chance for progress. The heightened federal oversight over urban affairs as well as the rights revolution left a divided legacy in Birmingham and elsewhere.[1]

Local government, under the leadership of Mayor Albert Boutwell, had worked hard so that Birmingham "on the surface presents the illusion of dramatic racial progress." The city's attempt to ensure compliance with the Civil Rights Act of 1964 had been the centerpiece of that effort. The Chamber of Commerce, which had had a tense relationship with the former commission government, took the lead in presenting a more moderate face to the nation. In the weeks before the passage of the historic civil rights bill, Chamber officials composed an eight-page memo detailing its potential impact on government and private businesses. Still the Chamber trod lightly. In his cover letter to more than three thousand community leaders and business owners, its president Frank Newton wrote, "It is not the intent of the Chamber to indicate a course of action for anyone." Nonetheless, "It is in the best interest of all to be prepared with a course of action that fits your situation which has been carefully thought out and adequate plans for its execution prior to the effective date of the act." Beyond the cautious bureaucratic wording, Newton's messages were elemental: don't mess up; avoid conflict.

Though it came far from embracing a more equal, idealistic racial order, the Chamber missive nevertheless highlighted the ascension of the Birmingham business moderates in the aftermath of the mayor-council and Albert Boutwell electoral victories. As a national newsweekly noted, "Crisis had taught Birmingham that token desegregation was the price of racial peace and economic progress." Moderates sought the appearance of calm even as they grudgingly tolerated new federal laws. The Chamber's directive acknowledged that African Americans would be ready to test the law and that cities such as Birmingham, Montgomery, Albany, and St. Augustine would draw the closest press scrutiny. "If any conclusion can be reached from general observation," Newton wrote, "it is that disorder begets unrest in other areas nearby. Preparedness is, as of now, possibly the only reasonable recourse which might preserve not only the public peace, but the economic health of the Jefferson County area as well." Bill Hamilton, Mayor Boutwell's top aide, distributed the report to the state's congressional delegation and to other southern mayors. The Chamber also organized a day-long seminar about the law for businessmen, union leaders, local government officials, and interested residents. Preparedness and begrudging public acceptance by many whites allowed the enactment of the civil rights legislation to occur without turmoil.[2]

Beneath the veneer of calm, injustice continued to run deep. The indignities ranged from the cold refusal of whites to accept equality of blacks before the law to fatal racial callousness. Throughout the summer of 1964, several county judges enforced segregated seating in their courtrooms. The county jail remained segregated until the spring of 1966; only then did city hall make its first meaningful attempt to hire blacks for Birmingham's police force, a topic of interracial discussion for more than fifteen years. By the mid-1960s, Birmingham remained the only sizable southern city without African Americans on the police force, and officers continued to harass blacks. In August 1966, medical college officials complained to the mayor after patrolmen interrupted an integrated soccer game that included residents, technicians from the X-ray department, and visiting physicians from Finland and Argentina. The police left after several minutes, but "this happening no doubt helped confirm some of the opinions they (and I) had about some of the Birmingham police," wrote a medical resident. At times, the stakes were graver. In October 1965 a man died after a white ambulance driver refused to transport him to a hospital and the "Negro ambulance" arrived too late.[3]

Although the pace of change remained slow throughout the 1960s, the federal regulatory revolution (and demographic pressures) continued to rearrange Birmingham's socioeconomic order and political landscape. Moderates who sought to dictate events soon found themselves overwhelmed by factors beyond their control. To an unprecedented degree, federal bureaucrats now supported the demands made by African American protesters. Washington's leverage flowed from the practical power generated by the expansion of grant-in-aid programs as much as it did from the moral authority of the black-led movement for racial equality. By 1964, civil rights protest in Birmingham joined the Southside health and education complex to the racial politics that had engulfed the rest of the South's iron and steel capital. Not surprisingly, University Hospital, the University of Alabama Medical College's teaching hospital and Jefferson County's primary indigent care facility, pulled the medical center into the ongoing civil rights disputes. University Hospital's ultimate desegregation further reveals the shifting political pressure in Birmingham in the mid-1960s.

The story of University Hospital, which relied on federal grants, demonstrated the government's ability to break down clear barriers to access. A year after the new civil rights law, the hospital could no longer separate patients by race. But Washington's ability to effect change was murkier in its more limited attempts to forge a more equitable economic order. The city's experience with Model Cities in 1968 showed that the political clout of African American residents was growing, yet, for the most part, their power was negative, checking or blocking programs or policies they found objectionable. And as black influence increased, whites began to abandon Birmingham for the suburbs. In the 1970s, Birmingham became smaller, blacker, and poorer when compared to its outlying suburbs. Steady growth at the medical center (and the establishment of a full-service, urban university there in 1966) broadened its role in the community. To be sure, its imprint ran deeper, and it offered more opportunities for minority students than other major state schools. But its hiring practices reflected the ways in which low-income and African American residents were getting left behind in Birmingham. The election of a black mayor, Richard Arrington, in 1979, signaled a political muscle by blacks that outpaced their economic gains.

While administrators charted the medical college's physical expansion in early 1963, University Hospital administrator Matthew McNulty planned to reduce the number of patient beds in his facility, a trend since the 1950s, because of budgetary shortfalls. Federal grants had spurred the tremendous growth of the college's research and education pursuits, but declining local aid for indigent medical care created a bind at the hospital that served twin charity and teaching functions. Joseph Volker, the medical school's top official, knew that shrinking patient space would complicate the hospital's efforts to desegregate. In 1963, the school had taken limited steps toward integration, ending discriminatory practices in several research buildings. The school held an integrated meeting of the American Psychiatric Association and, after years of deliberations, granted privileges to a black physician who practiced at Birmingham's Holy Family Hospital. The physician, Dr. James Montgomery, would be invited to join the school's staff the next year.[4]

Volker considered the steps cautious but felt reluctant to outpace change in the state and the city. The vice-president of health affairs had written to former University of Alabama chancellor Oliver Carmichael of the "dilemma" of being caught between opposing forces: the fairness rules attached to Washington grants and local pressures to defend the social status quo. The school still received nearly one-quarter of its operating budget and about one-third of its capital budget from Alabama sources. Yet passage of the Civil Rights Act tightened Washington's administrative oversight, propelling the medical school and University Hospital along with the stricter standard. Months before the historic law, federal appeals judges knocked down the legal supports for segregation in Hill-Burton facilities.[5]

Volker tried to guide the school between two eras. He organized an advisory committee of local blacks, telling them that college officials wanted to desegregate their facilities, including University Hospital, without coercion from federal bureaucrats. The committee featured members of the city's African American professional elite, a group heretofore willing to compromise on racial matters. It included Arthur Shores; John Porter, minister at Sixteenth Street Baptist Church; John Drew, a leading black insurance executive at whose home King often stayed during his 1963 Birmingham campaign; and Louis Willie, A. G. Gaston's second in command at the Booker T. Washington Insurance Company, the city's most prosperous black-owned business. Volker's blueprint lacked a specific integration timetable, but he did make a series of general pledges throughout early 1964, including one to allow blacks to enroll at the college's extension center in the fall. Not all black leaders accepted Volker's vague schedule. In May the Alabama Christian Movement for Human Rights and its attorney Oscar Adams, who a decade earlier had helped to fight Birmingham's 1953 urban renewal project, pondered a lawsuit against the medical college. Previously, Adams had worked for Southside homeowners and the NAACP. Now he represented the ACMHR, and his new clients wanted a clear end to segregation, not better terms in an unequal society as the homeowners had sought.[6]

The task of desegregating University Hospital fell to McNulty, who quickly felt trapped between the school's overstressed budget and a federal ruling that ended the Hill-Burton Act's separate-but-equal history. The only feasible way to integrate the patient wards, which along with the waiting rooms, nursery, obstetrical, and other services remained divided by race, would be to have all private rooms, according to McNulty, a Boston native who had moved to his present job from the VA Hospital in 1955.

Desegregating the larger wards, both the administrator and Volker believed, would drive away paying white patients, further shrinking the facility's tight operating margins. Overcrowding at the hospital made the plan impractical, so school officials gravitated to another solution: an addition funded by a Hill-Burton grant. Shifts in federal policy, however, stymied this traditional and time-consuming reform strategy. In the wake of the civil rights law, medical center officials faced pressure from both local protesters and bureaucrats at the Public Health Service, which had just issued a regulation—"Title 45, Sub-title A, Part 80"—that required nondiscrimination in all aspects of federally assisted health programs. The rule, effective January 3, 1965, jolted McNulty and his colleagues, who had been snared in their own catch-22: the school required federal funds for an addition to desegregate, but it could not get the money unless it integrated. McNulty hurried off to Atlanta to talk with James Quigley, the PHS regional administrator. The meeting brought no reprieve; McNulty learned that the regulations would be "applied judiciously with understanding but with intent of eventual full implementation."[7]

The vise tightened on the school, which was dependent on Washington-based grants, as Volker's interracial advisory group refused to accept halfway measures. McNulty's post-Atlanta actions—opening private patient rooms and the sixteen-bed General Clinical Research Center to blacks and ensuring fair treatment at the emergency clinic—were not enough for Willie, Drew, and Porter. They wanted full desegregation, even if it meant fewer patient beds for blacks. In addition to the threat of the ACMHR lawsuit, Volker knew that current policies, which included separate wards, a partitioned cafeteria, and separate admitting offices, jeopardized funding for critical programs. The medical center had more than $10 million in pending federal grants for a new psychiatric clinic, a dormitory for nursing students, a rehabilitation clinic (with significant private funding contributed by Frank Spain), a third clinical building, and plans to renovate and add onto University Hospital. The threat to withhold funds was real. Earlier in the year, the PHS had stopped payments to five Alabama nursing homes slated for construction because of questions of equal access. College officials worried, however, that a dramatic stance for civil rights might risk offending Governor George Wallace, causing him to abandon support for an $8 million bond issue needed to match the federal grants. "In recent months, the sociological problems of the University Hospital have come to the point of major crisis," Volker wrote a senior University of Alabama administrator.[8]

The matter crossed a critical threshold even before Adams filed the ACMHR lawsuit in March 1965. Questions about inequality at the medical center that Adams raised with PHS bureaucrats during his case preparation, as well as a complaint filed by the Birmingham NAACP, prompted a cursory visit by federal investigators. Their report led the agency to place University Hospital (along with the Children's Hospital and the Crippled Children's Hospital) on the its noncompliance list in March. The designation automatically triggered a visit to Birmingham and a more thorough investigation by a PHS survey team. The threat of actual enforcement of stringent federal guidelines, which had the potential to derail millions of dollars in grant money, ended hesitation and delay over desegregation. During the second and third weeks of April, the hospital staff moved "as rapidly as possible . . . 24 hours a day, every day" to achieve the goals. Hospital employees renovated the facility's cafeteria and then reconfigured the nursery, obstetric, pediatric, and surgical wards. McNulty even moved the administrative offices elsewhere to make room for the changes. On April 25, 1965, "the University of Alabama Hospitals and Clinics are 100% 'non-segregated,'" McNulty reported. The hospital continued to separate patients by age, sex, paying status (minimizing contact between the races), and clinical discipline.[9]

The changes satisfied the PHS survey team, which visited University Hospital three weeks later, as well as Volker's own advisory committee. PHS regional director Quigley declared the hospital in full compliance with his agency's civil rights edicts; moreover, the review "thoroughly convinced [the committee] of the sincere efforts on the part of the hospital staff to provide equal facilities and service to all our people."[10]

The combination of new civil rights laws and stricter regulatory standards altered behavior in Birmingham, but it did not necessarily change existing attitudes. Medical center benefactor Frank Spain, who had been a key political ally in the school's expansion efforts and who had made substantial financial contributions for new buildings, fumed when a faculty member participated in the voting rights demonstrations in Selma. After reading a newspaper account about Frederick Kraus, a European-born Jew whose family had fled to the United States during the 1930s, the seventy-year-old lawyer wrote both Volker and Kraus to chastise the medical school professor for his public support for voting rights for blacks. Spain urged Kraus to keep the school out of "controversial and explosive issues" that could destroy the medical center's growth, especially since Governor Wallace continued to harass college officials for mixing white and black patients. Kraus's actions might anger Wallace, undermining the existing support in Montgomery for the state's bond issue for the hospital and the medical center urban renewal project, Spain argued. But his discomfort went beyond political pragmatism; Spain could not accept the new racial status quo. Let the Black Belt solve its own problems, he wrote Kraus, adding that blacks, like his "manservant," did not need the vote. In the civil rights era, however, administrators and politicians would have to act in accordance with new rules and regulations imposed by Washington, despite the persistence of traditional racial outlooks.[11]

Birmingham's Model Cities effort several years later further revealed both the federal government's more intrusive urban policy and the altered sociopolitical factors at work in the Alabama city. In the spring of 1968 the five-year-old Birmingham City Council drafted a Model Cities grant application. Part of the Demonstration Cities and Metropolitan Development Act passed by Congress in November 1966, Model Cities was a three-year, $1.2 billion comprehensive assault on urban woes. Ambitious in scope, the bill "sought to attack the human problems as well as the physical factors causing blight and decay." To do this, it would combine a slew of housing, education, antipoverty, and social welfare programs to rehabilitate decaying urban neighborhoods. The nine-member council selected a section of Ensley, hoping that the area, which was majority white when it was targeted for renewal efforts fifteen years earlier and was now majority black, would be one of seventy-five projects nationwide slated to receive demonstration funding.[12]

The Model Cities proposal quickly drew the ire of local blacks. Even the two dozen African American members of the mayor's task force objected. So did the NAACP's Ensley–Pratt City branch, whose officers contended that the proposal lacked sufficient new housing plans, job development programs, and local health facilities. They also felt shut out of the planning process, citing the planning commission's refusal to allow black task force members to comment on the proposal. Black leaders responded in two ways. The NAACP, funded by the national organization, hired its own consultants to comment on the community renewal plan. Furthermore, the NAACP hired Harvey Burg, Oscar Adams's law partner, to present its objections to both the city council and federal bureaucrats. Although Burg met with councilmen Allen Drennen and E. C. Overton, he also focused on Washington. In an April 1968 meeting with federal Department of Housing and Urban Development (HUD) officials, Burg claimed that Birmingham's application misrepresented the required "meaningful citizen participation" of local blacks. Ensley was also 75 percent black, an estimate half again greater than the one in the city's grant proposal, a discrepancy that was part of the city's deliberate attempt to limit black representation on the thirty-member task force, Burg told HUD officials. Blacks also demanded changes to the proposal's housing rehabilitation, job training, and health services components.[13]

Both the program's social intent and the political control over it were at stake. Federal bureaucrats had designed Model Cities as a grassroots antipoverty program, and Birmingham's black leaders contended that they had been cheated out of a chance both to run and to benefit from the program. At first, the council, after meeting with Burg and the Ensley NAACP in May 1968 and mindful of the federal government's demands, accepted greater community control. Then the council reversed course, deciding, in effect, to ignore black demands and to restore the original proposal as the official Model Cities plan.[14]

As the grant deadline approached, each side pleaded its case in Washington. Federal bureaucrats seemed sympathetic to the requests of the Ensley group. City officials and community activists lobbied Walter Farr, the national director of the Model Cities program, and a host of lesser bureaucrats. Burg also approached HUD secretary Robert C. Weaver, telling him that "as a matter of policy" Birmingham's government "refused to agree to any concept of a neighborhood citizens board [and] really did not grasp the concept of citizen participation." Quite simply, Ensley's blacks would oppose the plan if the city did not amend the application. Thirty-two years earlier, Weaver, a Harvard-trained economist, had met with officers of the Birmingham NAACP when he had been the Negro affairs adviser in the Public Works Administration. In 1936, the PWA had not supported the

NAACP's protest about the absence of black managers at a public housing project. Again Weaver, now enforcing a government policy that explicitly combined civil rights and urban issues, would decide the fate of Birmingham's application. This time, the opposition effectively torpedoed Birmingham's bid because its application lacked the support of a group the grant was intended to benefit. By the late 1960s, unlike the New Deal years, Washington bureaucrats no longer deferred to southern racial customs. Instead, agency officials now attempted to encourage grassroots activism, a legacy of the decades of coalition-building, from erstwhile urban grant programs.[15]

Birmingham's politicians sought federal funds, like the Model Cities grant and other War on Poverty programs, to offset economic stagnation and to reverse the continued concentration of black poverty. Between 1965 and 1975, federal grants grew from 10 percent of the city's $26 million budget to 18 percent of the $94.5 million municipal spending. City officials remained reluctant, nonetheless, to relinquish meaningful authority to local blacks. Mayor George Seibels, elected in 1967 to succeed Albert Boutwell, had been quick to appoint two dozen blacks to his Model Cities task force. Although he still expected city hall to run the program, black activists no longer accepted token participation in matters having a direct impact in their communities. In this case, the two sides stared each other down, refused to compromise, and both lost something to make a point. The Seibels-led municipal government refused to adjust black participation, while the Ensley NAACP, rebuffed in its demand for altered priorities, refused to endorse the project. HUD would not include Birmingham as one of the seventy-five demonstration grants without the NAACP's blessing of the project. HUD's decision to reject the plan gave the NAACP its victory, which carried a cost: blocking a program that could have brought useful services into the community. For the most part, blacks still held a form of veto power, the ability to block something objectionable, but had little capacity to propose and enact their own initiatives.[16]

Blacks also expressed their frustrations with local conditions by leaving Birmingham. The city's population fell 12 percent—and contiguous industrial towns Irondale and Fairfield lost 10 percent of their residents—in the 1960s as ten thousand blacks and thirty thousand whites left the city. Fewer blacks lived in both Birmingham and Jefferson County in 1970 than a decade earlier, indicating that they migrated elsewhere for new opportunities. Whites tended to leave for the city's suburban hinterlands. In the 1960s, for the first time, the region's suburban dispersion was not limited to the wealthiest residents. Mountain Brook and Vestavia Hills continued to grow, but so did the working-class and lower-middle-class towns of Gardendale, Fultondale, and Pleasant Grove to the north and west of the city.[17]

White flight reinforced the existence of two Birminghams—the city proper and the surrounding Jefferson County communities, which by 1970 had a larger population than the city. Suburban voters affirmed their separateness by twice rejecting annexation (in 1964 and 1971). Whites abandoned the city in droves in the 1970s, and Birmingham became a majority black city. The suburban outskirts grew larger and whiter; the urban core lost population and became blacker. In 1950 city dwellers had earned more than county residents; however, two decades later that pattern had been reversed (and brought in line with the national norms)—and those trends accelerated. By 1980, the racial composition of Birmingham was the mirror image of century-old norms; African Americans constituted nearly 60 percent of the city's population. The centripetal movement pulled wealth out of the city as well. Thanks to residential displacement and white flight, blacks moved into new parts of the city, for instance locating in areas of Ensley and West End abandoned by whites. The proportion of blacks living in super-majority census tracts (more than 75 percent of one race) declined to 38 percent in 1970 from 63 percent in 1960, confirming this dispersion. Moreover, in the 1970s, the black population increased by thirty thousand, reversing twenty years of decline. More than ever, blacks in the metropolitan region concentrated in Birmingham.

At the dawn of the demographic shock waves of the 1970s, Birmingham still drifted between its past and future. A carillon still rang "Dixie" throughout downtown on the hour, and the Federal Reserve Bank's district branch displayed the Confederate battle flag in its marble foyer. Eight blocks south of the bank, however, the sprawling Southside health and education complex offered evidence of change. "A new force is at work, slowly, perhaps irrevocably reshaping social attitudes and patterns of life in this one-time stronghold of segregation," a *New York Times* reporter noted. When the college finally acquired the forty-two-block urban renewal area in 1976, a decade after it had first applied for the land, it had a new name—and it made a broader and deeper imprint on the city. The former University of Alabama Medical College had become the University of Alabama at Birmingham. School officials frequently referred to their campus by its initials, UAB, consciously imitating California's UCLA. The new name came in 1969 when Governor Albert Brewer reorganized the University of Alabama System and established separate campuses in Tuscaloosa, Birmingham, and Huntsville. University of Alabama president Frank Rose had elevated the Birmingham Extension Center, first created in 1936, to the degree-granting College of General Studies in 1966.[18]

University College, as it was known after 1971 when it added a graduate program, grew quickly. By 1971, 4,418 students enrolled in classes, a 32 percent increase over the previous academic year. Degree and course offerings focused on career training, especially in the health services professions, education, and engineering. That same year 704 students enrolled in graduate classes, primarily in nursing or doctoral programs in biology and other health sciences. In contrast, there were only 100 students in each medical school class. Eight years after its creation, 2,800 students graduated with M.A.'s, including the nursing program, or Ph.D.'s. Undergraduate enrollment doubled in that period as well. By then, the college's business division had the most students, followed by the science and math, education, social sciences, engineering, and humanities divisions.[19]

UAB's employment growth and its growing reputation put the health and education complex front and center in the city's development policy. Commercial leaders believed that the school had "boosted the area's economy and [was] changing the attitude and prospects of the city." As a measure of both his and UAB's reputation, Volker earned a place in 1971 on the Chamber of Commerce's list of Birmingham's ten greatest businessmen. Medical center benefactors Spain and Frank Samford, Liberty National's chief executive and leader of the most recent urban renewal drive, also merited selections. As the iron and steel economy rapidly constricted—and Sloss-Sheffield's decision to close its downtown City Furnace in 1970 was a visible reminder—UAB rose in prominence. By 1976, it was Birmingham's largest employer and fourth largest statewide, with twelve thousand workers and a $100 million annual payroll. UAB officials noted that the university "has given some white collar balance to a city which long has been dominated by a blue collar" and highlighted the caliber of professionals it brought to Birmingham. John Kirklin, who left the Mayo Clinic to become the head of surgery at UAB, was an example of the infusion of top-flight talent they often cited. The *Post-Herald*'s editor Duard LeGrand agreed that a "somewhat more subtle but a potent influence nonetheless has been the introduction of highly educated, sophisticated people whose skills have influence far beyond the geographic limits of the center."[20]

The steady creation of jobs at the medical center ran counter to citywide employment trends. Most growth occurred in the suburban rings, and even that trailed regional boomtowns. A 1971 study of the twelve largest southern cities placed Birmingham last in most economic indicators, including population growth, hourly earnings, effective buying income, and retail sales growth. Metro Birmingham did add 60,000 new jobs between 1965 and 1973 (one-third came because the Census Bureau extended the region's boundaries). Yet those figures paled compared to Atlanta, which added 245,000 jobs in a similar period. The tepid economy meant the business leaders still talked in terms of potential. "Could we get the one big industry here that would result naturally in spin-offs rather than seeking developments that would come from our own ideas at a lot of effort?" Tom Fontana asked at a meeting of the Metropolitan Development Board, the Chamber's latest recruitment offshoot. Throughout the 1970s, employment in Birmingham was virtually stagnant, while the suburbs added 80,000 new jobs. Still, the area lost high-paying manufacturing jobs, which had accounted for 40 percent of all full-time positions in 1960 but fell to 30 percent in 1980. By 1983, U.S. Steel ranked as the area's eighteenth largest employer.[21]

The health sciences complex's importance as an employment center also reflected the boundaries of change in Birmingham. It offered an abundance of white-collar, service sector jobs. By 1970, blacks held about one-third of the nearly five thousand positions at UAB. Nonetheless, black employees mostly filled the menial, lower-wage positions. About half of the black workers held service jobs, which accounted for about three-fourths of all of those positions. As the educational requirements and pay levels increased, black workers held a smaller share. Twenty-five percent of the college's African American employees, for instance, worked as technicians (50 percent of that category) and 12 percent held clerical jobs (less than 25 percent of those spots). At the same time, fewer than one in six blacks were managers or supervisors (4 percent of that class). These same racial distinctions appeared among workers throughout the metro region. In 1980, blacks were three times as likely as whites to hold service positions, while just 10 percent of African Americans were managers or professionals of any sort compared to 25 percent of white workers.[22]

Job differences were directly reflected in the wealth of the black and white communities. Fully one-third of Birmingham's black families, compared to one in seven white families, lived below the poverty line in 1970. A persistent wage gap remained; the average income of a black family in Birmingham was just three-fourths that of a white family in the county throughout the 1970s. A yawning educational divide perpetuated the divergent racial paths. Whites were twice as likely as blacks to have completed a high school education. Still UAB's "dramatic contribution" to the black community offered some hope of creating a more equitable society. By 1970, 13 percent of its three thousand students were black, a far higher proportion than at Alabama's Tuscaloosa or Huntsville campuses or Auburn University, where black enrollment was below 2 percent. One African American student, thirty-two-year-old Fred Wallace, an air force veteran training to become a medical technician, exemplified University College's diverse population: one-third were veterans; 40 percent attended evening classes; and two-thirds held full-time jobs. Blacks also accounted for one in six graduate students, but the vast majority of those blacks studied for their master's degrees in education.[23]

By the mid-1970s, UAB—and the municipal government—was knee-deep in federal money. The legislature's flintiness magnified Washington's role at the medical center. In 1971, the Alabama government paid just 23 percent of the medical school's operating budget, about half the national average (40 percent). Alabama's share of medical school funding was the lowest in the South, whether measured in total dollars or as a percentage of the budget. No other medical school received a larger percentage of its funding from federal sources. The Birmingham campus received $3.41 from Washington for every dollar of state aid, nearly double the average at other state-supported medical colleges in the South. Despite the school's profile in Birmingham, its urban renewal plans dragged in the early 1970s because of its "inability to develop the financial resources to purchase" the land. A *News* editorial commented that UAB suffered because "the public—and the Legislature—fail to appreciate what this development means to the state." UAB officials had to lobby state legislators for more than three years before they released the $8.5 million from the state's coffers to buy the forty-two-block urban renewal tract. The back and forth over the land acquisition money was typical of the state's stinginess toward the Birmingham campus and higher education overall. A warning from federal regulators that the city would have to sell the land to private developers if the school did not buy it finally loosened the state's purse strings. UAB officials also revealed a $64.5 million expansion plan.[24]

Birmingham's efforts to cleanse its past through racial accommodation and the growth at UAB could not disguise the city's failure to forge a stable biracial order. The social costs of that failure remained high too. A federal study of the largest sixty-five cities in the mid-1970s ranked Birmingham second only to Jersey City, New Jersey, as having the lowest "standard of living" in the country. The report measured traditional economic indicators (per capita income, savings, retail sales), less typical ones (teacher pay, political turnout), and environmental factors (air and water quality, number of hospital beds, housing stock). To some, the statistics showed that there had been little real change since the demise of segregation. According to Chris McNair, whose daughter had been one of four girls killed in the 1963 Sixteenth Street Baptist Church bombing, "You can sit down and buy a meal anywhere you want—if you can afford a meal."[25]

At the end of the 1970s, city voters would call on black politicians to try to solve the decades-old problems. Forty-nine-year-old Richard Arrington, a Miles College professor, was elected mayor in 1979. The son of a TCI worker had been part of the city's first wave of elected black officials, winning a council seat in 1971. In 1968, then-mayor George Seibels had appointed civil rights attorney Arthur Shores to a vacant council seat. Blacks made up one-third of the electorate at the time, and the next year, Shores won the seat in a citywide election. Rapid white suburbanization made Arrington's victory possible. He won with less than 5 percent of the white vote. Arrington embraced the medical center as the city's future—calling it "by far the best thing this city has going for it"—and his plans for economic development and efficiency in government initially won him the support of the white business class.[26]

Yet Arrington led a different city than his predecessors. Even as Washington's research and grant funding remained fundamental to UAB's health, the federal government retreated from Birmingham, and other cities, in significant ways. The federal government's absolute contribution to Birmingham and its aid as a percentage of the city budget declined during the 1980s. Arrington's Birmingham had become "a reflection of urban American more generally." In Birmingham, as in cities across America, matters of race continued to intersect and dominate debates about poverty and welfare, urban renewal and public housing, job creation and affirmative action. All of America, and not just the South, now searched for solutions.[27]

# Conclusion

The Birmingham story defies neat explanation. In 1992, the University of Alabama at Birmingham was responsible for every seventh job in the metropolitan region, powerful testament to the transformative power of the health sciences complex—largely shaped by federal aid—and the ascendancy of the postindustrial service economy in the erstwhile iron and steel town. The city's economic reconfiguration was uneven, however. On average, African American families earned one-half the income of area whites, and nearly 28 percent of blacks lived below the poverty line, a percentage four times higher than for white residents. Blacks now controlled city hall, but, at times, local politics played out in absurd theater. That year, Mayor Richard Arrington, the city's first black mayor and then in his fourth of five terms, skirmished with federal prosecutors pursuing a corruption and graft investigation involving municipal contracts. As Arrington battled against contempt of court charges, some of his supporters donned chains and marched to city hall to symbolize the oppression that blacks still faced. Although Birmingham, with its explosive legacy, might draw closer scrutiny from the national press than comparable cities, its woes were not unique.[1]

The Birmingham story, in fact, extends beyond mere regional characterization. Observers often have struggled to label the Alabama city. Four decades ago *New York Times* columnist James Reston offered that "no generalization about Birmingham is safe," and historians, searching for explanations, have adopted paradoxical conclusions. Blaine Brownell once claimed that Birmingham had more in common with Youngstown, Ohio, than with any other southern city; later, he found that it shared a common ethos with its regional counterparts in the 1920s. Yet "in a perverse way Birmingham has always epitomized the national experience," as Henry McKiven speculated in his book about the formation of the city's working class. Recent studies of Atlanta, Detroit, Chicago, Portland, and Richmond, among others, which consider the impacts of national housing and urban renewal legislation, describe the powerful influence of federal policy in shaping the modern city, revealing motives and actions similar to those in the Alabama city.

UAB's rise, along with the surrounding medical center, through federal government programs for education, biomedical research, and health-related construction, tied Birmingham to nationwide trends too. Perhaps the city's combination of a rustbelt economy and southern social relations made it singular. More likely that context accounted for the city's peculiarly all-American burdens from the Depression through the civil rights era. As Thomas Sugrue's award-winning study of Detroit emphasizes, these were not mere southern concerns. The intersection of two distinctive but ultimately interrelated trends—industrial decline and the fight over segregation—put rare pressures on Birmingham. Not only did these factors define the burdens of Birmingham's past, they have been played out—at different paces—elsewhere.[2]

Historians have begun to document the critical impact of Washington's economic policy on the post–New Deal South. Numan Bartley highlighted the emergence of a moderate consensus that "brought to power in the South metropolitan corporate leaders who had much in common with their northern peers and who accepted the demise of strict Jim Crow segregation. Thereafter, the South became considerably more like the non-South." Washington's grant-in-aid bounty, the New Deal's fiscal legacy, animated and nourished groups with alternate visions, causing Birmingham to undergo significant and lasting metamorphoses that brought new elites to the forefront of city life, ended segregation, gave the city's African American community a meaningful political voice (and thus recast politics), and established a new economic foundation for Birmingham. "Whatever its economic effects, federal intervention in the South certainly catalyzed vast changes in politics and relations," according to Bruce Schulman.[3]

The slow, wrenching march of change began during the Depression, when the president, Congress, and agency bureaucrats made experimental efforts to restore the nation's vitality. In Birmingham, like the rest of the nation, the acceptance of federal aid—whether for unemployment relief, large-scale construction projects, or public housing—loosened the city's traditional economic, social, and political moorings. To be sure, "Washington became the focus of groups long on the margins of national politics," the historian Patricia Sullivan noted, creating openings, some of them temporary, to challenge the status quo. The Birmingham attorney Arthur Shores remembered that "the participation of blacks in New Deal programs prompted black leaders to look increasingly toward the federal government for support." In the 1930s, the building of the Smithfield Court housing project enabled African Americans to establish alliances with federal bureaucrats, bypassing obstinate city politicians and winning improvements at the 544-unit project for blacks. The coalition-building worked best during the 1930s, when Birmingham's blacks were pleading with Washington-based agencies for equal living conditions and less well when trying to guarantee blacks a percentage of the construction work or a role in the project's day-to-day operations. But for all of the New Deal's experimentation, its programs were compatible with segregation. They undermined traditional leadership claims without undoing them. In her study of "racial justice" during this period, even Sullivan underscores the circumscribed nature of liberal reform. While barely remembered later, "the activists of the earlier decades [1930s and 1940s] tilled the ground for future change."[4]

In the aftermath of World War II and the nation's economic rejuvenation the strain of New Deal interventionism that emerged triumphant was the idea of the "Keynesian state," according to the historian Alan Brinkley.

The winning formula allowed the federal government to use "the state to save the economy without intruding the state too far into the economy," a distinction with lasting impact. Grant-in-aid legislation, with its broad (and intentionally vague) policy prescriptions and decidedly local implementation, remained central to this governing philosophy. The postwar statutes with the most lasting imprint on Birmingham were the Hospital Survey and Construction (or Hill-Burton) Act of 1946 and the Housing Act of 1949, which unlike its Depression-era predecessor had a pro-development, downtown-building-over-housing slant. These programs did not go unnoticed. In his unpublished memoirs, Charles Zukoski, a trust officer at Alabama's largest bank, noted that "what may be termed the second period in the city's history began with the end of World War II." Hill-Burton helped build a fledgling medical center and later, in the 1960s, it—along with the burgeoning of health research grants through the National Institutes of Health—contributed to the emergence of a renowned institution on the Southside. City leaders even used the Housing Act to clear land to expand the medical complex, illustrating the complementary effect of the laws. The Housing Act would have a more equivocal legacy in Birmingham, but like Hill-Burton, it had the clear consequence of making local elites dependent on Washington for economic development initiatives.[5]

At first, the deepening dependence on federal funding sources was of little consequence to the pro-development business leadership in Birmingham. In 1950, elites viewed the acceptance of Hill-Burton grants as a way to avoid stricter scrutiny by Washington over race relations. Former congressman John Newsome convinced Chamber of Commerce types to pursue Hill-Burton funding for a hospital for blacks because it could reduce the need for local contributions, improve medical care for underserved blacks, and prove to the rest of the country that segregation was compatible with progress. The textile magnate Donald Comer, who chaired the subsequent fund drive, used that pitch when soliciting contributions. "This hospital matter is a real test of whether we mean it when we say we can handle our own problems," he wrote the mayor. A decade later, even though Elton Stephens, president of the Birmingham Downtown Improvement Association, still forwarded similar arguments in defense of an urban renewal proposal, the circumstances had changed, negating the earlier logic.[6]

To many in Birmingham, especially the city's rank-and-file voters, federal aid no longer came without strings attached. After *Brown v. Board of Education* (1954), any role for Washington was suspect. A series of citywide votes in the mid-1950s showed that Birmingham's business class and the city's lower-middle-class and blue-collar voters had split priorities. The business moderates, attempting to form a pro-growth consensus like their colleagues in other southern cities, put economic growth issues at the top of their agenda. But as the expansion at the medical college showed, those policies required Washington's support in the form of grants, which could mean regulation. A majority of the city's residents considered the defense of segregation, long used by working-class whites as an economic barrier against black competition in the district's manufacturing sector, more important. Further complicating matters as Birmingham's economy slumped in the 1950s were the fissures among the manufacturing and commercial elites, making the business class timid. These divisions stymied efforts for moderate reform in the 1950s, and Birmingham's business class, unlike their counterparts in many other southern cities, had lost control of day-to-day politics. The sports segregation balloting in 1954, the Avondale urban renewal vote a year later, the 1957 municipal elections, and the merger effort in 1959 were skirmishes in a battle for Birmingham.

These complex divisions give a fuller sense of Birmingham's struggles during the civil rights era. To be sure, as Schulman writes, "Cities that only lightly felt government-sponsored economic development and population growth—Memphis, Birmingham, Augusta, Saint Augustine—experienced explosive racial conflict. In booming cities like Atlanta, Dallas, and Huntsville, however, the civil rights struggle followed a more moderate course." The long-standing differences should not be overstated, however. While Birmingham had a deserved reputation for frequent bombings of black housing, its history of residential terror was matched in boomtown Dallas, Miami, and nonsouthern Detroit, for instance. Moreover, concerning Atlanta, Ronald Bayor argues that "policy decisions made decades ago to divide the races and maintain African Americans' status as second-class citizens had long-range and debilitating effects upon the city, although these effects were not always obvious at the time of implementation." Apparent racial harmony should not be confused with the absence of conflict or assumed to mean that local governments treated blacks and whites equally. For instance, neither Birmingham nor Atlanta was among the nation's twenty most racially segregated cities in 1940, yet they tied for eighth on the list by 1970.[7]

Concurrent with its bid for moderation, Birmingham became a target of the civil rights movement led by Martin Luther King Jr., obscuring the long-term factors that contributed to change in the Alabama city. Even before the city had been targeted by the SCLC, business leaders led by Sidney Smyer adopted a new strategy to assert their political control. Starting in 1961, Smyer shrewdly switched the nature of the power struggle away from the personal popularity of the three commissioners to one focused on the best way to provide local services. Couched as a battle about efficient municipal government—and not as a challenge to Connor's authority—voters supported a change-in-government referendum in the fall of 1962, choosing to replace the three-member commission with a mayor and a nine-member council. Thanks in large measure to unified African American voters, city residents twice picked the businessmen's candidate over Connor for mayor. Albert Boutwell's administration aligned Birmingham's future with UAB, reliant on federal agencies for its ongoing operations and capital building schedule. In the future, UAB administrators and city politicians accepted, at times reluctantly, the demands of local blacks, supported after 1964 by the new civil rights law, for equal access to facilities and a role in local decision making. Linking social regulation to decades-old economic policy gave blacks more specific authority than they had held decades earlier. Moreover, "white leaders desired civic harmony, federal aid, and continued economic advance so strongly that, if necessary, they would accede to racial change in order to secure them," Schulman found in his study of the federal government's impact on the South, especially through military spending.[8]

The inability of the 1964 civil rights law to address economic inequality has frustrated observers of the region. Some historians, like Sullivan, found possibilities for racial justice, evident in the New Deal and World War II eras, derailed afterward. Bartley concluded that while "the South was prosperous and progressive, and southerners were free to pursue personal self-fulfillment through career and achievement," poor and inner-city blacks had been left behind. Glenn Eskew, author of a study of the fight for racial equality in Birmingham, is unable to reconcile how the city that provided "the climax of the civil rights struggle" is also a place torn by poverty and violence among blacks. Although these observations should not obscure the real and lasting changes in places like Birmingham, they do emphasize the limitations of the grant state, which transformed the South. Grant legislation such as Hill-Burton, the Housing Act, or even Great Society efforts like Model Cities, had over time linked economic aid to social concerns but had never addressed the basic structure of the economy, which long had tolerated poverty and class inequality. Indeed, Steve Fraser and Gary Gerstle note that it is not possible to solve "problems of poverty—black or white—without more extensive state control of capitalist institutions and markets." However imperfect its development, Birmingham after the 1960s had been absorbed into the national mainstream. In that context, the Birmingham story may offer clues as to why Birmingham and other American cities continue to fight battles over race and poverty to this day.[9]

# Notes

ABBREVIATIONS USED IN NOTES

| | |
|---|---|
| ACCL | Atlanta Chamber of Commerce Library |
| AHCLA | Atlanta History Center Library and Archives |
| ASAH | Alabama State Archives and History Department, Montgomery |
| BPL | Birmingham Public Library Archives |
| FRC | Federal Records Center, Suitland, Maryland |
| HABD | Housing Authority of the Birmingham District Minutes |
| IRB | Intergroup Relations Board |
| LC | Library of Congress, Washington, D.C. |
| NARA | National Archives, Washington, D.C. |
| NARA II | National Archives, College Park, Maryland |
| PHA | Public Housing Administration |
| RG | Record Group |
| UAB | University of Alabama at Birmingham Archives |
| UAL | University of Alabama Libraries, Tuscaloosa |

## INTRODUCTION

1. *New York Times,* 20 September 1963, 32.

2. Brinkley, "Writing the History of Contemporary America"; Leuchtenburg, "Pertinence of Political History"; Crenson and Rourke, "American Bureaucracy since World War II," in *New American State,* ed. Galambos.

3. *New York Times,* 20 September 1963, 32.

4. *Time,* 15 December 1958, 16; Grantham, *South in Modern America.*

## CHAPTER 1. HOUSING AND THE PROMISE OF REFORM

1. H. M. Walker, "Pittsburgh Plus," *American Mercury* 12 (September 1927): 12–19; Hagur, *Commercial Survey of the Southeast; Birmingham News,* 8 April 1930, James M. Jones Scrapbook, 17.1.5.1.5, and *Birmingham News,* 30 August 1929, Jones Scrapbook, 17.1.4.1.4, BPL.

2. Smith, *New Deal in the Urban South,* 14–17; Atlanta Chamber of Commerce Industrial Bureau, *Facts in Figures about Atlanta 1936,* ACCL.

3. *Birmingham News,* 15 October 1934, 6; Pizitz to Jones, 1 December 1930; Jones to Pizitz, 10 December 1930, Box 6, Jones Papers; Jones to John Temple Graves, 8 February 1932, Box 5, Jones Papers, BPL.

4. George Leighton, "Birmingham, Alabama: The City of Perpetual Promise," *Harper's* 175 (August 1937): 225–42.

5. *Birmingham Post,* 7 May 1932, 1; Smith, *New Deal in the Urban South,* 36–41; LaMonte, *Politics and Welfare,* 70, 79, 89, 90, 114; Jones to Graves, 8 February 1932, Box 5, Jones Papers, BPL; "Final Report of Health Projects Paid by Federal Relief Funds, Nov. 15, 1933–Jan. 14, 1938," Dr. J. D. Dowling, and "Birmingham's Health," Jefferson County Board of Health, May 1940, Box 2, Health Organizations Collection, UAB.

6. *Birmingham News,* 1 April 1934, 1; 8 May 1934, 1; 1 September 1936, 6; 12 September 1936, 12; 14 November 1936, 4.

7. *Birmingham News,* 4 May 1934, 5; 3 October 1934, 6; 4 October 1934, 8; 5 June 1935, 7; and 4 September 1936, 1; Smith, *New Deal in the Urban South,* 114–17.

8. Frank Spain to R. A. Coale, 28 January 1939, Box 5, Jones Papers, BPL; "Relation of Substandard Housing to Crime," 5 December 1936, Box 2, Health Organizations Collection, UAB; W. D. Moore, "What Slum Clearance Means to Birmingham," 13 July 1935, Box 219, PHA Project Files (1933–37), RG 196, NARA II; *Birmingham News,* 19 June 1935, 8.

9. *Birmingham News,* 14 December 1937, Vertical Files, Southern History Room, BPL; *Hearings before the House Committee on Banking and Currency, House of Representatives,* 75th Cong., 1st sess., 249.

10. *Birmingham News,* 4 May 1934, 5; 3 October 1934, 6; 4 October 1934, 8; 5 June 1935, 7; 4 September 1936, 1; Smith, *New Deal in the Urban South,* 114–17.

11. *Birmingham News,* 31 August 1934, Vertical Files, BPL; *Birmingham News,* 2 September 1934, 2; 14 September 1934, 2; 3 June 1935, 6.

12. Robert Jemison to Robert Gregg, 21 March 1934, Robert Jemison Jr. Papers (uncataloged), BPL.

13. *Birmingham News,* 31 August 1934, Vertical Files, BPL.

14. Eugene Klabber to W. J. Wynn, 7 May 1934, Box 5, Jones Papers, BPL.

15. *News,* 20 May 1934, 2; 25 May 1934, 8; 2 June 1934, 2; 17 September 1934, 3.

16. Horatio Hackett to Hugo Black, 25 April 1935, Box 175, Black Papers, LC; "Analysis of Family Study for Federal Low Cost Housing Project," Box 3, Jones Papers, BPL; Jefferson County Board of Health, *Final Statistical Survey,* BPL; "Factors Related to Housing," Box 2, Atlanta Bureau of Planning Papers, AHCLA.

17. Board of Health, *Final Statistical Survey; Post,* 23 October 1934, Jemison Papers, BPL; Ivey, *Building Atlanta's Future,* 164, 175.

18. Hackett to Black, 25 April 1935, Box 175, Black Papers, LC; "Analysis of Family Study for Federal Low Cost Housing Project," Box 3, Jones Papers, BPL.

19. "Birmingham, Alabama," Box 214, PHA Files, RG 196, NARA II; Silver, "Racial Origins of Zoning."

20. *Birmingham City Directory 1932;* Dismuke, *The Other Side; Birmingham Reporter,* 9 January 1932, 1.

21. "Selling to Birmingham," *Business Week,* 9 May 1936, 34–36; Johnson, *Patterns of Negro Segregation,* 22.

22. "Report of the Proceedings of the Southern Conference for Human Welfare" and miscellaneous reports, Box 3, Jones Papers, BPL.

23. *Birmingham News,* 1 February, 13 August 1935, Vertical Files, BPL.

24. "Supplementary Data Concerning Members of the Housing Authority of the Birmingham District," Box 219, PHA Project File, NARA II; *Birmingham News,* 11 April 1934, 8.

25. *Birmingham News,* 1 May 1935, 2; 13 August 1935, 2; Russell to deHoll, 29 May 1935, Box 214, PHA RG 196, NARA II.

26. Petitioners to Hackett, 8 May 1935, and Russell to James Bacon, 26 June 1935, Box 214, PHA Files, RG 196, NARA II; *Birmingham News,* 18 July 1935, 26 July 1935, and *Birmingham Age-Herald,* 20 July 1935, Jones Scrapbook, 17.1.10.1.10, BPL; Eskew, *But for Birmingham,* 76.

27. *Birmingham Post,* 17 July 1935, Jones Scrapbook 17.1.10.1.10, BPL; deHoll to HABD, 30 July 1935, *Housing Authority of the Birmingham District Minutes—July 30, 1935 to June 14, 1938 Volume 1* (hereafter HABD Minutes), Housing Authority of the

Birmingham District Office, Birmingham, Alabama; J. C. deHoll to Horatio Hackett, 4 April 1935, Box 217, PHA Files, RG 196, NARA II.

28. Untitled petition, Inter-Denominational Ministers Alliance, Box 217, PHA Files, RG 196, NARA II; deHoll to Taggart, 6 May 1936, Box 5, Jones Papers, BPL.

29. Taggart to deHoll, 4 May 1936, deHoll to Taggart, 6 May 1936, Box 5, Jones Papers, BPL.

30. A. R. Class to deHoll, 22 June 1936, Box 217, PHA Files, RG 196, NARA II; Meetings of 20 and 27 April 1936, HABD Minutes; Untitled, Committee to Housing Authority of the Birmingham District, 21 September 1936, Box 2, Group I, Series G, NAACP Papers, LC.

31. Meetings of 17 and 21 September 1936, HABD Minutes.

32. McPherson to Walter White, 22 September 1936, McPherson to Adams, 23 September 1936, White to McPherson, 25 September 1936, Box 2, NAACP Papers, LC.

33. H. A. Gray to McPherson, 31 October 1936, Box 2, NAACP Papers, LC.

34. McPherson to Walter White, 24 November 1936, Box 2, NAACP Papers, LC; Autrey, "National Association for the Advancement of Colored People," 139–41; *Birmingham News,* 28 October 1936, 6; Smith, *New Deal in the Urban South,* 248.

35. Donald Jones to Administrator, 22 November 1937, Box 219, PHA Files, RG 196, NARA II.

36. Donald Jones to Mr. Latimer, 7 February 1938, Box 219; deHoll to Nathan Strauss, 29 January 1938, Benjamin Shaw to Nathan Strauss, 10 March 1938, Box 218; Weaver to Nathan Strauss, 29 January 1938, Box 217; PHA Files, RG 196, NARA II; HABD to City Commission, 15 February 1939, Box 5, Jones Papers, BPL.

37. *Birmingham Age-Herald,* 9 June 1938, Jones/City Commission Scrapbook 741.1.14.1.14, BPL; "A Resolution Concerning Public Housing," 7 June 1939, Box 5, Jones Papers, BPL.

38. Hodo to Jones, 22 June 1938, J. H. Shearer to Jones, 14 April 1938, and "A Resolution Concerning Public Housing," 7 June 1939, Box 5, Jones Papers, BPL.

39. E. M. Henderson to Black, 14 April 1937, Black Papers, LC; Fred Harper to Jones, 5 August 1938, Roy Copeland to Jones, 5 August 1938, Box 5, Jones Papers, BPL; "Labor," *Alabama,* 22 May 1938, 10.

40. *Birmingham Post,* 19 May 1931, Jones Scrapbook, 17.1.5.1.5, and *Birmingham Post,* 1 October 1930, Jones Scrapbook 17.1.4.1.4, BPL; *Birmingham News,* 30 September 1936, 12.

41. John Altman to Black, 7 June 1937, Box 195, Black Papers, LC; "Tough on Horatius," *Alabama,* 10 May 1937, 5; Nunnelley, *Bull Connor,* 9–22.

42. *Birmingham Post,* 20 April 1937, Vertical Files, BPL.

43. "Stormy Weather," *Alabama,* 17 May 1937, 5; "Introducing Alabama's Next Legislators," *Alabama,* 3 October 1938, 8.

44. Morgan to Spain, 23 August 1939, HABD Minutes, Vol. 3.

45. Kruman, "Quotas for Blacks," 37–51; Weaver, "Racial Policy," 149–61.

46. DeHoll to Gentlemen, 24 March 1939, Sidney Meer to D. W. Bateman, 29 March 1939, Box 1, Records of the IRB, RG 196, NARA II.

47. Spain to Jacob Crane, 20 April 1939, Alex Lawrenson to Walter Price, 25 May 1939, Daniel Bateman to Nathan Strauss, 2 June 1939, Price to Lawrenson, 7 June 1939, Box 1, IRB, RG 196, NARA II.

48. Clarence Johnson to Weaver, 1 August 1939, Leon Wofford to John Broome, 9 August 1939, Wofford to William Brown, 25 August 1939, and Clarence Johnson to Robert Weaver, 26 August 1939, Box 1, IRB, RG 196, NARA II.

49. Leon Wofford to Alex Lawrenson, 25 July 1939; Wofford to William Brown, 25 August 1939, Box 1, IRB, RG 196, NARA II.

50. Stenographic Transcript of Telephone Conversation between Robert Weaver and L. M. Gaillard, 11 October 1939; Weaver to L. M. Gaillard, 11 October 1939; Roy Copeland to Thomas Joy, 1 May 1940; H. V. Appen to Daniel Bateman, 25 June 1940; and Long Distance Telephone Conversation between Frank Horne, Clarence Johnson, and L. M. Gaillard, 2 August 1940, Box 1, IRB, RG 196, NARA II.

51. Weaver, "Racial Policy," 149, and Long Distance Telephone Conversation between Frank Horne, Clarence Johnson, and L. M. Gaillard, 2 August 1940, Box 1, IRB, RG 196, NARA II.

52. *Birmingham Post,* 19 October 1939, Vertical Files, BPL; Smith, *New Deal in the Urban South,* 234.

53. *Birmingham Age-Herald,* 17 October 1939, Jones/City Commission Scrapbook 741.1.15.1.15, BPL.

## CHAPTER 2. HILL-BURTON SUPPORTS TRADITION

1. "Defense Boom in Dixie," *Time,* 17 February 1941, 75–80; "Team Work Won for Birmingham," 16 February 1944, Box 9, Cooper Green Papers, BPL.

2. Kracke, undated, "Consideration in Favor of Locating a Medical School in a Metropolitan Area," and undated, "A Report to the Governor and the Members of the 1947 Legislature on the Development of Alabama's Medical Center," Box 51, Alabama Museum of Health Sciences Collection, UAB; "Summary of Developments of the Medical College of Alabama," Box 1, Dean Roy Kracke Administrative Files (Kracke Papers), UAB; interview with James A. Head, 19 January 1995, Birmingham, Alabama.

3. *Birmingham News,* 17 February 1944, 10; Carmichael, "Our Dean: Roy Rachford Kracke," 157–60; and M. Don Clawson to Kracke, 2 June 1948, Box 51, Health Collection, UAB.

4. "Annual Report for the Medical College of Alabama for the Twelve Months Ending 1 May 1946," and *Birmingham Post,* 6 August 1946, Box 1, Kracke Papers, UAB; "Alabama's Idea of a Medical College," *Southern Hospitals* 14 (November 1946): 23–24; *Birmingham News,* 15 July 1947; *Birmingham Post,* 29 January 1949, Vertical Files, BPL.

5. "A Proposal," January 1946 File, and "To: The Building Commission of the State of Florida," 8 February 1946, Box 1, Kracke Papers, UAB; *Birmingham News,* 11 February 1946, 12.

6. Harrison, "The Medical School of the University of Alabama," chap. 4, UAB.

7. "Report on Survey of the Medical College of Alabama, Birmingham, Alabama, August 26–30, 1946," Dr. Victor Johnson, Box 18, Records of the Department of Health, Education, and Welfare, RG 90, Hospitals and Medical Facilities Division, Accession No. 60-A-146, General Subject Files (1946–54), FRC.

8. "Health Crisis," *Alabama,* 24 November 1950, 14; "Education: Gout Again," *Alabama,* 2 January 1948, 10.

9. Crenson and Rourke, "American Bureaucracy since World War II," in Galambos, ed., *New American State,* 149.

10. Stevens, *In Sickness and in Wealth,* 222; Hill to Joe Holley, 11 November 1960, Box 245, J. Lister Hill Papers, W. S. Hoole Special Collections, UAL.

11. "Facts Concerning Hospital Facilities in the State of Alabama," Box 18, FRC; *Birmingham News,* 2 August 1946, 14.

12. Kracke to John Gallalee, 6 November 1947, W. D. Partlow to Kracke, 11 November 1947, Box 1, Kracke Papers, UAB; V. M. Hoge to L. W. Charters, 25 November 1946, Box 18, FRC.

13. *Birmingham News,* 20 August 1944, and *Birmingham Age-Herald,* 7 November 1947, Vertical Files, BPL; George Denison to Members, 27 August 1945, Box 9, Green Papers, BPL; Denison to Joseph Mountin, 20 November 1946, Box 18, FRC.

14. Kracke, "Summary of Developments of the Alabama Medical Center," 87; John Gallalee to Board of Trustees, 28 November 1949, Box 1, UAB; *Birmingham Post,* 3 June 1946, 11 April 1948, 19 May 1949, 13 May 1950, Vertical Files, BPL; Surgeon General to Laurie Battle, undated, Box 18, RG 90, FRC.

15. "Committee on the Location of the Children's Hospital," 1 November 1949, November–December 1949 File; Kracke, "A Summary of the Problem of the Children's Hospital," 8 August 1949, Box 1, Kracke Papers, UAB.

16. Kracke to B. G. Shaw, 7 January 1946, Box 1, Kracke Papers, UAB; interview with Kathryn Crossland, 20 July 1989, UAB Oral History Project, UAB; *Birmingham News,* 8 February 1946, 1.

17. Kracke to Shaw, 7 January 1946, Zukoski to Kracke, 15 January 1946, and Kracke to Zukoski, 16 January 1946, Box 1, Kracke Papers, UAB; *Birmingham News,* 24 March 1946, D2; *Birmingham Post,* 14 January 1943, and *Birmingham Post-Herald,* 29 May 1943, Vertical Files, BPL.

18. Charles Zukoski, "A Life Story," 200, BPL; Nelson C. Jackson to Lester Granger, 20 August 1951, Box A128, General Office Files, National Urban League Papers, LC; "Negro Participation," 11 June 1953, and "Minutes: Special Call Meeting," 2 March 1956, Interracial Committee Minutes and Related Documents File, 16.2.2.1.20, Jefferson County Coordinating Council Papers, BPL.

19. Kracke to B. G. Shaw, 7 January 1946, Box 1, Kracke Papers, UAB; *Birmingham News,* 19 May 1949, Vertical Files, BPL; "Facts Concerning Hospital Facilities in the State of Alabama," Box 18, RG 90,FRC.

20. Kracke to B. G. Shaw, 7 January 1946, Kracke to Zukoski, 16 January 1946, January Files, and Robert Durr to Kracke, 12 April 1946, Box 1, Kracke Papers, UAB.

21. Mr. Steinle to V. M. Hoge, 16 September 1947, Box 18, RG 90, FRC; *Birmingham News,* 17 March 1946, Vertical Files, BPL; *Chattanooga Times,* 20 September 1946, Box 63, Health Collection, UAB.

22. Kracke to Zukoski, 31 July 1948, Box 1, Kracke Papers, UAB; "The Mineral District Medical Society, June 2 Meeting," Group II, Series C—Branch Files, Box C2, NAACP Papers, LC; *Birmingham Age-Herald,* 1 July 1948, and *Birmingham News,* 7 September 1948, Vertical Files, BPL.

23. *Birmingham News,* 31 January, 2, 7 February 1950, Vertical Files, BPL; Eskew, *But for Birmingham,* 60–63.

24. Comer to Green, 29 June 1950, and Pizitz to Green, 14 June 1950, Box 10, Green Papers, BPL.

25. *Birmingham Post-Herald,* 11 Jan. 1954, Scrapbook, Jefferson County Health Department, Birmingham, Alabama; "For Negroes Only," *Time,* 30 June 1952, 64.

26. Jackson to Wiley E. Daniels, 22 February 1950, Group II, C—Branch Files, Box C2, NAACP Papers, LC.

27. "Protest Alabama Hospital Bias," 19 April 1951, Box C2, Ruby Hurley to Gloster Current, 20 August 1954, Report to Board for September Meeting, Box C224, NAACP Papers, LC.

28. Harrison to Brewer Dixon, 7 May 1951, Box 2, Tinsley Harrison Administrative Papers, UAB.

29. *Birmingham News,* 12 February 1950, 1; "Report of the Special Survey Com-

mittee," UAB; "Health Crisis," *Alabama,* 24 November 1950, 14; Durrett to D. G. Gill, 22 June 1953, State Board of Censors, Administrative Files of the State Health Officer, Container RG-7131, ASAH.

30. Zukoski to Harrison, 11 October 1950, Harrison Papers, September–October 1950, Box 2, UAB.

31. Harrison, "The Medical School of the University of Alabama," 9, UAB; *Birmingham News,* 12 February 1950, 1; "Report of the Special Survey Committee," UAB; *Birmingham News,* 11 January 1953, Box 2, Durrett Papers, UAB.

## CHAPTER 3. URBAN RENEWAL IN AN ERA OF DECLINE

1. Harold Martin, "The Cities in America: Birmingham," *Saturday Evening Post,* 6 September 1947, 21–25; "Boom-time in Dixie," *Time,* 17 February 1941, 75; George S. Perry, "The Cities in America: Atlanta," *Saturday Evening Post,* 22 September 1945, 26–52.

2. *Birmingham News,* 27 May 1937, James M. Jones Scrapbook, 17.1.12.1.12, BPL; "Certain Aspects in the History of the WPB Region 4," 14 September 1945, Box 588, Records of the War Production Board, RG 179, NARA II; *Birmingham News,* 15 April 1946, 1; *New York Times,* 22 April 1946, 16.

3. *Birmingham News,* 20 January 1946, 2A; 30 June 1946, 5A; 29 September 1946, 1C; 24 November 1946, 1C; George Banks to Green, 1 August 1945, Box 8, Green Papers, BPL.

4. *Atlanta Journal,* 24 May 1949, 1.

5. *Alabama,* 10 June 1949, 8; 9 September 1949, 5–6; 16 September 1949, 10–11; 25 November 1949, 2; D. W. LaRue to Green, 25 August 1949, Box 3, Green Papers, BPL; *Birmingham News,* 7 September 1949, 3; 14 September 1949, 1; *Alabama,* 19 November 1949, 10.

6. *Birmingham News,* 7 September 1949, 3.

7. "Slum Clearance under the Housing Act of 1949," Box 1, James W. Morgan Papers, BPL.

8. *Birmingham News,* 10 July 1945, Vertical Files, BPL.

9. Hill Ferguson to John M. Gallalee, 14 October 1949, Folder 152-A, Medical Center Development Papers, UAB.

10. *Birmingham News,* 13 January 1946, 2; 9 December 1949, 1; Harold Harper to City Commissioners, 17 January 1950, Box 14, Morgan Papers, BPL; Frederick Allen to HABD, 6 September 1950, Box 12, Green Papers, BPL; George Denison to City Commission, 10 November 1949, Box 8, Green Papers, BPL.

11. "Health as an Indication of Housing Needs in Birmingham, Alabama and Recommendations for Slum Clearance, Redevelopment and Public Housing,"

Jefferson County Health Department, 4 April 1950, Box 8, Green Papers, BPL.

12. Preliminary Report of the Birmingham Planning Board, 2 February 1952, Box 1, City Council Pamphlets, BPL; *Birmingham Post,* 20 April 1950, Vertical Files, BPL; *Birmingham Post-Herald,* 12 May 1951, and *Birmingham News,* 24 October 1951, Health Scrapbook; Notes Covering Meeting in Dean Durrett's Office, 28 February 1952, HABD Archives, BPL.

13. J. J. Steiner to HABD, 24 March 1953, Notes Covering Meeting in Dean Durrett's Office, 28 February 1952, and "Medical Center, Site A," HABD Archives, BPL.

14. *Birmingham News,* 20 March 1952, Vertical Files, BPL; "A Statement of Activities Relative to Title I Redevelopment Program in the Medical Center Area," Box 12, Morgan Papers, BPL.

15. Preliminary Report, Slum Clearance and Redevelopment, Medical Center Site A, and "Meeting with Birmingham Planning Board," 5 November 1962, HABD Archives, BPL.

16. "Transcript of the Public Hearing, 30 March 1953," Title I File, HABD Archives, BPL.

17. Notes Covering Meeting in Dean Durrett's Office, 19 June 1953, Title I File, HABD Archives, BPL; Program Review Committee, 22 May 1953, Box 278, RG 207, NARA.

18. Interview with Oscar Adams, 3 June 1994, Birmingham, Alabama; *Birmingham News,* 23 February 1997, B1; *Birmingham Post-Herald,* 23 February 1997, B1; "An Appraisal of the Redevelopment Plan, Medical Center Site A," Birmingham Branch of the NAACP, Group II, Series A, General Office Files, Box A306, NAACP Papers, LC.

19. Ruby Hurley to Lucille Black, 23 April 1952, Box C222, NAACP Papers, LC; *Birmingham World,* 24 May 1953, 6, and 29 May 1953, 6.

20. "Statement for NAACP by Ruby Hurley," 15 October 1953, NAACP Birmingham File, 1951–55 (microfilm), BPL.

21. "Objections to Proposed Slum Clearance," Box 12, Morgan Papers, BPL.

22. *Birmingham World,* 12 June 1953, 1; 26 June 1953, 1; 28 July 1953, 1; To Albert M. Cole, 15 June 1953, Box A306, NAACP Papers, LC; "Re: Conversation, Washington," 29 June 1953, HABD Archives, BPL.

23. "Re: Discussion with Robinson," "Conversation," 29 June 1953, and "Conversation," 29 June 1953, HABD Archives, BPL; Morgan to Lister Hill, 28 September 1953, Box 450, Hill Papers, Hoole Collection, UAL.

24. *Birmingham News,* 24 July 1953, Health Scrapbook; *Birmingham Post-Herald,* 23 July 1953, Vertical Files, BPL; Adams interview.

25. Maxwell Rabb to Mr. White, 16 November 1953, Box A306, NAACP Papers, LC; Maxwell Rabb to B. T. Fitzpatrick, 13 November 1953, Box 73, RG 207, NARA; James Follin to Harper, 25 November 1953, Box 25, Morgan Papers, BPL; Ruby Hurley to Gloster Current, 11 June 1954, Box A306, NAACP Papers, LC; attachment in Harper to Morgan, 31 January 1955, Box 25, Morgan Papers, BPL; *Birmingham Post-Herald,* 1 December 1956, Health Scrapbook.

26. "Well, What Do You Think of the Connor Case?" *Alabama,* 11 January 1952, 5–6.

27. Eskew, *But for Birmingham,* 96–102.

28. *Birmingham News,* 20 January 1954, Health Scrapbook.

29. *Birmingham News,* 27 January 1954, Planning Scrapbook.

30. *Alabama,* 2 April 1954; Corley, "Quest for Racial Harmony," 89.

31. See American States Rights Association advertisements in *Alabama,* 2 April 1954; McWhorter, *Carry Me Home,* 86–100.

32. "No Mingling," *Alabama,* 3 June 1954, 10.

33. "Application for Recertification, 1956," Community Renewal Application File, Box 668.1.39, Planning and Zoning Records, BPL.

34. Alton McWhorter to George Denison, 29 November 1954, Planning and Zoning Records, Box 668.1.19, BPL; *Birmingham News,* 20 January 1955, and *Birmingham Post-Herald,* 29 June 1955, Health Scrapbook.

35. "Avondale, Site C, Planning Studies," undated, HABD Archives, BPL; *Birmingham News,* 2 August 1955, Health Scrapbook.

36. "Workable Program for Community Redevelopment," Box 14, Morgan Papers, BPL; "4 Years, 4 Principles, 4 Points," Jefferson County Health Department, Box 13, Morgan Papers, BPL; James Waggoner to C. B. Holliman, 22 January 1958, Box 5, James T. Waggoner Papers, BPL.

37. James Waggoner to James Biller, 5 December 1960, Box 6, Waggoner Papers, BPL; Ben Englebert to James Morgan, undated, Box 24, Morgan Papers, BPL; "Relocation of Families Through 9/55," Box 620, RG 207, NARA.

38. "Population," undated, Box 1, Chamber of Commerce Pamphlets/Reports, BPL; "1960 Census of Population Final Counts," File 668.242, Planning and Zoning Papers, BPL.

39. Lamar Coffin to Editor, 12 May 1962, Box 6, Arthur Hanes Papers, BPL; "Number 1 Test Market of the Deep South," Box 1, Chamber of Commerce Pamphlets, BPL.

40. *Birmingham Post-Herald,* 28 July 1956 (quotations) and 22 February 1956, Health Scrapbook; *Birmingham News,* 9 October 1958, 28 September 1958, Planning Scrapbook, BPL; *Birmingham Post-Herald,* 29 July, 1 August 1955, *Birmingham News* 28 July, 1 August 1955, Health Scrapbook.

41. *Birmingham News,* 3 November 1954, 1; *Birmingham Post-Herald,* 29 July, 1 August 1955, and *Birmingham News,* 28 July, 1 August 1955, Health Scrapbook; LaMonte, *Politics and Welfare,* 136.

42. *Union Labor News,* 11 August 1955, 1; "Special City Bond Election," 13 September 1955, City Clerk's Office, Birmingham, Alabama.

43. *Birmingham News,* 5 June 1957, 1; Corley, "Quest for Racial Harmony," 160–62; Nunnelley, *Bull Connor,* 179; *Union Labor News,* 8 May 1958, Box 22, Morgan Papers, BPL; "Recapitulation Sheet for the City of Birmingham for the Democratic Primary," 7 May 1957, City Clerk's Office, Birmingham.

44. Eskew, *But for Birmingham,* 128; McWhorter, *Carry Me Home,* 127–42; "A Survey of Resistance Groups in the South," Box 41.6.2.20, Southern Regional Council Papers, BPL; *Time,* 15 December 1958, 16.

45. *Birmingham News,* 8 May 1957, 1, 28 September 1958, and 3 October 1958, Planning Scrapbook, BPL.

46. *The Economy of Metropolitan Birmingham,* Hamer, Greene, Siler and Associates, October 1966, Box 1, Operation New Birmingham Papers, BPL; *Birmingham News,* 28 September 1958, 12 November 1959, Planning Scrapbook, BPL; *Birmingham News,* 12 February 1958, Chamber of Commerce Scrapbook, BPL; "Labor Force," undated, Urban Economy File, 668.4.7, Planning and Zoning Papers, BPL; *Union Labor News,* 17 November 1955, 1; "Model Cities Grant Application," 12 April 1968, Box 190, RG 207, NARA II; *New York Times,* 12 September 1963, 32.

47. Asa N. Green, "An 'Office-Park' in a Triple-A Suburb," *American City* 74 (1959): 75.

48. *Birmingham News,* 9, 10 April 1959, Planning Scrapbook; *Birmingham News,* 26 February 1961, Chamber Scrapbook, BPL.

49. *Birmingham News,* 13 April 1959, Health Scrapbook; *News,* 22 March 1959, and *Birmingham Post-Herald,* 14 April 1959, Planning Scrapbook, BPL; *Birmingham Post-Herald,* 17 April 1957, 1; "Population Review, 1960 Census," File 668.242, Planning and Zoning Papers, BPL.

50. James Morgan to Albert Cole, 5 July 1956, Box 668.1.39, Planning and Zoning Records, BPL; Paul Cooper to Emil Hess, 18 May 1956, Box 20, Morgan Papers, BPL; Eskew, "But for Birmingham," 95–97; *Birmingham Post-Herald,* 29 December 1955, and *Birmingham News,* 11 January, 1 August 1956, Health Scrapbook; Hugh Denman to Melvin Baldwin, 13 February 1959, Box 5, Waggoner Papers, BPL.

51. "The Birmingham Metropolitan Audit—Preliminary Report No. 2, The Personality of Birmingham," Southern Institute of Management, Box 6, Barber/Bishop Papers, BPL.

## CHAPTER 4. MEDICAL CENTER TURNS TO GRANTS

1. Interviews with S. Richardson Hill Jr., 6 April 1990, and Charles A. McCallum, 11 July 1994, Oral History Project, UAB.

2. James Durrett to D. W. Hodo, 23 March 1953, State Board of Censors, Administrative Files of the State Health Officer, Container SG-7131, ASAH; Harrison, "The Medical School of the University of Alabama," chap. 4, UAB.

3. T. Duckett Jones to James Durrett, 21 September 1953, Box 2, Duckett Papers, UAB; "Report of the Special Survey Committee," University of Alabama Medical Center, August 1954, UAB.

4. Interview with Matthew F. McNulty Jr., 25 January 1990, Oral History Project, UAB; *Birmingham News,* 13 April, 15 May 1955, Health Scrapbook.

5. "Report of the Special Survey Committee," University of Alabama Medical Center, August 1954, UAB.

6. "Public Meeting on the Medical Center," 30 March 1953, HABD Papers, BPL.

7. Interview with Ehney A. Camp Jr., 7 July 1989, Oral History Project, UAB; "Aggressive Liberty," *Alabama,* 6 December 1937, 9–11; Rogers, *Alabama,* 595.

8. Planning Committee Meeting, 25 August 1955, Medical Center Planning Committee, Box 4, Robert C. Berson Administrative Papers, UAB.

9. Berson to Lister Hill, 12 September 1956, Box 639, Hill Papers, Hoole Collection, UAL; *Birmingham News,* 5 January 1956, Jemison Papers, BPL.

10. Berson to Harper, 21 February 1956, and Harper to Berson, 3 March 1956, Box 7, Barber/Bishop Papers, BPL; *Birmingham Post-Herald,* 29 December 1955, Health Scrapbook.

11. Planning Committee Meeting, 4 January, 9 February 1956, Box 11, Volker Papers, UAB; Berson to Todd Wheeler, 29 November 1955, and Camp to Berson, 28 December 1955, Box 5, Berson Papers, UAB.

12. Meeting Between Representatives, 6 April 1956, Box 14, Morgan Papers, BPL.

13. Berson to Medical Center Advisory Board, 10 April 1956, and Planning Committee Meeting, 12 April 1956, Box 5, Berson Papers, UAB.

14. Berson to Amzi Barber, 25 April 1956, Box 7, Barber/Bishop Papers, BPL; "The Redeveloper's Viewpoint," Box 22, Volker Papers, UAB; Planning Committee Minutes, 2, 24 May, 12 June, 30 August 1956, Box 5, Berson Papers, UAB; *Birmingham Post-Herald,* 7 April 1956, Health Scrapbook; Bruce Wedge to Roy LeCraw, 28 May 1941, Atlanta Master Plan Survey, Box 4, Atlanta Bureau of Planning Records, AHCLA.

15. Berson to Lister Hill, 12 September 1956, Box 639, Hill Papers, Hoole Collection, UAL.

16. Camp to Richard Steiner, 23 May 1957, Box 5, Berson Papers, UAB.

17. Camp to Richard Steiner, 23 May 1957 (quotation), Box 5, Berson Papers, UAB; Camp to Richard Steiner, 11 July 1957, Box 6, Berson Papers, UAB.

18. *Birmingham News,* 10, 12 (quotation) July 1957, Planning Scrapbook, BPL.

19. Camp Interview, UAB; Bruce Wedge to Hugh Denman, 11 September 1957, Box 5, Waggoner Papers, BPL; Frank Spain to Joseph Volker, 17 June 1963, Box 22, Volker Papers, UAB.

20. *Birmingham News,* 17 August 1957, Planning Scrapbook, BPL; *Birmingham News,* 23 August 1957, Health Scrapbook.

21. "A Medical Center for Alabama: Information and Recommendations," 25 August 1955, UAB.

22. "Report of the Indigent Patient Committee," Medical Center Advisory Board, 3 May 1956, Box 11, Volker Papers, UAB.

23. Meeting of the Legislative Interim Committee, 27 September 1958, Box 15, Volker Papers, UAB; "Report of the Indigent Patient Committee," Medical Center Advisory Board, 3 May 1956, Box 11, Volker Papers, UAB; "Annual Report of the Medical College of Alabama, 1958–1959," UAB; "Year-End Balance, 1957–1958," Box 18, Volker Papers, UAB.

24. *Birmingham News,* 18 January, 16 June 1955, Health Scrapbook; Frederick Almer to Lister Hill, 27 March 1958, Box 639, Hill Papers, Hoole Collection, UAL; Minutes of a Special Meeting of the Board of Trustees of the University of Alabama, 8 April 1963, Trustees Record, Vol. 15, Hoole Collection, UAL.

25. Berson to Paul McNulty, 8 July 1960, Box 9, Berson Papers, UAB; President's Report to the Board of Trustees, 3 November 1961, Trustees Record, Vol. 15, Hoole Collection, UAL.

26. Starr, *Social Transformation of American Medicine,* 338–47; Geiger, *Research and Relevant Knowledge,* 179–85; "Development of UAB," undated, Box 136, Volker Papers, UAB.

27. McCallum Interview, UAB; *Birmingham News,* 7 September 1959, Health Scrapbook; "The Condition of the Medical Center, 1959–1961," Box 18, and Planning Committee Meeting, 8 March 1956, Box 11; Volker to Matthew McNulty, 26 September 1962 and Berson to State Board of Health, 6 August 1962, Box 21, Volker Papers, UAB; Berson to S. Richardson Hill, 20 May 1958, Box 7, Berson Papers, UAB.

28. "Medical," Medical Center Research and Grants File, Box 7, and Volker to Francis Schehl, 29 November 1956, Box 12, Volker Papers, UAB.

29. Berson to Volker, 21 March 1960, "Divisional Report," 1 May 1959–30 April 1960, Director of Research and Graduate Studies, and Medical Center Advisory Board Meeting, 7 January 1960, Box 9; Berson to Frank Rose, 15 December 1969,

Box 8, Berson Papers, UAB; "Divisional Report," 1 May 1961–30 April 1962, Box 66, Volker Papers, UAB; Minutes of the Special Meeting of the Board of Trustees of the University of Alabama, 23 April 1962, Trustees Record, Vol. 15, Hoole Collection, UAL; Lister Hill to Sidney Smyer Jr., 20 June 1960, Box 244, Hill Papers, Hoole Collection, UAL.

30. *Birmingham Post-Herald,* 23 September 1958, and *Birmingham News,* 2 June 1956, Vertical Files, BPL; Medical Center Advisory Board, 7 January 1960, Box 9, Berson Papers, UAB; Amzi Barber to Morgan, 15 January 1959, Box 2, Waggoner Papers, BPL.

31. "Report of the Medical Center Committee of the Board of Trustees," 3 November 1961, Board of Trustees, University of Alabama 1961 File, Box 10; "Financial Support for the Medical Center Operating and Capital Funds for Discussion with the Medical Center Advisory Board," 9 December 1960, Box 9, Berson Papers, UAB; "University of Alabama: A Financial Report on Your University and Its Immediate Needs," Box 67, Volker Papers, UAB; Minutes of the Special Meeting of the Board of Trustees, 8 April 1963, Hoole Collection, UAL; Minutes of the Medical Center Advisory Board, 4 June 1963, Box 4, S. Richardson Hill Papers, UAB.

32. "Report of the Survey of the Medical College of Alabama Liaison Committee of Medical Education," December 1960, Box 9, Berson Papers, UAB; Harrison, "Medical School of the University of Alabama," chap. 10, 9, UAB; Report of the Medical Center Committee of the Board of Trustees, 3 November 1961, Trustees Record, Vol. 15, Hoole Collection, UAL.

33. "Employment Statistics," March 1963, and Volker to O. C. Carmichael, 5 December 1963, Box 22, Volker Papers, UAB.

## CHAPTER 5. BIRMINGHAM CHANGES ITS GOVERNMENT

1. *New York Times,* 12 April 1960, 1; 13 April 1960, 1; and 4 May 1960, 1; "Salisbury Stake," *Newsweek,* 25 September 1960, 68, and *New Republic,* 11 July 1960, 10; McWhorter, *Carry Me Home,* 157–60.

2. *New York Times,* 4 May 1960, 1.

3. *Birmingham Post-Herald,* 29 December 1955, and *Birmingham News,* 11 January, 1 August 1956, Health Scrapbook; *Birmingham Post-Herald* 22 August 1956, 7 January 1961, and *Birmingham News,* 29 August, 7 November 1956, 7 April 1961, Planning Scrapbook, BPL; Hugh Denman to Melvin Baldwin, 13 February 1959, Box 5, Waggoner Papers, BPL.

4. *Birmingham News,* 18 April 1957, Planning Scrapbook, BPL; *Birmingham Post-Herald,* 16 May 1957, and "Proposal and Objectives of the Downtown Improvement

Association," Jemison Papers, BPL; "BDIA Bulletin," Box 2, Waggoner Papers, BPL; and "Industrial Recruitment Data," Industrial Bureau, Atlanta Chamber of Commerce, 19 February 1954, Box 1, Atlanta Plan Papers, AHCLA.

5. "BDIA Bulletin," Box 2, Waggoner Papers, BPL.

6. *Birmingham News,* 13 October 1959, Planning Scrapbook, BPL; Hugh Denman to Sen. John Sparkman, 11 July 1958, Box 5, Waggoner Papers, BPL; Minutes of the Birmingham Planning Commission, 6 May 1959, Box 21, Morgan Papers, BPL; Clarence Hanson to James Waggoner, undated, Box 5, Waggoner Papers, BPL.

7. *Birmingham News,* 23, 30 November, 13 December 1958, Planning Scrapbook, BPL; "Greater Birmingham Committee," 27 November 1958, Box 40, Albert J. Boutwell Papers, BPL; *Birmingham News,* 7, 14 October 1958, and *Birmingham Post-Herald,* 10 March 1959 (quotation), Planning Scrapbook, BPL.

8. Elton B. Stephens Interview, 18 January 1995.

9. Miss Cusack to Robert Jemison, 27 February 1959, George Taylor to Gentlemen, 14 May 1959, and Citizens for Merger Committee Pamphlets, Jemison Papers, BPL.

10. Allen Wood to William Engel, 14 April 1959, and "Statement," Box 1, Waggoner Papers, BPL; *Birmingham News,* 31 March, 10, 18 February 1959, Planning Scrapbook, BPL.

11. W. B. Hartsfield to Mr. ——, 14 April 1959, File 1.16, Box 1, Waggoner Papers, BPL; BIRMINGHAM Needs Us and We Need BIRMINGHAM!, Jemison Papers, BPL; Hartsfield, 14 April 1959 (memo), File, Box 1, Waggoner Papers, BPL; *Birmingham News,* 10 February 1959, Planning Scrapbook, BPL.

12. *Birmingham News,* 15 April 1959, Planning Scrapbook, BPL; James Simpson to All My Fellow Citizens, undated, Box 40, Boutwell Papers, BPL; "Registration of Negro Voters in Alabama," 1954, Box 41.2.16.3.37, and "Conference on Voting Restrictions in Southern States," Voting Restrictions File, Box 41.1.6.2.31, Southern Regional Conference Papers, BPL; *Birmingham News,* 20 April 1958, 10; *Birmingham World,* 4 March 1959, 6.

13. Untitled voting report, Box 500, Hugo Black Papers, LC.

14. *Birmingham Post-Herald,* 24 October 1958, 9 February 1959, Planning and Zoning Scrapbook, BPL; William Silsbee to Robert Ryan, 9 April 1959, Box 40, Boutwell Papers, BPL; *Birmingham News,* 8 October 1952, 10.

15. *Who's Kidding Whom,* Citizens Information Committee, undated, and William Silsbee to George Taylor, 15 April 1959, Box 40, Boutwell Papers, BPL.

16. *Union Labor News,* 21 May 1959, 1; *Birmingham News,* 13 May 1959, Jemison Papers, BPL.

17. William Silsbee to Morgan, 14 April 1959, Box 40 Boutwell Papers, BPL; Newman Waters to Charles Zukoski, 12 May 1958, and Milton Fies to Robert Jemison Jr., 6 April 1959, Box 5, Operation New Birmingham Papers, BPL.

18. *Birmingham Post-Herald,* 20 March, 26 November 1959, and *Birmingham News,* 19, 25 August 1959, Planning Scrapbook, BPL.

19. Elton B. Stephens to Fred Taylor, 14 December 1959, and William Silsbee, "Recap of Activities Relative to Red Mountain Feasibility Study," 23 March 1960, Box 5, Operation New Birmingham Papers, BPL; "Resolution," Birmingham Downtown Improvement Association, 16 October 1962, Box 3, Arthur Hanes Papers, BPL; John Steinichen to William Silsbee, 22 January 1959, Box 40, Boutwell Papers, BPL.

20. "Events Leading Up to 6 January 1960," BDIA, Urban Renewal File, Box 668.4.8, and "Resolution," 12 January 1960, Box 668.4.10, Planning and Zoning Papers, BPL; *Birmingham Post-Herald,* 15 December 1960, Planning and Zoning Scrapbook, BPL; "Minutes of the Meeting," 2 March 1961 (quotation), Planning and Zoning, 2 March 1961–28 April Box 6, Waggoner Papers, BPL.

21. *Birmingham News,* 4 January, 15, 16 February 1961, Planning Scrapbook, BPL.

22. *Birmingham News,* 4 January, 15, 16 February 1961, Planning Scrapbook, BPL; *Birmingham Post* 11 November 1934, Jones Scrapbook 17.1.9.1.9; *Birmingham News,* 8 October, 1952, 1; "New Deal," *Alabama,* 13 June 1953, 8, "Bow-out by Bull," *Alabama,* 6 March 1953, 10; "Greater Birmingham Committee," 27 November 1958, Box 40 Boutwell Papers, BPL; *Birmingham News,* 8 September 1958, Planning Scrapbook, BPL.

23. *Birmingham News,* 22 February 1961, Planning Scrapbook, BPL; *Birmingham News,* 26 February 1961, and *Birmingham Post-Herald,* 11 February 1961, Chamber of Commerce Scrapbook, BPL; "Report of a Committee of the Birmingham Bar Association," October 1961, Box 40, Boutwell Papers, BPL.

24. Hemphill, *Leaving Birmingham,* 286–89; David Vann to author, 27 February 1995; McWhorter, *Carry Me Home,* 202–35.

25. *Birmingham News,* 8 January 1962, 1; 9 February 1953, 5; 15, 22 May 1961, Chamber Scrapbook, BPL; "Resolution," 18 May 1961, Box 7, Waggoner Papers, BPL; *Wall Street Journal,* 26 May 1961, 1; Committee of 100 to Lister Hill, 22 May 1961, Box 376, Hill Papers, Hoole Collection, UAL.

26. Nunnelley, *Bull Connor,* 92–111; *Birmingham News,* 27 March 1961, and *Birmingham Post-Herald,* 3 May 1961, Vertical Files, BPL.

27. *Birmingham News,* 31 May 1961, Vertical Files, BPL; "Report of a Committee of the Birmingham Bar Association," October 1961, Box 40, Boutwell Papers, BPL.

28. "Birmingham: Brinksmanship in Race Relations," *Christian Century,* 30 May 1962, 689; "Busting Up Ball Games," *New Republic,* 12 February 1962, 10–11.

29. *Birmingham News,* 31 May 1961, Vertical Files, BPL; Travis Wolfe to James Waggoner, 4 December 1961.

30. Wolfe to Waggoner, 4 December 1961, and T. W. Aitken to Arthur Hanes, 29 December 1961, Box 7, Waggoner Papers, BPL.

31. "Joint Statement Issued by the City Commission On 17 January 1962," Box 5, Hanes Papers, BPL.

32. *Birmingham News,* 14 March 1962, Chamber Scrapbook, BPL; James A. Head interview, 18 January 1995; Corley, "Quest for Racial Harmony," 232.

33. Branch, *Parting the Waters,* 592; Eskew, *But for Birmingham,* 194–99; "Brinksmanship," *Christian Century,* 689; Joe David Brown, "Birmingham, Alabama: City in Fear," *Saturday Evening Post,* 3 March 1961, 11–19; Robert G. Corley, "In Search of Racial Harmony: Birmingham Business Leaders and Desegregation, 1950–1963," in Jacoway and Colburn, eds., *Southern Businessmen,* 184–90.

34. "Birmingham's Problems, Causes, and Suggested Solutions" and "Statement of Policy," undated, Richard Puryear to Dear Members, 19 September 1962, and Clarence B. Hanson Jr. to Richard Puryear, 26 September 1962, Box 2, Hanes Papers, BPL; Smyer interview in Raines, *My Soul Is Rested,* 165.

35. Vann to the author, 3 August 1993; and Vann, "Events Leading to the 1963 Change from Commission to Mayor-Council Form of Government."

36. *Birmingham Post-Herald,* 26 July 1962, Chamber Scrapbook, BPL.

37. Newman Waters to William Spencer, 5, 28 March 1963, Box 2, Waggoner Papers, BPL; *Birmingham Post-Herald,* 5, 19 September, 19, 24, 27 October 1962.

38. J. T. Waggoner to Newman Waters, 29 March 1963, Box 2, Waggoner Papers, BPL; *Birmingham Post-Herald,* 19, 31 October, 2 November 1962.

39. City Elections File, Box 5, George G. Seibels Jr./City Council Papers, BPL.

40. Branch, *Pillar of Fire,* 26.

41. City Elections File, Box 5, George G. Seibels Jr./City Council Papers, BPL; *Union Labor News,* 28 February 1963, 1; Brown, "Birmingham," *Saturday Evening Post,* 11–19; *New York Times,* 4 April 1963, 24; Stephens interview.

42. For a fuller discussion of the Birmingham movement, see Eskew, "But for Birmingham," 262–399; Branch, *Parting the Waters,* 688–802; McWhorter, *Carry Me Home,* 303–422.

43. *New York Times,* 23 May 1963, 36; "Federal Aid as Percent of State and Local General Revenue—1963 Fiscal Year," April 1965, Box 24, Volker Papers, UAB.

44. Boutwell to My Fellow Citizens, 16 July 1963, Box 3, City Council Papers, BPL; *Union Labor News,* 21 February 1963, 1; *Birmingham News,* 19 March 1963, Box 13, Boutwell Papers, BPL.

45. Morgan, *A Time to Speak,* 2; Untitled Report, Box 66, Volker Papers, UAB.

46. *Wall Street Journal,* 28 June 1963, Box 640, Hill Papers, Hoole Collection, UAL; "Employment Statistics," March 1963, Box 22, Volker Papers, UAB.

47. *Washington Post,* 21 April 1963, Box 13, Boutwell Papers, BPL; Matthew McNulty to Volker, 19 September 1964, Faculty Council/Medical College of Alabama, 10 September 1963, and Spain to Volker, 23 April, 17 June 1963, Box 22, Volker Papers, UAB; "Planning Committee Meeting," 18 April 1963, Box 5, Hill Papers, UAB.

48. Volker to Boutwell, 13 April 1963, Box 13, Boutwell Papers, BPL.

49. Henry Goodrich to James Mills, 18 September 1962, Goodrich to Albert Boutwell, 18 July 1963, George Brownwell to William Spencer, 14 March 1963, Box 3, City Council Papers, BPL; *Eastern Sun (Birmingham),* 1 August 1963, HABD Scrapbook, BPL.

50. Frank Newton to Boutwell, 25 September 1963, Box 3, City Council Papers, BPL; LaMonte, *Politics and Welfare,* 185–93.

51. Sidney Smyer Jr. to Volker, 15 June 1964, Box 6; Planning Committee Meeting, 24 March 1964, Box 10, Hill Papers, UAB; *Birmingham News,* 2 March 1964, Planning Scrapbook, BPL.

52. "Mayor's Speech," 24 December 1964, Box 64; *Birmingham News,* 25 December 1964, Box 23, Volker Papers, UAB; *Birmingham Post-Herald,* 23 February 1965, University Hospital Scrapbook, UAB.

53. "Mayor's Committee on the Medical Center," Box 64; Boutwell to Dear Friend, 26 January 1965, Box 23, Volker Papers, UAB; *Birmingham Post-Herald,* 30 December 1964, Planning Scrapbook, BPL; "Mayor's Committee for Expansion of the Medical Center," 23 February 1965, and Jack McSpadden to Volker, 3 August 1965, Box 23, Volker Papers, UAB.

54. "Meeting of the BDIA Steering Committee," 20 November 1964, Box 2, City Council Papers, BPL; First Annual Report—1964, Box 14, City Council Pamphlets, BPL; Bruce Wedge to Hugh Denman, 1 June 1965, Box 668.1.24, Planning and Zoning Papers, BPL; Boutwell to William Slayton, 22 December 1965, Box 2, Council Papers, BPL.

## CHAPTER 6. CHANGE AND ITS LIMITS IN BIRMINGHAM

1. Paul Good, "Birmingham Two Years Later," *Reporter,* 2 December 1965, 21–27.

2. *Newsweek,* 11 December 1964, 32; Donald Newton to Boutwell, 25 June 1964, and W. C. Hamilton to Franklin D. Roosevelt Jr., 23 September 1965, Box 39, Boutwell Papers, BPL; "An Information Memorandum with Regard to 'The Civil Rights Act of 1964,'" 23 June 1964, Box 7, Hill Papers, UAB.

3. Charles Whitfield to E. L. Oden, 9 August 1966, and Paul Brann to William Hamilton, 10 August 1966, Box 1, William C. Hamilton Papers, BPL; James T. Montgomery to M. E. Wiggins, 26 June 1964, Box 2, City Council Papers, BPL; William Hamilton to Legal Department, 4 March 1966, Box 12, Boutwell Papers, BPL; *New York Times,* 13 March 1966, 45; *Birmingham Post-Herald,* 7, 8 October 1965, and *Birmingham News,* 7, 8 October 1965, University Scrapbook, UAB.

4. Matthew McNulty to Thomas Bradford, 23 March 1964, Box 3, City Council Papers, BPL.

5. *Simkins v. McCone* 323 F. 2d 959; Volker to O. C. Carmichael, 5 December 1963, Box 22, Volker Papers, UAB.

6. Volker to Frank Rose, 6 May 1964, Box 23; McNulty to Volker, 8 May 1964, Box 25, Volker Papers, UAB.

7. McNulty to Volker, 22 October 1964, Box 22; Volker to Jefferson Bennett, 30 July 1964, Box 23, Volker Papers, UAB; interview with Louis J. Willie, 10 October 1989, UAB Oral History Project, UAB; "Compliance Forms under the New Civil Rights Legislation," Box 13, Hill Papers, UAB; McNulty to Volker, 21 December 1964, Box 22, Volker Papers, UAB.

8. Memorandum for Senator Lister Hill, 2 February 1964, Box 245, Hill Papers, Hoole Collection, UAL; Volker to Jefferson Bennett, 31 October 1964, and Volker to Luther Callahan, 4 December 1964, Box 23, Volker Papers, UAB.

9. McNulty to Jefferson Bennett, 5 November 1964, Box 22; Volker to McNulty, 10, 12, 16 April 1965, and McNulty to Volker, 17, 25 April 1965, Box 24, Volker Papers, UAB.

10. McNulty to James Quigley, 18 May 1965, and John Drew to McNulty, 17 May 1965, and Henry Cottrell to Alex Pow, 29 July 1965, Box 24, Volker Papers, UAB.

11. Hugh Maddox to McNulty, 26 May 1966, Box 26; Spain to Frederick Kraus, 9, 12 March 1965, and Volker to Spain, 11 March 1965, Box 24; Frederick Kraus to Spain, 12 March 1965, Box 68, Volker Papers, UAB.

12. *Birmingham News,* 29 February 1967, 1 August 1968, 1; Alan Drennen to James White, 22 February 1968, Box 13, City Council Papers, BPL; "Birmingham, Alabama: Model Cities—Application for Planning Grant," 12 April 1968, Box 3, RG 207, Records of the Department of Housing and Urban Development, NARA II.

13. "Memorandum," 16 May 1968, and "Neighborhood Citizens Proposed Agenda," 18 May 1968, Box 13, City Council Papers, BPL; Harvey Burg to Seibels, 23 May 1968, Box 32, Seibels Papers, BPL.

14. "Citizens Proposal," 31 May 1968, Box 13, City Council Papers, BPL.

15. Burg to Walter Farr, 27 May 1968, and Burg to Weaver, 14 June 1968, Box 13, City Council Papers, BPL; Seibels to Burg, 4 June 1968, and Seibels to Walter Farr, 6 June 1968, Box 32, Seibels Papers, BPL.

16. Weaver to Burg, 1 July 1968, Box 32, Seibels Papers, BPL; "Statement of Complaint," 14 June 1968, Robert Conkling to Seibels et al., 6 November 1968, and Allen Drennen to Ralph Taylor, 12 November 1968, Box 13, City Council Papers, BPL.

17. James White to Tom Bradford, 9 June 1971, and *Birmingham News* 1 June 1971, Box 32, Volker Presidential Papers, UAB.

18. *New York Times,* 7 May 1970, Box 79, Volker Papers, UAB; "The Medical Center: University of Alabama in Birmingham," Box 74, Hill Papers, UAB.

19. Volker to Ehney Camp, 6 April 1971, Box 33, Volker Papers, UAB; "Medical Center—Special Commencement Issue," 1977, Box 8, Hill Papers, UAB.

20. *Birmingham Post-Herald,* 9 May 1972, and *Birmingham News,* 9 January 1969, Medical Center Scrapbook, UAB; *Birmingham Post-Herald,* 18 May 1974.

21. *Birmingham News,* 6 January 1971, University Scrapbook, UAB; Joseph Fontana to Members of the MDB Brainstorming Session, 23 February 1971, Box 33, Volker Papers, UAB.

22. "Table I: Equal Employment Opportunity (By Race)," April 1973, Box 49, Volker Papers, UAB.

23. "A Brief Report on University College," Box 36, Hill Papers, UAB.

24. *Birmingham News,* 5, 14 July 1967, 27 June 1971, and *Birmingham Post-Herald,* 17 February 1972, Medical Center Scrapbook, UAB; "Federal Obligations to the 100 Universities and Colleges Receiving the Largest Amounts," 16 June 1978, Box 58; miscellaneous reports, Box 93, Volker Papers, UAB.

25. *Birmingham Post-Herald,* 22 September 1975, A2; Larry Johnston to Stephen Smith, 12 November 1979, Box 32, Hill Papers, UAB; "Birmingham," *U.S. News and World Report,* 19 September 1983.

26. Franklin, *Back to Birmingham,* 134–97.

27. LaMonte, *Politics and Welfare,* 239.

## CONCLUSION

1. *Birmingham News,* 30 October 1992, 1D; *New York Times,* 18 January 1992, 6; 20 January 1992, 12; 24 January, 1992, 12; 26 January 1992, 12; 18 August 1992, 6.

2. Brownell, "Urbanization in the South" and *Urban Ethos; New York Times,* 20 September 1963, 32; McKiven, *Iron and Steel;* Sugrue, *Origins of the Urban Crisis.*

3. Bartley, *New South,* 461; Schulman, *From Cotton Belt to Sunbelt,* 208.

4. Sullivan, *Days of Hope,* 4, 275; Smith, *New Deal in the Urban South,* 248.

5. Brinkley, *End of Reform,* 266; Charles Zukoski, "A Life Story," 113, BPL.

6. *Birmingham News,* 31 January, 2, 7 February 1950, Vertical Files, BPL; Donald

Comer to Cooper Green, 29 June 1950, Box 10, Green Papers, BPL; *Birmingham Post-Herald,* 10 March 1959, Planning Scrapbook, BPL.

7. Schulman, *From Cotton Belt to Sunbelt,* 208; Bayor, *Race and the Shaping of Twentieth-Century Atlanta,* 256.

8. Schulman, *From Cotton Belt to Sunbelt,* 209.

9. Sullivan, *Days of Hope;* Bartley, *New South,* 470; Eskew, *But for Birmingham,* 338; Fraser and Gerstle, eds., *Rise and Fall of the New Deal Order,* xix.

# Bibliography

Abbott, Carl. *Portland: Planning, Politics, and Growth in a Twentieth-Century City.* Lincoln: University of Nebraska Press, 1983.

——. *Urban America in the Modern Age: 1920 to the Present.* Arlington Heights, Ill.: Harlan Davidson, 1987.

Abrams, Douglas. *Conservative Constraints: North Carolina and the New Deal.* Twentieth-Century America Series. Jackson: University Press of Mississippi, 1992.

*Alabama Official and Statistical Register.* Alexander City: Outlook Publishing Co., 1959.

Alabama State Planning Commission. *Alabama: A Guide to the Deep South.* New York: Charles R. Smith, 1941.

Argersinger, Jo Ann E. *Toward a New Deal in Baltimore: People and Government in the Great Depression.* Chapel Hill: University of North Carolina Press, 1988.

Autrey, Dorothy A. "The National Association for the Advancement of Colored People in Alabama, 1913–1952." Ph.D. diss., University of Notre Dame, 1985.

Badger, Anthony. *The New Deal: The Depression Years, 1933–1940.* New York: Hill and Wang, 1989.

Balogh, Brian. *Chain Reaction: Expert Debate and Public Participation in American Commercial Nuclear Power.* Cambridge: Cambridge University Press, 1991.

———. "Reorganizing the Organizational Synthesis: Federal-Professional Relations in Modern America." *Studies in American Political Development* 5 (1991): 119–72.

Banfield, Edward C., and James Q. Wilson. *City Politics.* New York: Vintage Books, 1963.

Bardach, Eugene. *The Implementation Game: What Happens after a Bill Becomes a Law.* Cambridge, Mass.: Harvard University Press, 1977.

Bartley, Numan V. *The New South, 1945–1980.* Baton Rouge: Louisiana State University Press, 1995.

———. *The Rise of Massive Resistance: Race and Politics in the South during the 1950s.* Baton Rouge: Louisiana State University Press, 1969.

Bauman, John F. *Public Housing, Race, and Renewal: Urban Planning in Philadelphia, 1920–1974.* Philadelphia: Temple University Press, 1987.

Bayor, Ronald H. *Race and the Shaping of Twentieth-Century Atlanta.* Chapel Hill: University of North Carolina Press, 1996.

Bell, Daniel. "Notes on a Post-Industrial Society (I)." *Public Interest* 6 (1967): 24–35.

———. "Notes on a Post-Industrial Society (II)." *Public Interest* 7 (1967): 102–11.

Bernard, Richard M., and Bradley R. Rice, eds. *Sunbelt Cities: Politics and Growth since World War II.* Austin: University of Texas Press, 1983.

Biles, Roger. *The New Deal and the South.* Lexington: University Press of Kentucky, 1994.

———. "The Urban South in the Great Depression." *Journal of Southern History* 56 (1990): 71–100.

Blakely, George. *Hard Times and New Deal in Kentucky, 1929–1939.* Lexington: University Press of Kentucky, 1986.

Braeman, John, Robert Bremmer, and David Brody, eds. *The New Deal: The State and Local Levels.* Columbus: Ohio State University Press, 1975.

Branch, Taylor. *Parting the Waters: America in the King Years.* New York: Simon and Schuster, 1988.

———. *Pillar of Fire: America in the King Years, 1963–1965.* New York: Simon and Schuster, 1998.

Bremner, Robert H., and Gary W. Reichard, eds. *Reshaping America: Society and Institutions, 1945–1960.* Columbus: Ohio State University Press, 1982.

Brinkley, Alan. "The Antimonopoly Ideal and the Liberal State: The Case of Thurman Arnold." *Journal of American History* 80 (1993): 557–79.

———. *The End of Reform: New Deal Liberalism in Recession and War.* New York: Knopf, 1995.

——. "Writing the History of Contemporary America: Dilemmas and Challenges." *Daedalus* 113 (1984): 119–35.

Brown, Ellyn R. "The Hill-Burton Act, 1946–1980: Asynchrony in the Delivery of Health Care to the Poor." *Maryland Law Review* 39 (1979–80): 316–75.

Brown, Joe David. "Birmingham, Alabama: A City in Fear, Racial Violence Smolders in This Deep South Tinderbox." *Saturday Evening Post,* March 3, 1963, 11–19.

Brownell, Blaine. "Birmingham, Alabama: New South City in the 1920s." *Journal of Southern History* 38 (1975): 1–31.

——. *The Urban Ethos in the South, 1920–1930.* Baton Rouge: Louisiana State University Press, 1975.

——. "Urbanization in the South: A Unique Experience?" *Mississippi Quarterly* 26 (1973): 105–20.

Bullard, Robert D., ed. *In Search of the New South: The Black Urban Experience in the 1970s and 1980s.* Tuscaloosa: University of Alabama Press, 1985.

Carmichael, Emmett. "Our Dean: Roy Rachford Kracke." *Quarterly of the Phi Beta Pi* 45 (November 1948): 157–60.

Carter, Dan T. *The Politics of Rage: George Wallace, the Origins of American Conservatism, and the Transformation of American Politics.* Baton Rouge: Louisiana State University Press, 1995.

Chafe, William H. *Civilities and Civil Rights: Greensboro, North Carolina, and the Black Struggle for Freedom.* New York: Oxford University Press, 1980.

Chapman, Herman H., et al. *The Iron and Steel Industries of the South.* Tuscaloosa: University of Alabama Press, 1953.

Clark, E. Culpepper. *The Schoolhouse Door: Segregation's Last Stand at the University of Alabama.* New York: Oxford University Press, 1993.

Cobb, James C. *The Selling of the South: The Southern Crusade for Industrial Development, 1936–1980.* Baton Rouge: Louisiana State University Press, 1982.

Connerly, Charles. "Federal Urban Policy and the Birth of Democratic Planning in Birmingham, Alabama, 1949–1974." Paper presented at Society for American City and Regional Planning History, Richmond, Virginia, November 1991.

Cooper, Weldon. *Metropolitan County: Survey of Government in the Birmingham Area.* Birmingham: Birmingham Printing Co., 1949.

Corley, Robert G. "The Quest for Racial Harmony: Race Relations in Birmingham, Alabama, 1947–1963." Ph.D. diss., University of Virginia, 1979.

Critchlow, Donald, ed. *Federal Social Policy.* University Park: Pennsylvania State University Press, 1988.

Daly-Bednarek, Janet R. *The Changing Image of the City: Planning for Downtown Omaha, 1945–1973.* Lincoln: University of Nebraska Press, 1992.

Daniel, Pete. *Breaking the Land: The Transformation of Cotton, Tobacco, and Rice Cultures since 1880.* Urbana: University of Illinois Press, 1985.

Davies, Richard O. *Housing Reform under the Truman Administration.* Columbia: University of Missouri Press, 1966.

Derthick, Martha. *The Influence of Federal Grants: Public Assistance in Massachusetts.* Cambridge, Mass.: Harvard University Press, 1970.

Dismuke, Otto, and Robert Norrell. *The Other Side: The Story of Birmingham's Black Community.* Birmingham: Birmingfind, n.d. Copy in BPL.

Eskew, Glenn. "But for Birmingham: The Local and National Movements in the Civil Rights Struggle." Ph.D. diss., University of Georgia, 1993.

——. *But for Birmingham: The Local and National Movements in the Civil Rights Struggle.* Chapel Hill: University of North Carolina Press, 1997.

——. "Demagoguery in Birmingham and the Building of Vestavia." *Alabama Review* 42 (1989): 192–217.

——. "The Freedom Riot and Political Reform in Birmingham, 1961–1963." *Alabama Review* 49 (1996): 181–220.

——. "Why Birmingham: Postwar Racial Strife in the 'Johannesburg of the South.'" Paper presented at the meeting of the Southern Historical Association, Louisville, Kentucky, November 1993.

Evans, Peter, Dietrich Rueschemeyer, and Theda Skocpol, eds. *Bringing the State Back In.* Cambridge: Cambridge University Press, 1985.

Fairbanks, Robert B. *Making Better Citizens: Housing Reform and the Community Development Strategy in Cincinnati, 1890–1960.* Urbana: University of Illinois Press, 1988.

Feagin, Joe R. *Free Enterprise City: Houston in Political and Economic Perspective.* New Brunswick: Rutgers University Press, 1989.

Foley, Michael. *The New Senate: Liberal Influence on a Conservative Institution, 1959–1972.* New Haven: Yale University Press, 1980.

Franklin, Jimmie Lewis. *Back to Birmingham: Richard Arrington, Jr., and His Times.* Tuscaloosa: University of Alabama Press, 1989.

Fraser, Steve, and Gary Gerstle, eds. *The Rise and Fall of the New Deal Order, 1930–1980.* Princeton: Princeton University Press, 1989.

Freedman, Leonard. *Public Housing: The Politics of Poverty.* New York: Holt, Rinehart, and Winston, 1969.

Funigiello, Philip. *The Challenge to Urban Liberalism: Federal-City Relations during World War II.* Knoxville: University of Tennessee Press, 1978.

Galambos, Louis. "The Emerging Organizational Synthesis in Modern American History." *Business History Review* 44 (1970): 179–90.

———. "Technology, Political Economy, and Professionalization: Central Themes of the Organizational Synthesis." *Business History Review* 57 (1983): 471–93.

———, ed. *The New American State: Bureaucracies and Policies since World War II.* Baltimore: Johns Hopkins University Press, 1987.

Garrow, David, ed. *Birmingham, Alabama, 1956–1963: The Black Struggle for Civil Rights.* Brooklyn: Carlson, 1989.

Geiger, Roger L. *Research and Relevant Knowledge: American Research Universities since World War II.* New York: Oxford University Press, 1993.

Gelfand, Lawrence, ed. *Changing Patterns in American Federal-State Relations.* Iowa City: University of Iowa Press, 1985.

Gelfand, Mark I. *A Nation of Cities: The Federal Government and Urban America, 1933–1965.* New York: Oxford University Press, 1975.

Gillette, Howard, Jr., and Zane Miller. *American Urbanism: A Historiographical Overview.* Westport: Greenwood Press, 1987.

Goings, Kenneth, and Raymond Mohl. "Toward a New African American History." *Journal of Urban History* 21 (1995): 283–95.

Goldfield, David. *Black, White, and Southern: Race Relations and Southern Culture, 1940 to the Present.* Baton Rouge: Louisiana State University Press, 1990.

———. *Cotton Fields and Skyscrapers: Southern City and Region, 1607–1980.* Baton Rouge: Louisiana State University Press, 1982.

———. "The Urban South: A Regional Framework." *American Historical Review* 86 (1981): 1009–34.

Grafton, Carl, and Anne Permaloff. *Big Mules and Branchheads: James E. Folsom and Political Power in Alabama.* Athens: University of Georgia Press, 1985.

Graham, Hugh D. *Civil Rights and the Presidency: Race and Gender in American Politics, 1960–1972.* New York: Oxford University Press, 1992.

Grantham, Dewey W. *The South in Modern America: A Region at Odds.* New York: HarperCollins, 1994.

Graves, John Temple. *History of the Southern Research Institute.* Birmingham: Birmingham Publishing Co., 1955.

Hagur, John. *Commercial Survey of the Southeast.* Washington, D.C.: GPO, 1927.

Hamer, Greene, Siler, and Associates. "The Economy of Metropolitan Birmingham." BPL.

Hames, Carl. *Hill Ferguson: His Life and Works.* Tuscaloosa: University of Alabama Press, 1978.

Hamilton, Virginia Van der Veer. *Lister Hill: Statesman from the South.* Chapel Hill: University of North Carolina Press, 1987.

Hanchett, Thomas W. "Federal Incentives and the Growth of Local Planning,

Thomas, James D., and William H. Stewart. *Alabama Government and Politics*. Lincoln: University of Nebraska Press, 1988.

Thomas, Robert D. "Cities as Partners in the Federal System." *Political Science Quarterly* 101 (1986): 49–64.

Thomas, Robert D., and Richard W. Murray. *Progrowth Politics: Change and Governance in Houston*. Berkeley: IGS Press, 1991.

Tindall, George B. *Emergence of the New South, 1913–1945*. Baton Rouge: Louisiana State University Press, 1967.

Underwood, Anthony P. "A Progressive History of the Young Men's Business Club of Birmingham, Alabama, 1947–1970." M.A. thesis, Samford University, 1980.

Vann, David. "Events Leading to the 1963 Change from the Commission to the Mayor-Council Form of Government in Birmingham, Alabama." BPL.

Volker, Joseph. *The University and the City*. New York: Newcomen Society, 1971.

Walker, David. *Toward a Functioning Federalism*. Cambridge. Mass.: Winthrop Publishers, 1981.

Warren, Kenneth. *The American Steel Industry, 1850–1970: A Geographical Interpretation*. Oxford: Clarendon Press, 1973.

Weaver, Robert. *Dilemmas of Urban America*. Cambridge, Mass.: Harvard University Press, 1965.

———. "Racial Policy in Public Housing." *Phylon* 1 (1940): 149–61.

Wilson, James Q. *Urban Renewal: The Record and the Controversy*. Cambridge, Mass.: MIT Press, 1966.

Wilson, Michelle, and John Lynxwiler. "The Federal Government and the Harassment of Black Leaders." *Journal of Black Studies* 28 (1998): 540–60.

Wilson, William J. *The Declining Significance of Race: Blacks and Changing American Institutions*. Chicago: University of Chicago Press, 1978.

———. *The Truly Disadvantaged: The Inner City, the Underclass and Public Policy*. Chicago: University of Chicago Press, 1987.

Woodbury, Coleman, ed. *Housing Officials' Yearbook 1936*. Chicago: National Association of Housing Officials, 1936.

Wright, Deil S. *Understanding Intergovernmental Relations*. Chapel Hill: University of North Carolina Press, 1988.

Wright, Gavin. *Old South, New South: Revolutions in the Southern Economy since the Civil War*. New York: Basic Books, 1986.

Zimmerman, Joseph. *Federal Preemption: The Silent Revolution*. Ames: Iowa State University Press, 1990.

Zukoski, Charles. "A Life Story." BPL.

# Index

1941–1948." *Journal of the American Planning Association* 60 (spring 1994): 197–208.

———. "Sorting Out the New South City: Charlotte and Its Neighborhoods." Ph.D. diss., University of North Carolina, 1993.

———. *Sorting Out the New South City: Race, Class and Urban Growth in Charlotte, 1875–1975.* Chapel Hill: University of North Carolina Press, 1998.

Harden, Victoria A. *Inventing the NIH: Federal Biomedical Research Policy, 1887–1937.* Baltimore: Johns Hopkins University Press, 1986.

Harris, Carl V. *Political Power in Birmingham, 1871–1921.* Knoxville: University of Tennessee Press, 1977.

Harrison, Tinsley R. "The Medical School of the University of Alabama: Some Reminiscences." University of Alabama, Birmingham Archives.

Harvey, A. McGehee, Gert Breigger, et al. *A Model of Its Kind: A Centennial History of Medicine at Johns Hopkins.* Baltimore: Johns Hopkins University Press, 1989.

Hawley, Willis D., and Frederick D. Wirt. *The Search for Community Power.* Englewood Cliffs, N.J.: Prentice-Hall, 1968.

Hemphill, Paul. *Leaving Birmingham: Notes of a Native Son.* New York: Viking Penguin, 1993.

Hill, Patricia. "Origins of Modern Dallas." Ph.D. diss., University of Texas–Dallas, 1990.

Hirsch, Arnold. *Making the Second Ghetto: Race and Housing in Chicago, 1940–1960.* Cambridge: Cambridge University Press, 1983.

Holley, Howard. "Medical Education in Alabama." *Alabama Review* 7 (1954): 245–62.

Holmes, Jack. *A History of the University of Alabama Hospitals.* Birmingham: University Hospital Auxiliary, 1974.

Horwood, Edgar M., and Ronald R. Boyce. *Studies of the Central Business District and Urban Freeway Development.* Seattle: University of Washington Press, 1959.

Ivey, John, Jr., et al. *Building Atlanta's Future.* Chapel Hill: University of North Carolina Press, 1948.

Jackson, Kenneth. *Crabgrass Frontier: The Suburbanization of the United States.* New York: Oxford University Press, 1985.

Jacoway, Elizabeth, and David Colburn, eds. *Southern Businessmen and Desegregation.* Baton Rouge: Louisiana State University Press, 1982.

Jeffries, John W. "The 'New' New Deal: FDR and American Liberalism, 1937–1945." *Political Science Quarterly* 105 (1990): 397–418.

Johnson, Charles S. *Patterns of Negro Segregation.* New York: Harper and Brothers, 1943.

Karl, Barry. *The Uneasy State: The United States from 1915 to 1945*. Chicago: University of Chicago Press, 1983.

Katz, Michael, ed. *The "Underclass" Debate: A View from History*. Princeton: Princeton University Press, 1993.

Keith, Nathaniel S. *Politics and the Housing Crisis since 1930*. New York: Universe Books, 1973.

———. "Urban Redevelopment—A Challenge to the Cities." *Planning 1949* (1949): 40.

Kelley, Robin D. G. *Hammer and Hoe: Alabama Communists during the Great Depression*. Chapel Hill: University of North Carolina Press, 1990.

Kirby, John B. *Black Americans in the Roosevelt Era: Liberalism and Race*. Twentieth Century Series. Knoxville: University of Tennessee Press, 1980.

Klarnan, Michael J. "How *Brown* Changed Race Relations: The Backlash Thesis." *Journal of American History* 81 (1994): 81–118.

Kracke, Robert R., and William G. Kracke. "The University of Alabama Medical Center; The Past—The Present—The Future." *Alabama Lawyer* 28 (1967): 78–88.

Kracke, Roy R., and J. W. MacQueen. "Developments in Medical Education in the Medical College of Alabama." *Southern Medical Journal* 39 (January 1946): 8–12.

Kruman, Marc W. "Quotas for Blacks: The Public Works Administration and the Black Construction Worker." *Labor History* 16 (1975): 37–51.

LaMonte, Edward S. *Politics and Welfare in Birmingham, 1900–1975*. Tuscaloosa: University of Alabama Press, 1995.

Lave, Judith R., and Lester B. Lave. *The Hospital Construction Act: An Evaluation of the Hill-Burton Program, 1948–1973*. Washington, D.C.: American Enterprise Institute, 1974.

Lawson, Stephen F. *Black Ballots: Voting Rights in the South, 1944–1969*. New York: Columbia University Press, 1976.

Lepawsky, Albert. "Government Planning in the South." *Journal of Politics* 10 (1948): 536–67.

Lesher, Stephan. *George Wallace: American Populist*. New York: Addison-Wesley, 1994.

Leubke, Paul. *Tar Heel Politics*. Chapel Hill: University of North Carolina Press, 1991.

Leuchtenburg, William J. "The Pertinence of Political History: Reflections on the Significance of the State in America." *Journal of American History* 73 (1986): 585–600.

Levine, Charles H. *Racial Conflict and the American Mayor: Power, Polarization, and Performance.* Lexington, Mass.: D. C. Heath, 1974.

Lewis, Benjamin. *VA Medical Program in Relation to Medical Schools.* Washington, D.C.: GPO, 1970.

Lotchin, Roger. *Fortress California: From Warfare to Welfare.* New York: Oxford University Press, 1992.

Markusen, Ann R. *Profit Cycles, Oligopoly, and Regional Development.* Cambridge, Mass.: MIT Press, 1985.

Matusow, Allen J. *The Unraveling of America: A History of Liberalism in the 1960s.* New York: Harper Torchbooks, 1984.

McConnell, Timothy J. *The Wagner Housing Act: A Case Study of the Legislative Process.* Chicago: Loyola University Press, 1957.

McEntire, Davis, and Nathan Glazer, eds. *Studies in Housing and Minority Groups.* Berkeley: University of California Press, 1960.

McKiven, Henry M., Jr. *Iron and Steel: Class, Race, and Community in Birmingham, Alabama, 1875–1920.* Chapel Hill: University of North Carolina Press, 1995.

McMillen, Neil. *Remaking Dixie: The Impact of World War II on the American South.* Jackson: University Press of Mississippi, 1997.

McWhorter, Diane. *Carry Me Home: Birmingham, Alabama, the Climactic Battle of the Civil Rights Revolution.* New York: Simon and Schuster, 2001.

Mead, Manson. *The Miracle on Hawthorne Hill.* Winston-Salem: Wake Forest University, 1988.

Mohl, Raymond. "Making the Second Ghetto in Metropolitan Miami, 1940–1960." *Journal of Urban History* 21 (1995): 395–427.

Mohl, Raymond, and Arnold Hirsch, eds. *Urban Policy in Twentieth-Century America.* New Brunswick: Rutgers University Press, 1993.

Mollenkopf, John C. *The Contested City.* Princeton: Princeton University Press, 1988.

Moore, Geraldine. *Behind the Ebony Mask.* Birmingham: Southern University Press, 1961.

Morgan, Charles. *A Time to Speak.* New York: Harper and Row, 1964.

Murray, William W. *Thomas W. Martin—A Biography.* Birmingham: Southern Research Institute, 1979.

Nash, Gerald D. *The American West Transformed: The Impact of the Second World War.* Bloomington: Indiana University Press, 1985.

National Resources Planning Committee. *Regional Factors in National Planning and Development.* Washington, D.C.: GPO, 1935.

Neride, Inc. "The Consortium: A Concise History of Blacks in Medicine." University of Alabama, Birmingham Archives.

Newbill, Robert S. "A Study of the Growth of the City of Birmingham's Corporate Boundaries, 1871 to the Present." N.p., 1980. BPL.

Norrell, Robert J. "Caste in Steel: Jim Crow Careers in Birmingham, Alabama." *Journal of American History* 73 (1986): 669–94.

———. "Labor at the Ballot Box: Alabama Politics from the New Deal to the Dixiecrat Movement." *Journal of Southern History* 57 (1991): 201–34.

Nunnelley, William A. *Bull Connor.* Tuscaloosa: University of Alabama Press, 1991.

O'Connor, Thomas. *Building a New Boston: Politics and Urban Renewal, 1950–1970.* Boston: Northeastern University Press, 1993.

Oliver, Leavy W. "Zoning Ordinances in Relation to Segregated Negro Housing in Birmingham, Alabama." M.A. thesis, Indiana University, 1951.

Patterson, James T. *Grand Expectations: The United States, 1945–1974.* New York: Oxford University Press, 1996.

———. *The New Deal and the States: Federalism in Transition.* Princeton: Princeton University Press, 1969.

Radford, Gail. "Modern Community Housing: New Responses to the Shelter Problem in the 1920s and 1930s." Ph.D. diss., Columbia University, 1989.

Raines, Howell. *My Soul Is Rested: Movement Days in the Deep South Remembered.* New York: Penguin Books, 1977.

Robinson, Armstead, ed. *New Directions in Civil Rights Studies.* Charlottesville: University Press of Virginia, 1991.

Rogers, William W., et al. *Alabama: The History of a Deep South State.* Tuscaloosa: University of Alabama Press, 1994.

Schlesinger, Arthur. *The Coming of the New Deal.* Boston: Houghton Mifflin, 1959.

Schneider, Lawrence. "Provisions of Free Medical Services by Hill-Burton Hospitals." *Harvard Civil Rights–Civil Liberties Review* 8 (1973): 350–83.

Schulman, Bruce J. *From Cotton Belt to Sunbelt: Federal Policy, Economic Development, and the Transformation of the South.* New York: Oxford University Press, 1991.

Schwartz, Joel. *The New York Approach: Robert Moses, Urban Liberals, and Redevelopment of the Inner City.* Columbus: Ohio State University Press, 1993.

Scott, Mel. *American City Planning since 1890.* Berkeley: University of California Press, 1969.

Scribner, Christopher M. "Federal Funding, Urban Renewal, and Race Relations: Birmingham, Alabama, in Transition, 1950–1955." *Alabama Review* 48 (1995): 269–95.

———. "The Quiet Revolution: Federal Funding and Change in Birmingham, Alabama, 1933–1965." Ph.D. diss., Vanderbilt University, 1996.

Seeley, Bruce. *Building the American Highway System: Engineers as Policy Makers.* Philadelphia: Temple University Press, 1987.

Seham, Max. "Discrimination against Negroes in Hospitals." *New England Journal of Medicine* (October 1964): 940–42.

Silver, Christopher. "The Racial Origins of Zoning: Southern Cities from 1910–1940." *Planning Perspectives* 6 (1991): 189–205.

———. *Twentieth-Century Richmond: Planning, Politics, and Race.* Knoxville: University of Tennessee Press, 1984.

Sinclair, Barbara. *The Transformation of the United States Senate.* Baltimore: Johns Hopkins University Press, 1989.

Skowronek, Stephen. *Building a New American State: The Expansion of National Administrative Capacities, 1877–1920.* Cambridge: Cambridge University Press, 1982.

Smerk, George, ed. *Readings in Urban Transportation.* Bloomington: Indiana University Press, 1968.

Smith, Douglas. *The New Deal in the Urban South.* Baton Rouge: Louisiana State University Press, 1988.

Spinney, Robert G. "World War II and Nashville, Tennessee, 1938–1951: Social Change and Public Sector Expansion." Ph.D. diss., Vanderbilt University, 1995.

Staples, John H. "Urban Renewal: A Comparative Study of Twenty-Two Cities." *Western Political Quarterly* 23 (June 1970): 294–304.

Starr, Paul. *The Social Transformation of American Medicine: The Rise of a Sovereign Profession and the Making of a Vast Industry.* New York: Basic Books, 1985.

Stevens, Rosemary. *American Medicine and the Public Interest.* New Haven: Yale University Press, 1971.

———. *In Sickness and in Wealth: American Hospitals in the Twentieth Century.* New York: Basic Books, 1989.

Stocking, George W. *Basing Point Pricing and Regional Development: A Case Study of the Iron and Steel Industry.* Chapel Hill: University of North Carolina Press, 1954.

Stone, Clarence. *Regime Politics: Governing Atlanta, 1946–1988.* Lawrence: University Press of Kansas, 1989.

Sugrue, Thomas J. *The Origins of the Urban Crisis: Race and Inequality in Postwar Detroit.* Princeton: Princeton University Press, 1996.

Sullivan, Patricia. *Days of Hope: Race and Democracy in the New Deal Era.* Chapel Hill: University of North Carolina Press, 1996.

Sundquist, James L. *Making Federalism Work: A Study of Program Coordination at the Community Level.* Washington, D.C.: Brookings Institution, 1969.

Teaford, Jon C. *The Twentieth-Century American City: Problem, Promise, and Reality.* Baltimore: Johns Hopkins University Press, 1986.